Capitalism, Dependency and Ultra-imperialism

Political Economy of the Capitalist International System

Capitalism, Dependency and Ultra-imperialism

Political Economy of the Capitalist International System

HARTMUT ELSENHANS

KNOWLEDGE WORLD
KW Publishers Pvt Ltd
New Delhi

ISBN 978-93-94915-01-5 Hardback
ISBN 978-93-94915-03-9 ebook

Published in India by Kalpana Shukla

KNOWLEDGE WORLD

KW Publishers Pvt Ltd
4676/21, First Floor, Ansari Road
Daryaganj, New Delhi 110002
Phone: +91 11 43528107
Marketing: kw@kwpub.in
Editorial: production@kwpub.in
Website: www.kwpub.in

Printed and Bound in India

Contents

Introduction

On the Genesis of a Heterodox Approach

The globalisation of rent is an impending threat. Globalisation itself is linked to increasing state intervention. Most often, this is done in an effort to improve the position of national economies within the international division of labour. It also aims at increasing national income if the competitiveness of highly promising sectors of production appears to be blocked.

On the surface, this might look like the globalisation of profit. In fact, it represents the globalisation of rent. The state's role in the global economy and in international relations is expanding right now. Only superficially does this constitute a process of 'capitalist' economic globalisation.

Rent is surplus, which is appropriated through market imperfections and ultimately through political mechanisms. Profit, on the other hand, is appropriated without political intervention in markets that are, in principle, characterised by perfect competition.

Rents can be used to increase incomes for a variety of purposes. Under the conditions of international rivalry, rent can also be used for subsidising new promising production lines. These may not yet be competitive at the existent level of development. Rent can be used for this purpose by developing economies as well as by leading developed economies. The latter may suffer from specialisation in old leading technologies. They may be prevented from transforming existing productivity advances in most modern technologies into comparative advantage. The cause of this lies in their high exchange rates, which are determined by high earning exports of older products (Elsenhans 2020a, b, c).

Rent provides financial resources in an attempt to change a particular economy's position in the international division of labour. In a global capitalist world system, profit derives from competitive sales on the world market. If comparative advantage is favourable, then profit triggers the production structure to be continuously adapted to the most technically promising production lines.

National economies can benefit from profit or rent. If profit is predominant, state intervention is limited. If profit is weak, then the tendency to appropriate rent will be strong. If rent is strong, then there are several possible outcomes. One of these is the state's subsidisation of particular economic activities in order to increase profitability.

The behaviour of states is determined by their position in the international division of labour as well as their internal structures and the opportunities offered by both. If they gain in competitiveness, then their economies can be profit-oriented. However, if an economy cannot achieve competitiveness in promising production lines, then its economy will surely be rent oriented. This is especially the case if the capitalist mechanism of profit depending on rising mass incomes is not deliberately launched on the internal markets of such economies. Such an initiative depends on non-profit oriented development strategies.

Clearly, then, I do not believe that capitalism is the inevitable outcome of the development of productive forces—that is, of human control over nature through technology. Capitalism results from rising mass incomes. This is the condition of cost-reducing technology. The contrast here is with the quality-augmenting technologies of, for example, ancient civilisations.

Cost-reducing technologies open the way for the physical creation of products that were earlier merely a pipe dream. Indeed, such technology not only allows for the invention of such products—it renders them accessible. We need only consider the respective technological intricacies and origins of, for example, the Taj Mahal and an aeroplane.

Nonetheless, not all economies have access to the most efficient and cost-cutting technologies. This is due to unequal specialisation.

Specialisation follows comparative advantage. An economy specialises in those products where it enjoys *relative* superiority—even if it remains less sophisticated than more advanced economies. In most technologies, for example, China is not yet superior to the established capitalist countries. However, China is cheaper. China's costs correspond to its low international labour costs, which are low because of its exchange rate, ultimately because of low average productivity of its economy. Until recently, the established industrialised countries enjoyed a comparative advantage in the most advanced production lines. To be sure, not all of these countries had comparative advantage over established industrialised countries. In laggard countries, most modern technologies were simply not available. Their introduction was immediately hamstrung because they were out competed by more advanced countries.

States endeavour to promote technical development by mobilising financial resources in order to subsidise innovation. In the realm of military technology, this has been the case more or less since the dawn of history. At the level of contemporary technical performance, state-subsidised technological innovation occurs across an extensive variety of economic activities. States can promote technical innovation by diverting resources resources away from lagging and unpromising sectors of production. They can divert these resources into more promising branches, even if they remain backward in relation to leading economies. States burden some non-innovative industries with additional costs. They appropriate surplus through political means. This is rent. Raw material rents are only a special case.

International systems are characterised by two principal types of states. On the one hand, we have leading economies that are well-positioned to benefit from capitalist mechanisms. On the other hand, we have lagging economies that operate on the basis of rent appropriation, whether they try to catch up or accept their predicament.

The behaviour of states within such a heterogeneous system is determined by several factors. These include their internal structure, their positioning in the international division of labour and the opportunities available to them for changing (or defending) their position.

This book intends to present this overall approach in more detail. It does so by bringing together several major papers. These were written during the process of developing my theory of the heterogeneity and hierarchical structure of the international system.

The first paper is entitled "*The International System at the Crossroads between Rent and Profit.*" This chapter summarises the current status of my theoretical approach. It focuses on current global trends in particular.

My intellectual career began with a challenge to the conviction that increasing capital accumulation is necessary for overcoming underdevelopment. Whatever divides them, both Marxist and neoliberal thinkers share this basic orthodoxy. However, capitalism is not necessarily capital deepening. It fails to be so if the labour values of directly employed labour—that is, the labour which produces the final products is compared to the labour value embodied in the stock of plant and equipment. The latter is known as capital. In labour value terms, the relation between directly employed labour and capital does not increase. This is amply demonstrated by the constant capital output ratio. In fact, the notion that capitalism is dependent on capital accumulation is actually a class-biased statistical misinterpretation. It serves to facilitate the upper strata's class war against the lower orders. The fact that this ruling class campaign enjoys theoretical backing from orthodox Marxists is a bitter irony indeed.

The second paper presented here is "*Equality and Development, The European Experience and Today's Underdeveloped World.*" This was one of the first formulations of my theory that capitalism requires rising mass incomes. It followed earlier formulations of the basic argument.[1]

For certain economies, the mechanism of deriving net investment, accumulation and profit from rising mass incomes is not directly accessible. These economies suffer from unequal specialisation. They are at a comparative disadvantage in terms of technology-triggering final productions and technology production. They may be highly competitive in production lines that depend on imported technology, or which do not require innovative technology. In order to facilitate their economic transformation, they draw on incomes imposed on competitive exports for subsidising industrial diversification. The oil-producing countries attempted this with oil rents.

Appropriating and channelling rent can only be accomplished by institutions that are not bound to the profit rate as signalled by the market. In order to expedite the process of catching up, these institutions may intervene in structuring the economy through investment. In order to explain the origins and functioning of these structures, I developed my theory of state classes.[2]

The third contribution assembled here illustrates this argument: "*Dependency, Rent, and Autonomy: The Controversy about the Role of the Third World State in its International Setting and the Paradigm of Rent-financed State-class Dominated Bureaucratic Development Societies.*" I also engage heavily with theories of imperialism. The legacy of these theories partly explains the centrality of the concept of "dependency" within much (supposedly) "progressive" writing on the international system. Certainly, state classes can play a positive role in developing economies. They can invest rents in order to restructure these economies according to mass needs. However, the state classes also constitute a danger. The fact that they can mobilise (and monopolise) such resources may inhibit them from undertaking an aggressive and ambitious program of economic restructuring. They fail not so much because they are dependent, but because they are so frequently unable to deviate from their short-term interests. These include self-privilege and desire for stability.

From the perspective of our analysis, the collapse of the Soviet Union towards the end of the 1980s had a highly detrimental effect on the power of two key groups—labour in developed capitalist countries and the social reformist state classes of the Global South. This theme is taken up in the fourth contribution: "*Ultra-imperialism, Ultra-reaction and Ultra-Stability: The Political Economy of the International System in the 21st Century: The Demise of National Liberation Movements and the Decline of Social Democracy at the Global Level.*" What happens when the forces that provide voice to the poor are weakened? This chapter shows how, in both the West and the Global South, this weakening results in particular adaptations that are ultimately harmful to the expansion of a capitalist world economy. The developed capitalist countries come to be characterised by underconsumption. The state tries to fight this through some degree of redistribution to newly marginal sections of the population. In this way, these marginal elements are rendered dependent on the state. Such demographics have lost their voice because they no longer have their ultimate bargaining chip—the possibility of exiting the labour market and depriving capitalism of their labour. Meanwhile, in the underdeveloped world, we also see underconsumption. However, because the secular state classes have failed to deliver on their promises, the social groups most adversely effected by these new trends increasingly turn to new, cultural-identitarian movements (Elsenhans 2012, 2015a).

At the global level, the logic of both types of systems leads to cooperation among the great powers. This comprises a sort of collective imperialism designed to stymy the demands of the South. A hundred years ago, this was referred to as "ultra-imperialism" by Karl Kautsky (1914). We are currently witnessing the emergence of a new great power system. These powers preside over large internal markets. They can launch new technologies with rapidly decreasing unit costs through economies of scale. These great powers organise regional spheres of influence around themselves and engage in trials of strength with other regional powers.

The last chapter is entitled "*A Fissured, Not-So-Capitalist World System.*" This essay studies the mechanisms that operate in such a world system. This system is characterised by regional hegemony, fragmentation and—from the perspective of the great powers—readily available political instruments. These big powers have the ability to alter the integration of the capitalist world system to their advantage. They do this in order to optimally benefit from the world market in their race to the top of the international division of labour. The great powers are undertaking a permanent modification of the international division of labour. However, smaller powers also participate in this process. All involved aim to improve their relative position by mobilising internally or externally appropriated rents.

Recent decades have seen a precipitous decline in the position of labour. Its claims to redistribution—both at the national and world level—have been severely weakened. Against this background, I deduce an enhancement of the role of rent in total surplus. Productivity increases continue to grow potential or actually produced surplus. This was the consequence predicted by Keynes in case of excessively high surpluses relative to investment opportunities. Governments and businesses will not opt for economic depression. As a solution for liquidating uninvested surplus, this is politically difficult to apply. And so the privileged will intensify rent appropriation—with the political support of labour. Maybe this will contribute to climate protection. The powerful may invest in more costly production technologies, or they may undertake expensive compensatory investment to protect against climate change. These rents may, however, also serve to increase the incomes of the rich and powerful (Elsenhans 2020d).

By presenting these papers, I hope to contribute to a better understanding of this heterodox approach beyond the contours of political economy. I aim to show the relevance of my theory for a critical international political economy. At present, such a critical approach is largely conspicuous by its absence. This owes to the dominance of the discussion by various ideologies—both Marxist and non-Marxist—which, despite their differences, all tend to advance two key points. First, that the struggle in the international system is linked to the accumulation of financial resources; second, that the result of this struggle for more financial resources determines the position of an economy in the international division of labour.

Notes

1. Elsenhans 1975 [1974], 1976b, c, 1982c.
2. Elsenhans 1976e, 1996b [1981], 1982a.

1

The International System at the Crossroads of Rent and Profit*

1. The basic political economy argument

Do we stand before an impending civilizational turn within the international system towards a law-based multilateralism? I argue here that this will not happen. The emergence of an interest-based multipolar structure, such as that which arose following the Treaty of Vienna in 1815, is far more likely.

The dominant discourse proceeds as follows: the international system will inevitably become more civilised due to a greater diffusion of civilisational norms. These norms will virtually guarantee a free trade regime, engineer a basic consensus among participating states, and give rise to myriad middle-class non-governmental organisations that promote universal values. These predictions are analogous to an international narrative largely dominated by the transnational outgrowths of mainly Western-based NGOs. To all intents and purposes, such organisations are the scriptwriters of world public opinion. Their message is entirely compatible with political and economic liberalism.

However, these forces are increasingly faced with competition. This competition emanates from new powers, which first arose in the economic sphere. These powers support a state-led correction of the spontaneous international division of labour, though they often do so surreptitiously. Their aim is to upgrade their position in the international hierarchy of technical competences. They, thus, serve to legitimate the ruling classes,

* Text written for this book.

whose overriding goal is to defend their political privileges against an increasingly educated class of direct producers. These producers claim some sort of political participation and freedom for themselves. Such demands must be met, at least formally.

Clearly, then, we are faced with myriad attempts to maintain political and economic inequality by non-market means. These are not the key concerns of the following article, however. The basic argument here is that these emerging rivalries are rooted in the immediate interests of ruling groups/strata/classes. These interests cannot be deduced from the so-called "social cultural heritages" of these groups. In fact, they result from the respective positions of these groups within the international division of labour. Ultimately, they result from the viability of the rent-based economic systems that these groups dominate and profit from.

The dominant discourse is based on a neoclassical interpretation of capitalist growth. According to this model, capitalism incessantly pushes for the integration of new production sites into its orbit. It does so on the basis of comparative advantage and accumulation of capital. The better capitalism performs this function, the less it is impeded by non-economic structures, such as redistributive governments or organised labour. Such forces are considered to be hindrances to this process of maximising general welfare, because they divert scarce financial resources from the most efficient avenues of investment. This limits accumulation and growth.

As mentioned, there are rivals to this neoliberal discourse. These are generally based on a nationalist identification with the attempts of rising states to enhance their technical competence in order to modify the international division of labour. This is achieved by mobilising additional financial resources beyond market-based profit-for-investment. Neoclassical authors are, of course, inclined to grumble about the supposed losses implied by such "economically inefficient" investment.

Some economic discourses hold that developed capitalist economies are essentially self-steering. Apparently, state intervention into this process constitutes a loss of growth. Even more egregiously, such intervention threatens to jeopardise the interests of other participants in this basically neoliberal world system, because it threatens the spontaneity and flexibility of the international division of labour. As it happens, opponents of this model do not deny the second implication. However, they postulate that overall positive growth effects are already unevenly distributed among the participants within the international division of labour. Those who want to correct their position must add financial resources to their investment spending beyond those which their companies can appropriate under perfect competition through sales to anonymous markets.

These resources are rents, that is surplus which is not appropriated under conditions of perfect competition. Their appropriation and their allocation for investment requires political instruments and therefore political coalitions to make use of them. These coalitions have historically shown considerable variety—they may include populist, nationalist and leftist political forces, or even a mixture of all three. The purpose of this article is not to delve deeper into the debate over these variations. Its goal is to investigate the political economy of, on the one hand, the "open", neoclassical economy and, on the other, the interventionist structures which are typical of partial integration into the world economy.

The political economy of these rivalries is based on the emergence of rent due to the weakness of profit. In this article, I concentrate on the reasons for the strength of profit, the reasons for its weakening, and the reasons for the emergence of rent. This last development has occurred despite intensified integration into a market-dominated world economy. I do not intend to draw the traditional dichotomy between free traders and protectionists. These two positions do not fully reflect the global conflicts that are increasingly in evidence for two reasons:

- The existence of nations that have recourse to rent appropriation. By "nation" I mean an economically integrated territory with a more or less articulated ideological representation of this integration. Profit-oriented states, seeking to impose profit domination on the global economic system, increasingly choose for rent appropriation as a result of their historical experience and ideological preferences.
- Economies which have historically lagged behind in terms of technology use principles of free trade in order to advance their

position in the international division of labour. They do this on the basis of rent mobilisation, enjoying new rents as a result of changes in international patterns of specialisation.

The overarching argument of this contribution is as follows in today's international system, the spontaneous behaviour of all participating economies serves to facilitate the generalisation of rent. This is the case whether these economies are profit or rent oriented. Indeed, a rent-based international system is on the horizon (Elsenhans 2019). The alternative lies in the transformation of the economies of the Global South into capitalist economies. This can only proceed through the empowerment of their labour and a possible ensuing rise in mass incomes (Elsenhans 2021a: chap. 8).

This argument is based on a Keynesian interpretation of the emergence, growth and possible future of capitalism, as opposed to neoclassical and Marxist interpretations (Elsenhans 2015b). There are clear differences between these two schools in terms of the problems they identify in the international system, and even more so in terms of the solutions they advocate. But despite these apparent divergences, both approaches agree that profit results from the capacity of capitalists to extract surplus from labour. This article thus follows a Keynesian—and ultimately a Kaleckian—approach to profit. This holds that profit is dependent on investment spending by capitalists (Kalecki 1942), irrespective of the available surplus. Profit cannot be reduced by redistributive measures of labour if incomes appropriated by non-capitalists are used for spending on products produced by capitalists.

Thus, the paper begins with the articulation of a theory of profit and rent. This is followed by a demonstration of the inevitability of the permanent emergence of rent, either in the Global South or in the West. This is unavoidable as long as the capitalist mechanism of making profit as a result of investment spending is not generalised. The mobilisation of such rents may drive rent-based economies to the dominance of profit *if* labour is empowered by economic tendencies of demand, or if it empowers itself through political mobilisation. Under contemporary conditions, the ongoing climate and environmental crises may result in a strengthening of profit by additional demand for preserving the environment and resulting investment. Politically, however, it might as well strengthen rent as a politically appropriated income. This spending is not necessarily distributed evenly as wages, and it may not be democratically controlled.

In order to drive economies to the dominance of profit via empowerment of labour, equality of income distribution leading to high multipliers of spending are helpful. If these are applied, the dominance of profit may be facilitated by labour-friendly measures, and by measures for reducing poverty.

The contemporary pattern of international specialisation is characterised by shifts in the distribution of comparative advantage. In contrast to nineteenth-century globalisation, rent-based economies with high pockets of labour marginality are becoming increasingly competitive in branches of production with high price and income elasticity of demand. Many of these economies are important for employment in profit-dominated societies. The result is a disempowerment of labour in the profit-dominated societies, but one which is not necessarily compensated by an empowerment of labour in the rent-based societies. Wherever we look, labour is growing weaker.

Economic developments or political activity can lead to scarcity of labour. But when this scarcity is no longer sufficient to ensure empowerment of labour, globalisation will result in the domination of rent rather than profit. Consequently, those forces which want to maintain the advantages of capitalist systems must unite on a transnational basis. The most important element of this cooperation is the involvement of labour representatives, whether western or southern, employed or marginal. However, there is no ideological framework from which such coalitions can be forcefully launched. This would first require the critical acceptance of capitalism as a possible mechanism for empowering labour. Naturally, this implies a rejection of both neoclassical and Marxist approaches. For the former, there is no need to empower labour; for the latter, the idea of empowering labour in order to defend capitalism is anathema.

As a result, I believe that the so-called capitalist world economy will increasingly devolve into a rent-based system managed by great powers. The sub-systems of this greater organism will probably be oriented, to greater or lesser degrees, to state-dominated structures. These will closely resemble the old tributary modes of production of the great Asian civilisations. I refer to these systems as modernised tributary modes of production, whereas others as feudalism (Varoufakis 2021).

The alternative would be the concerted empowerment of labour, which can be achieved through collective action. This would imply the abandonment of the Marxist distinction between bourgeois and socialist revolutions (Marx 1972 [1844]: 388). The empowerment of labour is the very factor which enables the bourgeois revolution, while the bourgeois revolution creates space for the empowerment of labour.

2. The peculiarities of profit and the universality of rent

Profit is a form of surplus which is appropriated on an anonymous market under conditions of perfect competition (Kalecki 1942). Let us make the usual assumptions (i.e. a balanced government sector, balanced foreign trade, all wages, but only wages used for consumption goods purchases). Under these conditions, positive profits in consumption goods industries require a demand out of wages from another economic sector. These can only be wages paid in net investment goods production (for details, see Elsenhans 2021a, chap. 2, section 3). Capitalists get what they spend, and they are compelled to reduce unit costs (Bortkiewicz 1907: 455-459). Consequently, the only investments that increase total demand for labour are those triggered by expanding demand, demand for new products that do not replace old products, or defensive investment in technologies. These become competitive only in case of increasing wages, because they aim to save on increasingly expensive labour by using more advanced technologies. These more capital-intensive technologies would not have been competitive at lower labour costs. Other investments are rationalisating costs that reduce total income paid in relation to total production.

Capitalist investment that does not reduce the demand for labour thus depends on rising labour incomes. I disagree here with Kalecki here, and instead follow Rosa Luxemburg (1951 [1912]: 104) in arguing that capitalists cannot unilaterally increase their consumption. This would render them uncompetitive. They cannot replace mass consumption, which must rise if capitalists want to continue accumulating. I thus conclude that capitalist growth depends on rising mass incomes (Elsenhans 1983c, 2021a: chap. 2, section 2, and chapter 3 in this volume).

I do not argue that capitalists perceive this interest in raising mass incomes and proceed to raise the incomes of workers. This is not necessary, assuming that labour is empowered and able to impose higher wages in line with productivity (and terms of trade) increases. It suffices if labour follows its own most immediate interests. Empowerment of labour results from its scarcity, hence its capacity to organise and to resist domination by the bearers of mainstream economic ideas.

Empowerment of labour is an important consequence for the structure of the system of relative prices. With scarcity of labour, wages rise all across the economy at the rate of the growth of average productivity, not at the rate of growth of the specific form of employment (Salter 1960: 161). Hairdressers' wages increase because, otherwise, hairdressers will find jobs in car factories, where productivity increases are higher and companies are willing to pay higher wages. If we want to continue to have our hair cut, the only solution is to raise the price of labour in haircutting, even if there is no increase in productivity in this particular branch.

The monetary product sought by capitalist investors thus converges, despite increases in physical productivity being chaotically different. This convergence is called structural homogeneity; it is realised by changes in relative prices (see below chap. 3)

In non-developing economics, the lags in productivity differ in relation to developed economies. This is called structural heterogeneity (Amin 1973: 188; Nohlen/Sturm 1982: 99). Substituting imports in lagging behind activities appears as costly and is economically possible only if such productions are subsidised or massively protected. Activities with low backwardness appear remunerative and have the potential to become leading export branches. Normally, however, these do not transform the rest of the economy. This is because such products have low price and income elasticities on the world market, much like older products or raw materials.

The Global South's lag in agricultural raw materials has always been relatively limited, because such products cannot be produced to the same degree under the climatic conditions of the industrial West. In mineral products, the Global South became competitive when (originally rich) deposits near the centres of industrial production in the West were exhausted. Because of decreasing transport costs, it was possible to tap the still-rich deposits of the unexploited regions of the—by definition, non-industrialised—South.

In case of low price elasticity of demand, the seller can increase his total sales by limiting supply. This is the basis of all attempts to limit supply, from associations of landowners to marketing boards and international raw material cartels. Indeed, the marketing boards of the late colonial period indicate the existence of rents (Cooper 2002: 22 ff.). By tapping undeveloped mineral deposits from the Global South, owners were able to charge the same price as high-cost marginal producers in the global West. The condition for this was that production in the West was necessary to satisfy total solvable demand. Producers with richer deposits earn an additional income beyond profit at an average rate and their different costs of production. This is, in effect, a mineral rent.

The collapse of the Eastern Bloc rendered the West insensitive to the argument that the South might withhold raw materials (beyond the key area of oil). Rent from raw materials mostly disappeared. Raw material-rich countries were compelled to follow raw material-poor countries (for example the Asian tigers) by engaging in manufacturing exports. With the disappearance of rent in raw materials, many countries found that their comparative cost advantage in raw materials simply disappeared. They were required to specialise in labour-intensive exports initially, which was entirely in keeping with neoclassical foreign trade theory.

The prospect of rent appropriation emerged here as well. Rent in raw material exports is only a special case of the effects of unequal specialization on technically lagging economies. The new export products also had very low price elasticities on the world market. Exporting countries saw the attraction of increasing prices in order to finance diversification into new activities. These new activities were less intensive in unskilled labour, but they could, if initially subsidised, contribute to further growth of production, export and employment. The most obvious case is Singapore's taxing of enterprises with low per capita wages. This revenue was used for skill formation in technically more demanding lines of production (Holtgrave 1987: 74 f.). Local content rules imposed on multinational affiliates are merely another form of rent appropriation,with relatively automatic channelling into not-yet competitive activities.[1]

Underdeveloped countries suffer from structural heterogeneity, but they nevertheless perpetuate it. Singer (1950: 482) has already criticised the tendency of underdeveloped countries to divert export earnings into diversification during economic booms as a waste of resources, and as an attempt to invent something that already exists. Lewis (1978: 13), however, demonstrates that the vulnerability of export earnings among non-developing economies is due to their lack of productivity increases in non-exporting activities. These activities provide a safety net to which they can turn if export prices should fall.

Rents are available for investment in diversification. Given the dominance of world market prices for assessing profitability, such investments are not profitable for an individual entrepreneur. The channelling of rent into not-yet-profitable activities requires the intervention of a non-market controlled agent, or some kind of state structure.

Rent is a form of surplus that is appropriated on the basis of natural or politically created market imperfections or open political power. Historically, this has been the dominant form of surplus. For its appropriation, there is no need for reinvestment in productivity increases, because productivity increases are of no direct concern to the gatekeeper of rent. Given the limits to diversification under the conditions of unequal specialisation, rent is both a chance and a danger. It can be used for investing in employment and skill creating activities, even if these are not currently profitable. That said, there is no microeconomic mechanism that guarantees such use of rent.

3. Failure to transform rent without simultaneous bourgeois and socialist revolutions

The victorious anti-colonial forces that won independence after World War II were immediately confronted with structurally heterogeneous economies. From the early nineteenth century, these anti-colonial forces had linked economic backwardness with the withdrawal of surplus by the colonial powers. This exploitation had purportedly deprived their economies of the necessary financial resources for investing in technical innovation and industrial growth.[2] This argument seemed to be substantiated by the world economic depression of the 1930s, when incomes in the Global South were halved due to the decline of raw material prices (and not so much because of quantities of raw materials exported, Singer 1949: 18 f.).

The discourse on imperialist exploitation was reflected by the conviction that overcoming underdevelopment required additional financial resources. These, it was believed, could be drawn partly from the big landowners. Ultimately, however, most of these resources had to be drawn from rising raw material prices and the appropriation of differential rents taken by Western mining companies.

During the Cold War, these anti-colonial programs were partially successful, especially with respect to oil prices. However, nationalisations of other raw material concessions and differential rents were less successful,[3] while consumer rents appropriated on the basis of agricultural raw materials must be judged to have failed. "Investing" in industries had to deal with existing, but overall narrow, markets for advanced industrial products, as well as inexistent and not very dynamic markets for mass consumption goods because of the generalised poverty of the populations of these countries.[4] The spill overs from such market constrained industries into local production of investment goods industries buyers proved to be minimal. Investment goods for the high-income industries were too complicated, and investment goods for mass consumption goods industries were suffering from the absence of economies of scale in these mass consumption goods industries. Profit was not created on the basis of local investment goods spending, as it is in capitalist systems. In these countries, both high-income goods industries and mass-consumption industries were undynamic. Because of high incomes from raw material production, the exchange rates were still high. Given the general restrictions for productivity growth, this explains the cost of locally produced industrial products.

Profit, due to structural heterogeneity, could not be a guide for selecting those investments that would allow for an economic restructuring in order to fulfil rising mass incomes on the basis of local technology production. State appropriation of surplus as rent led to the emergence of a somewhat privileged class—a state class (Elsenhans 1996b: 173-254, and ahead in this book's chap. 3). This class quickly proved that there is nothing inevitable about the emergence of a traditionally progressive bourgeoisie. This should not have come as a surprise—historically, bourgeois progressivism owed to the fact that the bourgeoisie was controlled by the market. As a result, it was required to invest in projects for which there was a demand in society (though, admittedly, a demand which frequently emanated from privileged social groups).

The appropriation of rent and its allocation to investment projects are dependent on political structures, and on the ability to acquire influence within these structures. Needless to say, these structures are not subject to the laws of the market. Their protagonists are driven by the desire for power, prestige or resources—and not by the desire to achieve efficiency in satisfying mass needs for consumable material products, as would be the case in a market-dominated system.

The places where such structures have historically dominated have given rise to a particular type of productive apparatus. This did not develop the necessary dynamism in terms of generating the capacity to produce local investment goods. The process of accumulation remained dependent on technology imports. The emerging industry did not earn foreign exchange; it lived on the foreign exchange still earned by the raw material exporting sector (Bruton 1998: 919; Felix 1969: 277). The internal embeddedness of the state-promoted industry did not substantially modify the pattern of integration of these economies into the international system. When the rents from raw material exports disappeared, there ensued an inevitable crisis in the import-substituting industrialisation that had been promoted by the state class.

This lack of dynamism in internal production is due to the existence of marginality. Underdeveloped countries are characterised by the fact that certain sections of their labour forces produce less than is required for their survival (i.e. a labour surplus) (Lewis 1954). This is due to diminishing returns in agriculture, as well as increased labour involvement without technical innovation. Standard development theory has linked the emergence of marginal labour to demographic growth. Famines are a permanently recurring crisis in all pre-capitalist societies. They indicate that marginality is not specific to the Third World. British history is characterised by constant state intervention in order to remove the manifestations of marginality—that is, to shed marginal labour. The English poor laws were a major instrument for achieving this (Elsenhans 1992a).

In the Global South, the distribution of comparative advantage and the inefficiencies of the newly launched industries apparently pointed to one solution. This was due to the economy's ongoing shift towards exporting manufactured products. Indeed, this is the entire story of export-oriented manufacturing, which began in East Asia with the tiger economies of Singapore, Hong Kong, Taiwan and South Korea. Neoclassical economics generally hails this as a victory of capitalism over state-led development, of profit over rent. However, export-oriented manufacturing is a variant of rent-based economic development. To be sure, it has proven more successful than import-substituting industrialisation. Nonetheless, it is still essentially based on the capacity to generate rent locally (Elsenhans 2021a: chap. 5, section 4, 2001b).

At first glance, it appears that success is dependent on cheap labour. This translates into real wages that are less than one-twentieth of those earned by average workers in the developed countries. Nobody in the developed countries could survive with a wage that is one-tenth those of an average worker in these countries. Consequently, the purchasing power of such a wage in the production sites of the Global South must be higher than its purchasing power in an industrial country. This is evident from the many statistics on the difference between per capita income at the exchange rate and per capita income in purchasing power parity.

When we compare developed countries to one another, this difference is fairly marginal. Ultimately, exchange rates reflect purchasing power parity. Should the products cost less in one country than in another, the cheaper country would export them to the first country and, ultimately, to the world market.

It has been shown that the purchasing power of the wage of an average Beijing household is between six and ten times as high as it is in a Canadian supermarket (Chen/Gordon/Zhiming 1994). If labour incomes have higher purchasing power on the local market than on the world market, then additional workers—including additional export workers—obviously cannot buy as much on the world market as they can on the local market. There must be a locally provided surplus that cannot be exported. The difference in real wages between industrially leading economies and real wages in the low labour cost production sites of the Global South is about six to one (Lafay 1996: 948; Strack/Helmschrott/Schönherr 1997). This is not considerably higher than the differences observed in the late nineteenth century between Mumbai and British textile workers (Lokanathan 1935: 358; Morris 1965: 22).

As a result, the new competitiveness of labour in the Global South is not the result of lower real wages. It derives from the capacity of these economies to devalue their currencies below purchasing power parity (Elsenhans 1996a). At low levels of mass incomes, the most important item is food, which is between 40% and 60% of household spending.[5] Other items include housing, textiles, traditional household equipment, various items like cigarettes and bus tickets, and some modern products such as refrigerators, TVs, cookers, and probably cell phones also. Each of these categories represents about 10% of total spending, or about 20%

of non-food spending (Lembke 1980: 173; Meo/Jambes/Guerrero 1985: 56). Most of these products, including the modern items, are produced locally in most of the underdeveloped countries, though not in sub-Saharan Africa.

Despite their high price in foreign exchange, there is only one good reason for reserving these products for local consumption: export difficulties. The blockage of food exports is thus a central condition. Transport costs, market regulations with public distribution systems, but also outright government monopolies on the international food trade may be relevant mechanisms here. Many industrial products, such as housing, cannot be exported. Similarly, the qualities of most industrial mass consumption goods are adjusted to the preferences of poor households, so these cannot be exported.

Preventing food producers from selling their products abroad at higher world market prices implies extracting an income from agricultural producers. If they had access to the work market, or if they had been permitted to engage in cash crop production, then agricultural producers would have earned this income for themselves. High prices for cash crops comprised a major incentive for farmers in many underdeveloped countries. Consequently, they produced food only for their own household needs. It offered an alternative to increasing food production for the internal market.

The cheap international price of labour in the exporting countries is the result of the success of the Green Revolution. This raised yields per hectare to more than 300% of the yields achieved in the immediate aftermath of World War II.[6] A rent generated in local wage goods production subsidises additional labour employed in export production. At best, a country endowed with thriving agriculture and a dynamic informal sector can devalue below purchasing power parity to levels where proceeds from exports cover the cost of imported equipment and inputs.

In neoclassical terms, this is unwise. There is no reason to employ labour which does not add to national wealth. In Marxist terms, this is exploitation. It contributes to the flight of labour value, which is subsequently unavailable for accumulation. According to my model, this is an efficient instrument for bringing labour into employment and creating mass incomes. At a low exchange rate, this may trigger local production of investment goods, especially of "appropriate technology". Employing people in manufacturing also constitutes an accumulation in skills, even if the respective activities are of a low-skilled nature. East Asia has shown that transforming textile workers into producers of electronic parts is easier then achieving the same result by merely mobilising rural labour.

The limits to devaluation-driven manufacturing exports, thus, lie in the exhaustion of the agricultural surplus and a consequent return to famines, and in the absorption of marginal labour (Elsenhans 2000b: 29, 2002: 67-73). The higher the multipliers of additional incomes created in the export sector in the wake of reasonably increasing mass incomes, the higher the multiplier in the domestic market-oriented lines of production. Historically, those economies which succeeded in exploiting manufactured exports for growth all engaged in land redistribution. This resulted in the allocation of agricultural rents to small farmer households, which increased their production by supplying previously marginal work to their farms.[7] This added to production, at a proportionally lower level than the additional labour effort.

As in the case of import substitution, successful export orientation is linked to rising mass incomes without previous empowerment of labour. This is due to previously existing marginality. This empowerment explains the triggering of internal market-oriented industries through increasing incomes in the export sector.

It is precisely these multiplier effects which lead to full employment. But exchange rates may be still too high for these to be achieved, and the demand originating from additional employment in manufacturing exports is too low for launching internal demand to a sufficient degree.

From the perspective of competitiveness, the exchange rate is more important than real wages. For this reason, the Western polemic against cheap labour from China, Vietnam and the rest of the Global South is misguided. The challenge would be obviated if one of two conditions were met: either the agricultural surplus is eliminated (with a return to periodic famines), or marginal labour is absorbed by the growing industrial sector.

The only politically viable solution is thus the absorption of marginal labour into the export-oriented and local market-oriented manufacturing countries. Before this outcome can be achieved, however, the Global South can devalue, while the West cannot counteract through wage restraint.

4. Rent travels West

From a global perspective, the South does not experience growth due to export surpluses in trade with the West (with China an obvious and notable exception). In fact, the West does not have a balance of trade deficit with the South (again, with the notable exception of the United States). The Global South, on the other hand, replaces industrial processes that draw on labour with relatively high purchasing power for production processes that require labour with relatively low purchasing power. Moreover, the South does this *without* the effect of employment growth compensating the loss of purchasing power in the West. Based on the cheapening of previously expensive products, the export offensive of the Global South does not lead to foreign trade surpluses which would impose currency appreciations. In addition, China exports its capital globally. Beijing clearly anticipates that the Yuan will eventually appreciate, implying that the value of exported currency will decline anyway (Faujas 2008: 2; Yang 2012: 125). The West benefits from improving terms of trade and can expect further benefits from a decline in the value of debt contracted with China.

I have argued here that capitalism depends on expanding demand and not on the availability of appropriated surplus. In keeping with this argument, the West concentrates on the employment effects of these processes.

Technical progress is not capital intensive but skill dependent. Consequently, a higher availability of physical capital does not protect Western industry. In some industries, catching up in skills provides production sites in the Global South with comparative advantage, despite their continued lagging in technical terms. This is unproblematic, provided that they lag less than the average of their production. Comparative advantage does not imply that the leading country specialises in the new leading technologies, but rather that the leading country specialises in those products in which it has the most dominance.

If productivity depends on learning by doing, then an established, technically leading economy possesses considerable advantages in terms of production lines in which newly emerging economies have never engaged. If a totally new technology emerges, then the established, technically leading economies will inevitably be superior in producing it. However, if the established economy is unable to entirely transfer the productivity advances from the old leading technology to the new emerging technology, then its productivity advances in this new field will be lower than its productivity advances in the older technology. Despite its relative inferiority, the emerging economy has comparative advantage in the new leading technology. Germany specialises in luxury cars and machinery, but it has comparative disadvantage in new micro-electronic industries. The rise of East Asia is not linked to its superiority in these new industries, but to its relatively lower lag in these when compared with older technologies (Elsenhans 2020a, b, c).

In a nutshell, the leading industrial countries are superior to developing economies in both old and new technologies but, because they are *considerably* superior in old technologies, they tend to specialise in these. Conversely, developing economies tend to specialise in new technologies because here their inferiority is less marked. The established countries react to this configuration of comparative advantage with three principal strategies.

The first of these strategies involves tightening belts and keeping wages below productivity increases. Obviously, this has no impact on comparative advantage. The only result is that productivity growth comes to outstrip production growth (Erber/Hagemann 2012: 39; OECD 2018: 21). This is the standard configuration for under consumptionist crises and it largely explains sluggish growth in the West.

The second strategy comprises an attempted mitigation of the consequences of lacking demand, usually as part of an attempt to preserve mass income expansion. This is achieved by diverting resources from highly competitive production lines in order to subsidise labour thathas been out competed on the labour market. This is the basis for Rodrik's (2008) argument about globalisation being accompanied by increasing tax shares, and thus by state intervention.

It is not unskilled labour that is out competed by the Global South, but rather middle-income industrial labour. This group then out competes unskilled labour in production lines where their skills constitute a competitive advantage, even if they are not permanently required (Laaser/ Schrader 2009: 199).

A third strategy consists in the promotion of industries that are so complex that they appear immune from the threat of being transferred to low-wage production sites in the South at the rates of devaluation that the Global South could support. The use of this strategy accounts for the re-emergence of industrial policy in the West.

All of this amounts to the disestablishment of a key mechanism of a functioning capitalist system; labour's capacity to defend its position on the market on the basis of its scarcity. This market mechanism is increasingly being replaced by a purely political structure. To a greater or lesser degree, this structure takes care of labour (and is pressured by labour to do so). And yet this arrangement effectively entails that labour accepts the patronising solicitude of the powers that be. One of these powers is capital, which always has the option of moving its production sites to the Global South. In this system, capital thus has greater negotiating power than labour. The latter can kick and scream but it can't walk away from the negotiating table. In fact, precisely this constellation confronted labour in the tributary modes of ancient Asian civilisations, including those presided over by "benevolent emperors".

Green growth may imply enhanced state spending and justify an increasing role for the state in demand creation. Moreover, however, such growth may be linked to declining capital productivity. This is because it excludes environmentally unfriendly technologies with high capital productivity. It may imply rising complementary productions in order to compensate pollution (Elsenhans 2020d). It may also support profit by demand expansion and triggering net investment spending.

At the political level, green growth weakens the mechanism of labour being able to impose its income increases because of its scarcity without acquiring ideological hegemony in the explanation of capitalist growth. Green growth requires political decision-making and, thus, political organisation around more complex agendas than an exclusive focus on the struggles of labour might allow for. Indeed, the more complex the agenda of political organisations, the greater the danger that the "iron law of the oligarchy" (Michels 1925: 182) will come into operation.

5. The danger of a rent-based international system

The international system is increasingly determined by three characteristics. The first is the profound weakness of labour. This is intensified by globalisation and the new competitiveness of labour in marginality-ridden economies. The availability of rent is the second characteristic. This provides the basis for a new alliance between the state and big companies, which benefit from rent-collecting opportunities due to market imperfections. The third characteristic is the persistent jockeying of these public-private coalitions for the accomplishment of technical superiority. All the while, the market exerts ever weaker control over profit rates and political protection.

In such a configuration, what matters are big power bases, big internal markets and being first. Many important technology development programmes are conceived for security and prestige purposes. Space technologies are one example. Many nominally market-oriented technologies have important security implications: this is the case for infrastructures in communication. The cost of new technology can be spread over large production batches if there are large internal markets on which products can be sold in large quantities. In this way, the sunk costs of developing the technology are reduced per unit of output. Developmental costs are swallowing up ever greater shares of budgets. Consequently, economies that have a protected infant market for new technologies can recover these costs more easily. This aspect is reinforced for companies that make it to the table first and are able to sell on the world market, still at high costs (Smiley/Ravid 1983). Late comers find themselves fighting a losing battle against pioneers who have already recovered a substantial share of their development costs and are able to lower prices in the wake of economies of scale.

To repeat, being first matters. And the state has a clear interest in supporting the efforts of domestic players in being first. There are resources for financing such support for private enterprises, provided that rents are available for a politically organised entity. There is an incentive to keep such entities free from too much bureaucratic control in order that they might expand, in the hope that this may contribute to their innovativeness. It would be difficult to deduce economic efficiency from the capacity of such projects to land on Mars, destroy asteroids, or create spatial surveying systems for planet earth. Such projects are not competing with each other economically. They are selected politically, even if ostensibly economic arguments are advanced in order to justify their existence. They represent the superior unity of the community, like the expensive but economically superfluous religious monuments of the old tributary modes of production (Marx 1973 [1857-1858]: 299).

As already mentioned, public programs for fighting climate change are based on similar decision-making mechanisms. Certainly, these projects may enjoy more—at least apparent—democratic legitimacy.

Economies become politicised, and economic processes can become politicised. This may even be desirable. But it is not capitalism. The empowerment of labour in capitalism may be replaced by highly participatory mechanisms of decision-making. It is highly doubtful, however, that these mechanisms will serve to integrate ordinary people to the same degree as can be accomplished by the market mechanisms of capitalism. A community of activists, a kind of secular priesthood, comes to assume the regulatory role of the organised masses, which once imposed rising mass incomes under capitalist conditions.

Activists—or at least, rational activists—mobilise for interests shared by human beings from a range of diverse social categories. They do not generally defend narrow class interests. Even if they do restrict themselves to defending the interests of closely circumscribed groups, they present these interests as communal in nature. They address the public space as it is currently organised. In the twenty-first century, this means nations as lawmakers which operate within territorially circumscribed frameworks. Even when activists address themselves to nominally global interests, they invariably bring their pressure to bear on national governments. Activists thus need the state, either as a purveyor of norms or as an institution that is able to launch the diffusion of norms on a global scale.

Irrespective of the level of globalisation—that is, of the degree of international interaction—states remain the essential constituents of the system. The instruments by which states integrate individuals into a (state-supporting) human community also remain crucial. These instruments include feelings of identity and belonging, which can take the form of more or less exclusionary forms of nationalism. If these identity-creating discourses are exclusivist, then a tendency toward separatism may emerge within the territories controlled by the state. China's minorities are a striking contemporary example. Conversely, the Indian discourse on national unity is more inclusive, because it defines Indian identity less precisely.

The basic traits of this international state system will be left untouched by globalisation. Historically, some territorial spaces have inherited small states, whereas others have inherited large states. As long as the rent distributing programme of the state do not fundamentally discriminate against territorially circumscribed minorities, then separatism on the basis of material interests is unlikely to emerge. However, separatist tendencies may be strengthened if rent is based on sub-state regions as in the case of regionally restricted "ethnic nationalisms".

The race for rent appropriation and rent-based technology promotion favours larger territorial units with large internal markets. With the exception of the GAFA, the world market seems to present no qualitatively higher opportunity to benefit from economies of scale in introducing new technologies in comparison to the large regional markets, such as the United States or the European Union. China will soon reach this level, and other powerful large states may emulate them, like Brazil or perhaps Russia. Economically weaker states will be more reliant on state-driven rent appropriation than those that are economically more powerful, either because of their technical development or because of the dynamism of the internal market. However, all states will endeavour to complement their internal markets by exports.

If leading states are characterised by relatively homogeneous labour markets with a tendency to average wages, they will experience excessively high costs on the basis of their exchange rates in a large variety of productions. Due to high exports of high-technology products, their exchange rates are too high for these productions. If states are unable to disperse their wages so that salaries in lagging branches correspond to wages in technically lagging economies, then even leading states will engage in protectionist policies.

The system will be characterised by the simultaneous pursuit of contradictory policies. On the one hand, there will be an attempt to keep the world economy open for additional exports, especially in high-technology productions. States, on the other hand, will engage in limited protectionism in order to maintain domestically acceptable levels of employment. Trumpism, then, was not based on the whims of an unhinged president; it quite accurately reflected the position of the United States within the international division of labour. So too is China's combination of commitment to worldwide free trade coupled with state promotion of catching up in high technology. Increased emphasis on industrial policy within the EU may also be mentioned here.

In this setup, labour no longer appears as a progressive force for rendering capitalism dynamic, especially through the extension of the internal market for leading technologies. Instead, labour becomes a reactionary force, committed to the defence of parochial interests in economically inefficient branches of production.

Such a system will appear as a mildly open world economy. However, this openness will result from inter-state negotiations; it will not arise naturally from unfettered economic patterns. Politically, it will resemble the kind of balance of power system that came into being after the Napoleonic Wars (Elsenhans 2019).

Smaller states have to accommodate regional powers. However, the sovereignty of these small states allows them to attract support from sources other than the major powers. This will be successful if a hegemonic regional power acquires decisive relative advantages in relation to other major powers with respect to the domination of smaller states in their "spheres of influence". Smaller powers will therefore not give up their sovereignty. In a similar kind of system, the German principalities were able to maintain their sovereignty in the face of Prussian designs until 1866.

Internally, the major basis for conflict within both the major and the smaller powers will be nationalism. This will be combined with a discourse on moral economy, advanced as a justification for a limited degree of inequality between the middle classes and labour. At all times, the aim will be to support the incomes from which investment is financed in order to maintain international competitiveness. China's notion of "harmonious development" is an appropriate moniker for such an approach. This discourse gains in currency precisely because high inequality results from the weakness of capitalist structures (i.e. the lack of empowerment of labour). Developed countries will increasingly pursue similar courses as they, too, witness a weakening of their capitalist mechanisms.

I call such structures modernised tributary modes of production. Like the ancient tributary modes of production, they subscribe to a basically organic view of society. Such a view represses class organisation and class consciousness; it locates the lower orders according to the Prussian principle of "to everybody their due" and permits a degree of social mobility. This prevents potential climbers from engaging in potentially disruptive class-based organisation. This system is distinguished from old tributary modes of production because of its orientation toward technical rivalry. The uneconomical architectural or cultural monuments which Marx (1973 [1857-58]: 299 f.) identified as features of the ancient period are replaced by equally uneconomical technical achievements.

There is no large coalition in place to counter such developments. Such a coalition would have to be transnational, and it would have to guarantee access to the markets of the leading economies. This would enable catching-up economies to rapidly overcome marginality and become capitalist through empowerment of labour. The elements for such a transnational coalition are highly heterogeneous: they would presumably comprise the reformist Western working classes and the marginalised of the Global South. Whether the latter are exploited in sweatshop production facilities or merely excluded from the economy entirely is immaterial. These forces remain nation-state oriented. In the developed world, this orientation results from their need for some state protection, either from the rapacity of the world market or in the form of social benefits.

These forces may have been committed to secular nationalism in the Global South in the wake of the victory of an anti-fascist coalition in World War I (Ahmad 2008: 33 f.). Despite their political victory in freeing their countries from formal or informal colonial dependency, secular nationalists were unable to create the material conditions for integrating marginal elements. The latter thus turned either to the state, which was capable of pacifying them with material benefits, or to new cultural-identitarian movements, which promise not just material benefits but also a kind of particularistic dignity.

It thus seems safe to assume that the tendency towards the generalisation of modernised tributary modes of production is unavoidable. Any change in the course of history would necessitate a change in the discourses of political economy. These are needed in order to equip those forces that are open to an alternative course of history. They must be provided with a vision of the capitalist system's mode of operation. Given the existing situation, the task of the intellectual is to provide this ideological weaponry, rather than to become embroiled in political activism.

A central point of departure must be an end to the demonisation of capitalism. Marx's distinction between bourgeois and social revolutions must be overcome (Marx 1972 [1844]: 388). The bourgeois revolution did not lead to a worsening of the position of labour. There are debates about exactly when real wage increases got underway in Britain. However, when Engels (1972 [1845]) wrote "The Condition of the Working Class in England," they were certainly rising.[8] Whether the real living conditions of the working classes also improved is a different issue. Deteriorating working conditions may well be accompanied by the capitalist mechanism of rising mass incomes as a condition for profit and capitalist growth.

Rising mass incomes are not a threat to profit. Labour can redistribute rents, but it cannot redistribute the part of surplus that capitalists appropriate as profit by spending on net investment. Nor do rising mass incomes constitute a threat to international competitiveness, because international competitiveness depends on exchange rates. The pursuit of a vanguard position in capitalist development can only achieve temporary results. Certainly, economies—and especially those with large international markets—may enjoy productivity increases beyond those of their competitors. But their competitors can catch up through learning, and they can do so with low exchange rates that render them competitive with the leading economy. Furthermore, there is no definite falling behind if there is no marginal labour which prevents average labour from participating in productivity increases. In this way, labour contributes to the dynamic enlargement of internal markets.

But all this entails an acceptance of capitalism as an inherently progressive mode of production. In the last twenty years, labour opposed capitalism not because of insufficiently high wage increases and growing job losses, but because of the rent-oriented character of capitalist conduct. It is typical for middle-income critics of capitalism to point to "alienation" from the true meaning of human existence as the principal flaw of the system. However, this critique has never been widely shared by labour itself. This was well demonstrated by the fundamental opposition between the old and new lefts during the student movements of 1968.[9]

The reproach has been made that labour is incapable of mustering anything more than bread and butter strategies. This intentionally negates the fact that integration into any economy may provide satisfaction, but it does not constitute the realisation of some kind of transcendent human destiny. Profound harmony in one's own existence can be facilitated by the absence of material worries—but it does not guarantee it. Perhaps, in the future, young people will perceive the (short?) historical lifespan of capitalism as an exciting period, one which was open for innovative opportunities. Their elders will surely privilege the private harmony they have been able to achieve within the inegalitarian but stable structures of the modernised tributary modes of production.

Notes

1. Hodara 1985: 5-11; Posthuma 1995: 3 f.; Sherry 2013.
2. Digby 1901: 33, 222; Limaye 1989: 26; Dutt 1970 [1949]: 111.
3. Krasner 1977: 669; Wälde 1983: 240 f.; Sideri/Johns 1980.
4. Boeckh 2002: 523; Furtado 1965: 170; Ikonicoff 1973: 638.
5. China shows poor households (39% of all households) spending 47% on food and beverages against 36% in case of average households. The corresponding values for India show the lowest income households (84% of all households) spend 51% of their incomes on food and beverages as compared to average households spending 45% on food and beverages (World Bank 2020). Shares were higher 40 years ago.
6. Latin America yearly average 1948-1950: 1070 kg, Asia: 910 kg, Africa:730 kg, FAO 1955: 19. 2017-2018 Low and Middle Income Countries 2861 kg, China 3452 kg, India 3699 kg, World Bank, World Development Indicators.
7. Grabowski 2018: 359; Kay 2002: 1093; Shih 1968: 121.
8. Allen 2009: 2 and Passim; Mokyr 2009: 11; Vries 2008: 190.
9. Bantiguy 2008: 13; Bronfenbrenner 1970: 750; Denitch 1970: 44.

2

Equality and Development

The European Experience and Today's Underdeveloped World*

Several German scholars have developed a new approach to the debate on economic development. It consists in rewriting the economic history of the industrialised countries in order to identify guiding principles for new strategies aimed at overcoming underdevelopment.[1] This line of argumentation has been taken up by, among others, Dieter Senghaas (1982), who was initially close to dependency theory.[2]

The central argument of this approach can be summarised as follows: long-term economic growth is only possible if mass incomes increase. At the level of economic and social history, the approach is required to show that "primitive" accumulation in Europe and North America was not dependent on the immiseration of the local masses. At the level of historical relations between the developed West and the underdeveloped South, the approach is required to show that the exploitation of the Third World played only a marginal or negligible role in European and North American industrial development (without, of course, denying that such exploitation occurred on a massive scale).

Ultimately, this new approach aims to contribute to a reformulation of development strategies in the Third World. It attempts to operationalise

* Text published in French, slightly shortened: Elsenhans, Hartmut (1983): Égalité et développement. L'expérience européenne et le monde sous-développé d'aujourd'hui. In: *Cultures et développement* 15 (2), pp. 187-215.

these strategies under a specific historical condition: the coexistence of underdeveloped with more developed economies. The latter suffer from this situation but, under certain conditions, they may come to benefit from it. This remains so even if the reaction of the West is initially quite unfavourable from the perspective of economic development on the basis of mass consumption.

1. The historical specificity of the European experience: The difficult centralisation of the ruling class under European feudalism

Economic development can be defined as human's improving control over nature. The transition from hunter-gathering patterns of subsistence to settled agriculture was a critical first stage in this process. The increasing control over nature implies a gradual enhancement of productive forces. Even at a low level of economic development, this inevitably results in the production of a surplus. In low-productivity, communitarian modes of production, decisions over the allocation of worktime must account for the danger of unfavourable natural conditions of production. These might include, for example, uncertain and unstable weather. In order to guarantee survival, cautious producers will engage more worktime than is necessary for subsistence under average conditions. These producers cannot be sure that such conditions will prevail during the coming cycle of production.

Such processes thus result in a surplus. The appropriation of this surplus by a small group is always possible. In early agricultural societies, the struggle against social stratification comprised the periodic destruction of the surplus in order to prevent its appropriation. In such societies, where control over nature is unsophisticated, magic becomes important. But magic, too, favours the emergence of stratified social structures (Junge 1980: 190). These structures are reinforced by multiple mechanisms, such as long-distance trade, migratory movements and conquest. The appropriation of surplus is accomplished according to particular religious, political or military mechanisms. This is also true forlong-distance trade (where the monopolistic control of trade routes becomes important).

In this way, the development of productive forces also marks the genesis of dominant social classes and social stratification. This is evident from the difference between African "feudalism" and European feudalism.[3] Historically, African feudalism was linked to social differentiation and a more intensive centralisation of political and economic powers. This partly explains the transition from communitarian to tributary modes of production. Under the second system, centralised state classes squeeze peasant communities. Tributary modes of production also evince secondary characteristics, such as big public works projects (Wittfogel 1931: 415-455, 1969) as well as private property, in contrast to communitarian landholding (Tökei 1982: 299 f.). In fact, Marx popularised this concept of communitarian landholding on the basis of a historical falsification undertaken by the administrators of the British East India company (Dumont 1970: 163).

Overall, the emergence of surplus is not difficult to explain. Nor is it particularly hard to comprehend the resultant transition to tributary modes of production dominated by centralised state classes. These systems were responsible for a considerable development of productive forces. However, they did not bring about an Industrial Revolution in any of the lands where they predominated.

Technical progress rests on the achievement of two separate goals: the production of highly sophisticated products, as against the reduction of necessary work time per unit produced of relatively standardised products. At the level of craft production, this difference is not immediately apparent. The skills and instruments of the craftsman allow for the production of both types of goods. However, handcrafted products in tributary modes of production fall into three categories: urban craft products for luxury consumption of the state classes, rural craft products, and craft products linked to raw materials (such as salt or saltpetre) (Gadgil 1971: 45-47; Ghosal 1966: 3-7). The very limited development of rural crafts indicates that, overall, technical progress was oriented mainly to the production of ever more elaborate goods. These were protected from competition. Craft products in Europe, however, were increasingly directed towards the consumption patterns of the middle and lower income classes.[4]

The transition to tributary modes of production with highly skewed income distributions represents the normal course of development for productive forces and social stratification. We might then ask why certain tributary systems do not take the next step and develop into full capitalist systems. However, this is not the most perplexing or urgent question. In fact, the absence of this transition constitutes the historical norm. The fundamental question is: why there are historical examples that deviate from this norm? Why do we see the emergence of pre-capitalist societies that have relatively developed productive forces but are not dominated by centralised state classes?

The European case is the exemplary anomaly here. Several factors have contributed to. Europe's peculiar course of development. First, although tributary modes of production did indeed emerge under the Roman Empire, they were disrupted or destroyed by "barbarian" invaders. These "Germanic tribes" evinced a low level of social stratification and placed a heavy emphasis on lineages, rather than state-bound hierarchies. Land changed hands in antiquity primarily as a result of commercial development and long-distance trade. Consequently, feudalism established the rights of feudal lords in relation to the central authorities. In Western Europe, the rivalry between secular and ecclesiastical sources of authority led to a conflict within the ruling class.

These three historical factors significantly restricted the centralisation of the European ruling classes, and hence their capacity to appropriate surplus. Feudalism alone did not constitute the sole specificity of Western European history, of course. However, it definitely posed a critical obstacle to the kind of ruling class centralisation seen in most other parts of the world, and which lay at the heart of tributary modes of production.

The historical fragmentation of Western European power gave rise to an artisanal sector oriented around the needs of dominated social classes. This sector was linked to a mercantilist bourgeoisie that was partially recruited from the lower nobility. These forces developed within the feudal system. Only later, and somewhat belatedly, did the central authorities of Western Europe make some attempts at engineering the kind of absolutism that was more firmly established elsewhere.

2. Mechanisation as a form of economic development based on the growth of mass incomes

Differences in the orientation of technical progress become visible with the emergence of "industrial", machine-based production processes. Machines are only useful for repetitive steps. This explains the production of standardised goods, whose quality is initially quite low. If there is a growing market for average quality goods, then machines can be used. This also means that a significant share of final demand must be taken up by low-income classes. If a given society lacks the existence of such a mass market, then intellectual activity in that society is unlikely to be focused towards the invention of new machines.

In physical terms, accumulation of capital comprises the construction of machines. The need to shelter such machines even accounts for the construction of industrial buildings. Machines, and especially newer machines, are only built if unit costs of production decrease (Elsenhans 1981a: 152-158, b: 15-18). Otherwise, new technology is simply not profitable. New technologies diminish overall incomes at constant wages and average profit rates. There is a reduction in the purchasing power of workers (Bortkiewicz 1907). Rosa Luxemburg (1951 [1912]: 105 f.) showed that other social classes cannot compensate for the deficit of final demand. Emmanuel (1982: 168),[5] however, claims that this deficit can be compensated by rising investment spending, thereby launching growth based solely on increasing investment goods production. Any new investment creates new productive capacities. However, intermediate demand for investment goods can only temporarily absorb the deficit in final demand for consumption goods. Growth based uniquely on increasing investment goods production requires totally unrealistic growth rates of labour productivity or declining capital productivity.[6]

At a theoretical level, Pasinetti (1974: 138) has shown the necessity of a relatively stable relation between fixed capital and production. This excludes growth based exclusively on the production of investment goods. The history of developed capitalist countries shows relatively stable—or even declining—capital output ratios in the industrial sector.[7] Even Marxist authors have arrived at this conclusion (Gillman 1965: 159).

Thus, mechanisation requires a relatively equal distribution of incomes. Its expansion requires increasing mass incomes.

3. The Industrial Revolution in Britain

The Industrial Revolution in Britain, just as in Europe, confirms the link between industrial development and rising mass incomes. Here, we see no evidence of primitive accumulation. This would have entailed either capital concentration or mass impoverishment. The eighteenth century enclosures[8] were based on expanding labour absorbing food production, not on labour shedding wool production. Food production required additional labour. This was also true for labour-intensive investments in agriculture. Until the early nineteenth century, labour in British agriculture was increasing. Food production increased more rapidly than demographic growth. Both developments contradict the argument about the impoverishment of the British rural masses. To be sure, land concentration happened, but this was only after 1680. Marx was highly critical of the societal consequences of this process, which included rural unemployment and impoverishment. On the whole, however, this transpired only in the peripheral zones of Britain.

Moreover, the poor laws enacted from the end of the sixteenth century do not indicate mass impoverishment. In fact, they point to income redistribution (Elsenhans 1992a [1980], 1981b: 28-31). These laws required parishes to guarantee the subsistence of their poor inhabitants. In exchange, the poor were obligated to work. Farmers and other businesses paid wages that were too low to guarantee their minimum subsistence needs. The parishes made up the difference, naturally by taxing the rich. In an economy with low average productivity, marginal productivity may be lower than the cost of subsistence. In this case, maximum surplus is achieved at a level of employment that implies unemployment if the economy is organised along capitalist principles.

Georgescu-Roegen (1960: 33) warned of the dangers of a precocious introduction of capitalism.[9] Full employment in capitalist economies requires a minimum level of productive forces so that marginal product can be higher than the cost of subsistence. In Britain, this problem was tackled through redistributive measures. Landowners were taxed. The surplus drawn by landowners from their more "productive" workers was used to subsidise "less productive" workers. Total surplus diminished. The poor laws organised the decrease in surplus to the benefit of increasing popular consumption. They had the same result as we might expect from an egalitarian land reform. Such an undertaking necessarily diminishes marketable surplus in order to increase popular consumption. It would accept—at least temporarily—a decrease in labour productivity because of increasing worktime input in relation to output in agriculture.

Some writers have pointed to declining real wages since the sixteenth century and during the Industrial Revolution. These are based on urban salaries and food costs. However, these figures are not representative for the mass of the population (Woodward 1981; Thirsk 1978: 173). Their decline also reflects British agriculture's improving terms of trade. The masses were dependent on the produce of this sector. In fact, both Marx (1965 [1867]: 468) and Deane (1965: 30) identified the middle of the eighteenth century as a golden age for British rural labourers. Crafts (1980: 186), Flinn (1974: 405-409) and Tunzelmann (1979: 49) showed that, during the Industrial Revolution, real wages increased in England. Hartwell (1961, 1964) and Gilboy (1934a, b: 210-219) established the improving consumption of the English masses during the eighteenth century, while Davies (1973: 123-125) highlighted the end of food shortage and starvation. The core zone of the Industrial Revolution was the Midlands,[10] where the concentration of land was lowest and where mass incomes were relatively high, despite massive immigration into the region.[11]

Capital for industrial investment did not come from foreign trade, despite high profits in long-distance foreign trade. If the external sector did contribute materially to fixed capital formation, then we would expect one of two eventualities to obtain. First, British imports should have comprised mass consumption goods raw materials. This would have cheapened the production of (Marx's) variable capital, hence lowered wage costs. Alternatively, such imports should have comprised raw materials for the construction of (Marx's) constant capital, i.e. machines and raw materials for machine building (coal and iron ore). In fact, however, 70% of imports from Asia, Africa and South America, including the Caribbean, consisted of luxury consumption or amenities, such as sugar, coffee, cocoa, spices, china and luxury goods. Tea, and later on cotton, were the sole imported mass consumption goods.

These imports surely allowed the upper classes to satisfy their appetite for imported luxury goods. And certainly, this reduced the demand for British labour, which otherwise would have been employed in the production of such goods (Davey 1975: 44). But the explanatory power of these factors with respect to the origins of the Industrial Revolution in Britain is weak.

Furthermore, at this time, the markets of today's underdeveloped world were limited. The British economy was not particularly open in the eighteenth century (Bairoch 1969: 259). Of course, there is the statistical observation that overseas markets grew more rapidly than European markets. But this does not establish unequal specialisation between Britain and the underdeveloped world. The increasing share of all these markets in British exports is almost totally due to the growth of the North American market. This also explains the replacement of indirect exports to Latin America via Spain and Portugal.

As a result, there is little evidence that the Industrial Revolution in Britain was caused by colonial exploitation or impoverishment of the masses through "primitive" accumulation. In fact, primitive accumulation was never actually accomplished. Capital requirements for British industries were limited.

Big, state-owned manufacturing plants, the so-called manufacturies did not pave the way for industrialisation. They were a continental phenomenon. They were inefficient, and they had to be protected against competition from artisanal enterprises. They served as a source of income for the ruling classes of absolutist regimes.[12] In fact, industrial progress was promoted by small rural industries. These were in turn promoted by expanding mass markets, which were unfettered by the demands and restrictions of urban gilds.[13] Big financial capital from long-distance trade was largely absent from this process of innovation. It was mainly invested in safe assets, such as land. The demand for land allowed the British peasantry and lesser nobility to sell their land rights at good prices and invest the resulting earnings in more profitable industrial activities.

The concept of primitive accumulation loses all importance when we consider that any new technology reduces the unit costs of its products. In a medium-term perspective, problems of indivisibility and replacement periods can be neglected in a gradual process of investment. Let us take the entire period of production of a profitable technology, from its investment to its complete amortisation. During this timeframe, it uses less labour per unit of output in machine construction and in production of final products than the older technology it replaces. As productivity increases in the wake of innovations (and not only in industry), rising mass incomes guarantee sales of standardised and simple products. Labour required for the construction of machinery is automatically available because of the reduction of the final product's unit costs.

The Industrial Revolution, then, was not the consequence of an accumulation of financial capital in the wake of income concentration. In fact, it resulted from the expansion of mass consumption. This oriented technical progress to the achievement of decreasing unit costs for simple products of current consumption. The American miracle of the nineteenth century was to the result an early standardisation of consumer durables and machine simplification. This derived from the generalisation of such machines (Brady 1964: 180; Rosenberg 1969: 193).

4. The European economies as examples of catching up industrialisation in the work of Senghaas

In terms of the pattern of economic development described above, most of the countries of the Third World are rather badly positioned. Even before the colonial encroachments of the capitalist West, income distribution was highly inegalitarian. The bases of craftsmanship were relatively weak. Moreover, underdeveloped countries want to—and are able to—catch up their industrial backlog by benefiting from Western economic and technological experience. The rulers of these less developed countries assume that catching up can be accelerated through a deliberate policy of importing technology. This allows for certain developmental steps to be skipped.

Consequently, the link between economic development and mass consumption has to be adjusted. It must be tailored to economies which coexist with more advanced economies. The former are able to opt for a strategy of surplus maximisation in order to import Western know-how.

Senghaas (1982: 41-57)[14] tried to elaborate patterns of catching up development in an effort to identify possible strategies. He focused especially on the articulation between internal social and economic restructuring on the one hand, and opening to an external market on the other. He essayed a comparative analysis of continental European economies. This analysis explained European industrial development along similar lines to those postulated here. However, it further focused on the relationship within the world market between opening and delinking, stressing the importance of delinking.

Senghaas drew extensively on Ulrich Menzel's research on nineteenth century European industrialisation carried out by Ulrich Menzel. Based on this empirical foundation, he distinguished five developmental variants: disassociated development with internal dynamics (France, Germany, Austria, Belgium); associative development oriented to exports (Switzerland, Netherlands): associative-dissociative development (Scandinavian countries, countries of recent European settlement: Canada, Australia, New Zealand, but not the United States); dissociative development with state capitalism (Tsarist Russia, Japan); dissociative development with state socialism (Soviet Union, Eastern Europe after 1945); and newly industrialising countries.

Senghaas' typology creates more problems than it solves. He argues that the experience of small European countries is particularly important for the contemporary Third World, with its preponderance of small states. However, by invoking the international environment as an essential condition, he calls this exemplary case into question. He rightly insists on the context of economic expansion in Great Britain for associative development with export orientation. Scandinavian development is difficult to explain without accounting for the fact that up to 60% of the region's entire nineteenth century population rise, emigrated to the United States. This implies that labour market conditions on the American frontier had a certain influence on labour market conditions in the Scandinavian countries.[15]

Clearly, the countries of recent European settlement could not attract immigrants unless they could offer superior living conditions. Their natural conditions of production for mineral and agricultural raw materials were plainly better than in Europe. A differential rent could be distributed as mass income. Discussion of the Rothbarth-Habakkuk paradox (Rothbarth 1946: 383-390; Habakkuk 1962: 18) has tended to insist on this fact (Temin 1966: 285; David 1975: 88). If living conditions in the countries of the centre were relatively favourable for the masses, then it is highly unlikely that the countries of recent European settlement could have been populated without better living conditions. Incomes would have to be sufficiently high for creating important internal markets in which mass demand prevailed. And indeed, mass incomes in these countries were higher than in Great Britain. Labour costs were higher. Manufacturing had to be protected because technical advances were not as high as nature-bound productivities in raw material production. The essential condition for the associative/dissociative pattern was the existence of rich deposits and land in comparison to industrially more advanced countries.

It is highly unlikely that this condition will occur in densely populated regions. To a very large degree, the probability of fertile land and rich mineral deposits is a function of the surface of the country. It increases with the land/labour ratio. Most of the countries of the Third World lack the kind of emigration valve which existed in the Scandinavian countries of the nineteenth century. Moreover, no new surfaces are available, and there is no necessity to pay higher wages then in the centre.

Senghaas also offered an analysis of certain "capitalist" rentier economies, such as the southern slave states of the US. In this way, he approached the problem of rent. His reliance on economic modernisation theory is evident in his attribution of "irrationality" to latifundist structures. And yet, economies with high land concentration are characterised by investment. This is oriented to labour saving. Agriculture's export focus provides the highest rates of "profit" here (and, indeed, rent).

However, Senghaas neglects some analyses of rent. Benachenhou (1971), for example, concluded that both the damage caused by raw material richness and especially improving terms of trade constituted important causes of underdevelopment (Singer 1950: 484; Kenwood/ Lougheed 1971: 33). This reveals that some raw material rich countries suffered from blockage of their development process precisely because of their richness (Kindleberger 1961: 290; Mahajan 1960: 357-360). Indeed, this very tendency is still evident today, as in Norway and Great Britain after both began to export oil (Singh 1979: 206; Noreng 1980: 204-214.

The developmental trajectories of the Netherlands and Switzerland cannot be characterised without first considering their respective geographical predicaments. They were surrounded by fully developed or rapidly developing countries. It seems unlikely that labour conditions were very different in the smaller neighbours of large, developed countries. Similarly, the categorisation of Belgium as a case of dissociative development seems problematic. Senghaas points to two important factors here: the creation of an integrated network of railways, and the integration of the coal mining industry into the national economy. In the case of Belgium, railways were indispensable in giving rise to transit networks in coal production between the industrial centres of England, France and Germany. Moreover, the emerging Belgian railway network of 1870 was only 10% longer than Ireland's. The transformation of coal and iron ore only occurred locally during the nineteenth century. This was certainly not restricted to Belgium. No single nineteenth-century coal mining region became an enclave economy or turned to the export of raw materials. In fact, the really important factor here was the labour intensity of coal mining and iron production. This explains the absorption of surplus labour during the transition to capitalism.

Senghaas rightly supports Berrill's (1960: 356) argument on the dependence of the impact of raw material exports on the internal structure of the respective economies. However, Senghaas also suggests that processing raw materials locally could serve to improve the position of underdeveloped economies in the international division of labour. This is less convincing. Again, the expansion of the surrounding economies is crucial. Consider the respective developmental trajectories of Uruguay and Denmark. The latter could sell massive quantities of butter, cheese and ham to its British neighbours. Uruguay's export opportunities were somewhat less opulent.

Three of the developmental patterns identified by Senghaas are more thought-provoking. These are dissociative development with internal dynamism, dissociative development with state capitalism, and dissociative development with state socialism. In these patterns, Senghaas considers self-sustained growth to be much more important than externally triggered growth. Unhappily, the categorisation is only clear for forms of state socialism. I do not see common criteria for France, Austria and Germany, which are grouped under the category of dissociative development with internal dynamics. Even less clear is how they might be distinguished from Italy, Russia or Japan, which are grouped under the category of dissociative development with state capitalism.

In the first category, Germany offers the only successful case of catching-up industrialisation. It was the least protectionist of these countries. France and Austria on the other hand, had backlogs. An anomaly is presented here by the relative free trade policy of Prussia, which served as a political instrument for isolating Austria from the rest of Germany. According to Senghaas' theory, Prussian industries should have supported the inclusion of Austria into the customs union in order to expand the protected market. These dissociative elements in German development do not justify disassociation as a strategy of development. They only point to a limited dissociation, the limits and targets of which would have to be precisely defined. The manufacturing industries, which were the backbone of German economic development, were opposed to the type of customs taxes that protected agriculture and mining.

Surprisingly, there is no discussion of the characteristics of German protectionism. As early as the 1910s, Hilferding (1968 [1909]: 414-418)[16] showed that Germany gave priority to the promotion of the external growth of German industry (i.e., associate development). It did so by protecting the internal market, allowing German industry to earn monopoly profits and subsiding German exports. Webb (1980: 323-324) argued that this policy allowed Germany to sell internationally at lower prices than average costs. Ultimately, German heavy industry grew on the basis of a protected internal market and an external market that was at least partly conquered by dumping.

Senghaas categorises Japan alongside Tsarist Russia. This is precisely the same interpretation of the Japanese case advanced by American protagonists of modernisation theory. However, much Japanese research on Japanese economic history has insisted on relatively parallel developments in Japan and England.[17] Similar factors include favourable conditions for the peasantry, the emergence of an internal mass market, the initial importance of a network of small and middle enterprises, and the development of investment goods industries. By contrast, Russia neglected its agricultural sector, as well as an industrial network and the constitution of an internal technological basis. Japan shifted rapidly to exports—first of silk, then of manufactured goods, particularly textiles. As early as the 1920s, the Japanese were in a position to challenge European textile manufacturers on Asian markets. Between 1901/06 and 1926/29, Japan's external trade in manufactures increased by 139% (world trade increased by 35% during the same period). The growth of the production of Japanese manufactures compared to the growth of trade was 174% during this period, compared to a world average of 50.1%. It may be so that "Japan liberalised its external economic relations only after economic reconstruction following World War II" (like most OECD countries, Senghaas 1982: 51). Nonetheless, before the economic crisis of the 1930s,Japan was clearly more "associative" than most other industrial countries.

Senghaas's typology of contemporary developed economies does not have much explanatory power because of his concentration on foreign trade openness. He reiterates the importance of equality of income distribution for small and large economies. He shows that if small economies are enclosed between growth poles, they can dispense with dissociation or opt for weak dissociation. My argument regarding the harmful impact of a hidden rent applies to the regions of recent European settlement. It discourages industrial investment. In the case of today's raw material exporters, it can only be eliminated through currency devaluation. This is associated with taxing already competitive raw materials (Elsenhans 1981b: 57-63).

Above all, there is no proof for Senghaas' claim about the necessity of increasing state intervention in the economy in function of an increasing backlog, at least not with respect to the most advanced industrial countries (Gerschenkron 1962: 353; Menzel/Senghaas 1983: 87-88). He offers an analysis of dissociative development with state socialism. This, however, does not demonstrate the superiority of a state-directed strategy in the USSR under Stalin, or in the eastern bloc during the immediate post-war period. In the countries of "real existing socialism", a discussion of economic reforms became visible from the 1960s. This rather demonstrated the definitive exhaustion of the extensive growth model, and certainly not its character as an optimal solution.

However, the Soviet model demonstrates that growth can be promoted even without increasing mass consumption, provided that state instruments are sufficiently powerful and effective. There are certain parallels here with some countries of the Third World, such as India or Brazil. These economies have undertaken the necessary big push for import-substituting industrialisation. Obviously, they have not done so under the hammer and sickle.

Disassociation and intensification of state intervention have to be discussed in a more nuanced manner. Senghaas shows that both can promote development. He admits that they have to be transitory. But he does not give any indication of the optimal or necessary extent of state intervention. Nor does he relate these mechanisms to the fundamental mechanism of growth, i.e. the enlargement of internal mass markets. This could have shown that dissociation can lead directly to underdevelopment by creating rent for privileged classes. As certain OPEC countries have clearly demonstrated, these detrimental effects do not appear to occur just after the period of so-called necessary dissociation.

Catching-up development cannot be theorised without indicating the targets of dissociation and state intervention. This can allow for orientations and desirable limits. Such a theory cannot be elaborated on the basis of historical analogies. It has to start from the specific problems which an underdeveloped economy faces when trying to adopt the "mechanism of development by the increase of mass incomes." When these problems are clearly identified, combinations of associative and dissociative strategies can be traced. This can be based on the concrete conditions of particular cases, but rooted within a consistent general theory.

5. Elements of an egalitarian development strategy

Underdevelopment basically comprises the fundamental deformation of an economy. This deformation prevents the economy from mobilising the most important source of wealth which any country possesses: labour power (Elsenhans 1982c: 55). It is caused by sectoral differences in productivity—that is, the factors of production (Elsenhans 1996b [1981]: 91 f.). In developed market economies, such sectoral differences tend to disappear. As long as they continue to exist,the factors of production will shift to higher productivity branches. These trends, together with the concurrent increase in output in the high-productivity sector, result in lower prices. Productivity is declining as assessed by pricing. Conversely, prices in low-productivity branches increase when the decline in their workforce leads to scarcity of their products. The resulting equalisation of factor productivities is the very condition of economic flexibility; the capacity of the economy to rapidly and flexibly react to changes in demand.

Sectoral productivity divergences exclude economic flexibility within underdeveloped economies. This inflexibility negates any simple redistribution of incomes. Precisely such a redistribution would enable the launching of development through rising mass incomes, that the economy reacts flexibly to price signals, which it does not because of sectoral differences in productivity. Consequently, such a strategy requires the previous planned restructuring of the productive apparatus. Without this restructuring, rising mass monetary incomes will lead to inflation or balance of trade deficits (Bitar 1979: 259; Müller-Plantenberg/ Hinkelammert 1973: 223-225). Restructuring must be planned, as a private enterprise cannot invest in the future demand that may emerge as a result of uncertain political developments.

One might argue that sectoral differences of productivities are the result of the transfer of an external system of relative prices. This would point to the necessity of dissociation (Amin 1973: 188). However, Kohlmey (1958: 74, 1962: 80-91), an early analyst of unequal exchange, has expressed criticisms of dissociation without nuance. He argues that the external (i.e. global) market system of relative prices reflects productivity levels achieved in the most advanced countries. To use Senghaas' terminology, we might consider such economies to be at the top of the hierarchies of competences. Consequently, this system has to be the basis for investment decisions in catching up development. If these economies are unable to react to new challenges by launching local equipment production, then this external system of relative prices faces some well-known negative consequences.

When it comes to energy production, European productivity is low. This did not exclude the transformation of European energy supplies after the oil price increases. New technologies were developed. Flexibility can be achieved, provided that machine production is not the lowest category within the spectrum of potential sectoral productivities.

The inflexibility of underdeveloped economies is ultimately the consequence of the lack of a local technological base. If this existed, then the local production of hitherto imported goods would become competitive, even with locally produced equipment. Of course, relative prices would have to change, perhaps due to a deterioration of the terms of trade. The dependence of capitalist technical progress on rising mass incomes implies that a lagging economy risks not being able to catch up, even if it has not suffered from the effects of colonialism. Capital accumulation in the industrial countries is not linked to the increasingly "heavy character" of production. The capital output ratio in the informal sector of Calcutta is about the same as in West German machine construction (Bose 1974: 3-46; Krengel et al. 1982: 98). Conversely, the value of equipment per worker is higher in Germany than in the so-called modern industries of the Third World. However, this equipment is produced by better-paid workers.

Superficially, we might take this observation to indicate a specialisation between industrial countries and underdeveloped countries according to factor endowments. To reach this conclusion, however, we would have to show an increase in the number of working hours for equipment construction in relation to labour time directly engaged in the elaboration of final products. It would also be necessary to demonstrate an increase in the value of the capital stock in relation to wages paid. These relations are, however, relatively stable.

Empirical analysis further shows that export branches of industrialised countries are not necessarily capital intensive. Moreover, those branches in which the countries of the Third World became competitive may be characterised by high capital labour ratios. Of course, this is not always the case. It does, however, provide a vivid illustration of the Leontief paradox (Leontief 1956: 398). Let us assume only marginal changes over time in the ratios between capital and labour, as expressed either in labour values or in prices of the two factors of production. Under such conditions, comparative advantage does not depend on capital intensity, but by disparities in productivity across sectors of production. These derive from other factors.

Due to the structure of technical progress, the difference between more advanced and less advanced countries becomes most glaring in machine production. Labour productivity and total factor productivity increases are achieved by employing new machinery. It may appear that technical progress originates in the availability of sophisticated material. In fact, however, it is due to the conception of new machines. To be sure, more sophisticated machinery is required for better qualities of steel, better performing alloys, or more elaborate glass fibre cables. In fact, technical progress in machine building can be measured by the price that a monopolistic machine producer would charge for his product. He remains competitive only if he offers his new machine at a price which is lower than the old machine, taking into account all savings in materials and all additional earnings due to higher quality.

And yet, the benefits of technical progress do not accrue only to the machine builder. The decentralisation of machine production in all developed industrial countries leads to imitation. Competitors come to develop more or less similar contraptions. Innovative producers thus have to lower their prices. These ultimately fall to the level of the cost of production of the new machines, including the cost of necessary research for the next generation of machines, plus an average profit rate. Consequently, the introduction of new machines results in falling costs of production, or in productivity increases for the users of the new machinery. Technical progress is thereby diffused within a system of production. It takes the form of increasing productivity across any production line in which the new machines are introduced. However, the know-how acquired from the conception of new machinery remains with its producers. Thus, the over all increase in productivity (as measured in machine building prices) is lower than the capacity to innovate in this branch.

Only those economies engaged in the construction and conception of new machinery benefit from the "capital" of additional know-how. This can provide the basis for further innovations. Economies that rely solely on imported new technology and exploit new production techniques do not enjoy this benefit. However, such economies benefit from increasing productivity. This is the natural result of the new technology. Machinery importing countries can only escape this mechanism if they already possess a sophisticated technological basis. This is what allows them to easily assimilate the imported technology.

Less advanced economies thus suffer from a systematic comparative disadvantage in technology producing branches relative to technology using branches. If the state does not aggressively pursue the development of a domestic technological basis, then this comparative disadvantage inevitably reproduces itself. The more capital intensive a particular imported technology, the more it incorporates innovative foreign labour.

For those who only employ the respective technique, the possibilities of participating in technical progress are reduced.

There is a close link between policies designed to develop a domestic technological base and policies for restructuring the productive apparatus. An egalitarian development strategy benefits from both mechanisms (in more detail: Elsenhans 1982c). Certainly, demand out of low incomes is less diversified than demand out of high incomes. A similar sum is spent on a restricted spectrum of products, each of which is subject to increasingly higher demand. The growing homogeneity of demand reduces the number of production lines that are necessary, at least initially. It also improves the possibilities of benefiting from economies of scale in each production line. Furthermore, enhanced homogeneity of consumption demand allows more homogeneity in demand for intermediary products. The share of imports in consumption can therefore be reduced. It is also possible to employ simpler technologies. Perhaps these can even be locally produced.

A developmental strategy that aims at benefiting from increasing mass demand has the following implications. Food constitutes an important share of increased spending on the part of poorer social classes. The great mass of the poor lives in the countryside. Any increase in income among the poor requires a higher food production. This is made easier if there is an egalitarian distribution of land. The possible decrease in tradable surplus is acceptable, because the consumption of the rural poor can increase. This owes to their new access to land in the wake of land redistribution (Elsenhans 1979: 535-565). Taxation of the peasantry by marketing boards is abolished. If it is not, then peasants have no incentive to work their land more intensively. Underdeveloped countries are overpopulated in relation to the available means of production. Marginal rural labour certainly achieves a higher additional production in agriculture (Bhalla 1960: 309) than urban workers in urban state-owned enterprises. Indeed, the latter tend to raise the costs of production to be paid by the consumers. The Green Revolution has not eliminated the mechanism of small farms achieving higher yields than those produced on the estates of big landlords (Ahmed 1981: 122).

Peasants will be ready to intensify their work on investment programs (such as hydraulic works, reforestation, etc.).[18] However, this readiness is conditional on the prospect of receiving material compensation in the not too distant future. This necessitates the simultaneous launch of industrial production facilities for low-income, agricultural consumers. Moreover, land reform will lead to better results if it is combined with a simultaneous introduction of new inputs and new equipment. The demand for such products from small peasant agriculture differs from the demand articulated by big landlords. The latter are concerned with reducing costs, while the former are only concerned with increasing production.

Small peasants cannot consider their own incomes as costs of production, assuming that they have no other opportunities for increasing their incomes and yields. Agricultural modernisation rooted in the small peasantry initially requires less diversified inputs. Certainly, some of the equipment and some of the consumption goods for this undertaking can come from the informal sector. For this to occur, this sector must be rendered dynamic through the acquisition of appropriate technologies and some limited new inputs. Any elevation of the productive capacities of such a sector allows for the combination of market regulation and state promotion to be defined. This in turn enables for limits to be set on state intervention in those domains where it is most essential. The "modern" industrial sector can concentrate on the production of equipment and some basic products (ex.: fertilisers) as well as some consumption goods.

Such an egalitarian development strategy can be operationalised on the basis of two sets of empirical data. The key question relates to the volume and structure of future demand that is likely to emerge in case of rising mass incomes. Projections can be based on the consumption patterns of more privileged income groups. On the basis of projected future demand, it is possible to follow the chain of production from the final products through different intermediary steps. This enables us to identify the industrial lines that must be operational when mass incomes increase. This identification of the necessary capacities of production enables us to categorise them. This can be undertaken according to comparative disadvantage of the small and medium-scale industries in relation to the sector of local big enterprises, as well as comparative disadvantage of different production facilities in relation to imports. Finally, this leads to an optimisation of the utilisation of scarce foreign exchange. This allows us to define those areas where large, locally producing enterprises have to become active.

Research on the future structure of demand is linked with research on the availability of local equipment production. The last decade was characterised by intensive efforts on the part of the Third World to launch economic development. In many countries, investment shares in national income have increased. So too have rates of investment growth. The rates of growth in investment goods imports, however, have been higher than the rates of growth of investment. The latter have been still higher than the rates of growth of production, even in the most advanced sectors, such as manufacturing. This points to "indebted industrialisation"—which is, in fact, a pattern of industrialisation where there is no sufficient increase in local production of investment goods.

This points to the necessity of establishing a local sector of production for investment goods, even if only to avoid deficits in foreign economic relations. Even in the rich OPEC countries, simple technology transfer is not conceivable without a suitably advanced technological foundation (Elsenhans 1982b: 62 f., 1983b: 51-60). Lenin's (1960 [1899]: 54-69) prognosis proved misguided here. High capital output ratios in underdeveloped economies do not demonstrate the constitution of an internal market by higher capital intensity of production processes. In fact, they are proof of the inefficiency of large industrial complexes. This derives from the lack of mastery of imported technologies.

The experience of the industrial countries shows the necessity of know-how in the production of technologies that require the training of labour at all skill levels. This training must involve participation in production. Local production of equipment can (apparently) lead to excessively high costs. Limiting investment efforts to the mere consumption of imported equipment, especially by accepting balance of trade deficits, leads to devaluation. A 50% devaluation of the domestic currency in relation to the currencies of the major industrial partners equates to a doubling of the cost of imported equipment (Sandmeyer 1976: 67). An economy which engages in local equipment production may never realise its profitability. It may avoid a devaluation by remaining underdeveloped and relying on raw material exports.

The decision to produce machinery in an underdeveloped country impacts all other technological choices. The investment goods sector cannot be integrated into the economy if the rest of the economy does not employ its products. With competencies at a limited level, at least initially, locally produced machinery will be less efficient. Consequently, production processes in other sectors cannot meet the internationally highest standards of precision. If machinery using branches require such degrees of precision, then locally produced machinery cannot be employed in, for instance, the manufacturing of spare parts.

Naturally, countries try to avoid falling into technological dependence, which inevitably results from the absence of a local technological basis. This compels their governments to choose imported technology, but always with an eye on their ability to assimilate this new technology. These economies are forced to restrict themselves to importing technologies that are compatible with their own existing technological basis (after a reasonable delay). However, this also implies that certain advantages can be drawn from multiplier and accelerator effects. These result from the marriage between imported and local technologies.

We may see a mutually reinforcing dynamic here between the creation of a local technological base and a more egalitarian distribution of income. This arises from the greater homogeneity of consumption and lower quality requirements for investment goods. Such a strategy may initially lead to high capital output ratios. These result from the sheer volume of work time that can be incorporated in such locally produced machines. This is critical when it comes to increasing productivity.

In countries that primarily consume technologies, a high capital output ratio has to be evaluated differently from an investment goods-producing, catching-up economy. Here, it reflects learning costs. These are essential costs for catching up. Evaluating the effects of learning by doing enables for a clearer definition of the share of invisible benefits in different machine producing lines of production. Different choices can be graded according to their long-term social profitability. This facilitates the choice between local production and imports.

I have presented several perspectives of catching-up industrialisation here. These viewpoints enable us to more precisely identify the public sector's potential role. In any case, the public sector is expanding across the Third World. This reflects the growing extractive power of the "elites" of the Third World in their relation with Western countries. To be sure, public-sector expansion and planning are required for restructuring an economy. And yet it is doubtful that any expansion of the public sector in Third World countries would result from this necessity. Relevant here is a thoroughgoing critique of the social cost of public-sector expansion in bureaucratic development societies (Elsenhans 1982a: 15-18; Szentes 1971: 318 f.). This critique has clearly identified the desirable limits of state intervention in particular cases. Indeed, some underdeveloped countries with high degrees of planning have evidently started to become conscious of these limits (China, Algeria).

Catching-up development does not imply identical recipes for different Third World countries. Underdevelopment is characterised by structural deficits and blockages. These differ from one country to another. They can encapsulate human, industrial and material resources. While, the European example does not provide fool proof recipes here, it does point to a possible double perspective. The expansion of an internal mass market should be encouraged, and the creation of a local technological basis should be achieved. Such a basis must be adaptable to new technologies. This certainly requires elements of planning, as well as market regulation. While some dissociation from the world market is necessary, this does not exclude monitored cooperation.

These perspectives are not analogous with older debates about socialism/statism versus capitalism. This also not a conflict between dissociation and association, or dependence against modernisation. If we think in terms of these oppositions, the possible solutions elude us. Conversely, an analysis of concrete structural deficits and concretely available resources allows for a clear definition of development strategies.

Such strategies would minimise the cost of an accumulation of know-how by exploiting the skill-creating effects of production lines oriented to mass consumption. In the process, the local technological basis would be enlarged.

Such a strategy does not run the risk of undermining international competitiveness, despite rising mass incomes. Senghaas (1982: 26) elaborated on the apparent "paradox" of South Korea. This entailed the necessity of simultaneously rising real wages and internationally competitive prices. In fact, however, this paradox does not exist. Real wages can increase without international labour costs increasing in international currency, provided that productivity in wage goods production also increases. Some East Asian export manufacturers already appropriate rents from their exports to the world market (Morkre 1979; Blackhurst 1972: 350-362). Such a strategy will help to maintain a liberal world economy, because it will soak up the inexhaustible source of cheap labour that threatens to destroy the negotiating power of labour movements in the North. At the same time, however, it will directly and indirectly counteract the global tendencies towards underconsumption that characterise the contemporary economic crisis (Elsenhans 1981c).

Notes

1. Elsenhans 2007 [1976], 1976a, b, 1977, 1992b[1979], 1983c, cf. also 1975 [1974], 1982c.
2. Zinecker 2011: 138, cf. Senghaas 1972: 9, 1974: 7.
3. Beattie 1964; Smaldone 1972; Mährdel 1957/58: 131.
4. Rader 1971: 81; Musson 1978: 17-53; Becker/Gehrisch 1977: 1377; Nell 1967: 344.
5. Cf. my rejection in Elsenhans 1981d, 1996b [1981]: 362-369.
6. Here an unpublished book manuscript, Elsenhans 1983a was quoted, which at the time was under review at ENDA (Dakar). Despite being accepted, it was finally not published. The link to the text is available at https://hartmutelsenhans.net/unpublished-papers-2/.
7. Fabricant 1959: 37; Helmstädter 1969: 48, 259 ff.; Kendrick 1961: 166.
8. Jones 1974:96; Hoskins 1950): 13; Holderness 1976: 50 ff.; Kulischer 1965: vol. 2, 63; Campbell 1960: 71; Chambers/Mingay 1966: 202; Lord Ernle 1961: 60; Saville

(1969: 266) and Lazonick (1974: 23) defend the argument of Marx and insist on the increasing land concentration without discussing the level of living in the English countryside.

9. MacCloskey (1975: 145 f.) bases his explanations on the timing of enclosures and the same argument.
10. Mantoux 1905: 71; Rowlands 1975: 42; Gilboy 1934b: 198.
11. Deane/Cole 1967: 113; Ashton 1955: 10; Redford 1964: 62.
12. Barkhausen 1958: 235; van Klaveren 1964; Ludloff 1956: 69; Pollard 1968: 63.
13. Nef 1940: 13-30; Deyon 1972: 32; Kellenbenz 1963: 840; Thirsk 1978: 169; Musson 1978: 125.
14. Menzel had investigated the cases of Switzerland, Denmark, Sweden and Canada. The mostly unpublished work is listed in Menzel/Senghaas 1983: 95 f.
15. Riegler 1978: 31-33; Hodne 1975: 356; Liebermann 1970: 44.
16. On the German pattern of specialisation cf. also Howard(1907: 91): "There is no doubt that it was the home market which first demanded the cheap goods of German manufacturer, for the poverty and low income in that country 50 years ago necessitated the strictest economy in purchasing. With these same goods, the Germans spent looking for foreign markets and found that there was a greater demand ready to be created when these cheaper goods could be offered."This pattern of specialisation is in sharp contrast to the pattern of specialisation of France.
17. Nakamura 1966a: 63, b; Hanley/Yamamura 1977: 5; Yamamura 1979: 319; Smith 1968: 280.
18. This form of fixed capital formation had been important also in US economic history: Primack 1966: 358; Bidwell/Falconer 1968: 35.

3

Dependency, Rent and Autonomy

The Debate Over the Third World State's International Role and the Paradigm of Rent-financed State-class Dominated Bureaucratic Development Societies*

1. Preliminary remarks

The importance of State activity in the economic and social development of Third World countries is self-evident, and I will not spend time proving it nor shall I give further details in this article. The indicators typically deployed to illustrate this fact even lead to underestimating the role of the state in economic development in the South. The share of the public sector in total GNP may be low in a country with a low level of per capita income simply because economic surplus is low. However, the role of the state in the economy may even then be dominant. This is because the state may absorb total surplus and be the only source of investment. Legally free agricultural producers may be dependent on state marketing organizations for absorption of their produce. Furthermore, they may also rely on state monopolies for strategic inputs and machinery to an important degree. This is especially the case when investment decisions and economic situations

---

* Extended text originally prepared in 1987 for International Organization but then abandoned because of change of focus of the journal.

of particular independent enterprises depend on the ideas and whims of central and local instances of public agencies. Import monopolies, especially of equipment, can be used as an effective instrument for tightly controlling the industrial sector, even if it is entirely private.

The reasons for increasing state interventionism—and hence the "class character" of the Third World state, as well as the possible outcomes of state interventionism—are highly controversial, however. Originally, Marxist and Keynesian writings were highly enthusiastic about increasing State interventionism in the Third World (Hirschman 1958; Dobb 1951). There were only few early warnings. Baran (1952: 81) argued: "The injection of planning into a society living in the twilight between feudalism and capitalism cannot help but result in additional corruption; larger and more artful evasions of the law; and more brazen abuses of authority."

The economic version of modernisation theory, which can be traced back to Rosenstein-Rodan's (1943) seminal contribution, considered economic backwardness as a "vicious circle" equilibrium. Limited demand discouraged investment, resulting in a lack of opportunities for (more) productive investment, employment and increasing incomes. Private entrepreneurs cannot invest without being sure of adequate markets, and these adequate markets would only come into being through large-scale simultaneous investment. Therefore, the state has to co-ordinate all this investment. The controversy about balanced (Nurkse 1953) or unbalanced growth (Hirschman 1958) relates only to the ways of implementing this coordination.

Additionally, the official Soviet doctrine of development in the Third World, the so-called theory of the non-capitalist development path, emphasises the necessity of increased state interventionism and a large public sector. The Soviet theory regards a large, interventionist public sector as essential to achieving rapid growth and ultimately socialism. In the last decade, however, Marxist *dependencia* writing has severely attacked the state in the Third World.[1] They consider the state to be the agent of international capital or to be ruled by state or administrative bourgeoisies; a contradiction in adiecto (Elsenhans 1996b[1981]:

125-172). The more critical version of this argument is found in the concept of "renegotiated dependency"(Quijano Obregón 1971:11; Ianni 1974: 32), in the earlier versions of dependent-associated development (Cardoso/Faletto 1967: 37).The other more critical version can be found in the theory of the bureaucratic-authoritarian state (O'Donnell 1973). This has led James Petras (1980: 127) to speak of a neofascist state in the Third World. In these theories, continued dependence is linked to the state's necessarily increasing degree of repressiveness. More optimistic versions of dependent development in later Latin American (Cardoso/ Faletto 1977) and in those imitating Latin American writing (Evans 1979) underline more the new triple coalition between state, local private sector, and international capital. They also admit a certain openness of possible results. Their arguments are compatible with the description of the internal structures of these states as corporatist. This, in turn, is compatible with the view that there may be some degree of political participation.

On the other side, there is a newly affirmed liberal orthodoxy that considers state interventionism as an essential cause of continued underdevelopment in the Third World (Bauer 1981: 149). This liberal orthodoxy is shared by some Marxist authors who reject even the notion of dependency and underdevelopment (Warren 1973). Rejecting the underdevelopment variant of imperialism and the argument that foreign direct investment does not lead to overall development, they return to the orthodox Leninist (Lenin 1960 [1899]) vision of capitalism as being the most efficient way of developing backward countries.

In summary, there are three characteristics of the discussion of the state of the Third World in development writing:

- There is writing about what the state should do if it really wanted to overcome underdevelopment.
- There is writing about what states actually did, and these actions vary greatly.
- There is writing about the principal ambivalence of the state in the Third World, ranging from outward advocacy to complete condemnation.

This eclecticism and these controversies are not accidental. They relate to the high degree of freedom of action for economic units which appropriate rent.

Within a general theory, certain issues must all be controversial, namely the economic basis, the eclecticism of actual government policies and the results of state intervention. These three factors are controversial because they dictate the degrees of freedom allowed to centralised classes that experiment with different development strategies and are financed from rent.

The argument to be followed in this article can be summarised: Rent is an income which is not necessarily dependent on innovation. This income does not accrue to a producer who has been forced by market forces to accumulate fixed capital and does not generally contribute to the creation of growth-inducing mass markets. Its use depends on the political orientation of those who appropriate rent. There are strong incentives to waste rent. Additionally, the rent-connected inefficiencies of state-dominated industrialisation processes in Third World countries strongly influence international relations. As a result, however, there is a chance of influencing the states in the Third World in order to facilitate overcoming underdevelopment. Increased state interventionism is based on the emergence of rent as an important source of income in Third World economies—if they coexist with developed industrial economies.

In order to clarify this point, I must show that economic development in capitalist countries is not capital-deepening. In that case, no change occurs in factor endowment within capitalist countries. Hence, comparative advantage of Third World economies is not due to factor proportions. Rather than that, it is the result of varying degrees of backwardness in particular manufacturing lines relative to mature industrial countries. A production line is an assembly of different production steps that are combined for producing a tradable good. It is normally more restricted than a branch of production.

In a capitalist world, the system of relative prices of goods is adjusted according to differences in productivity increases. Productivity—as measured in prices of goods and inputs—tends to be equal in any productive use of factors of production. Certain economies participate only partially in the technical progress of the advanced capitalist countries and,nevertheless, are oriented by the dominant world-market price system. These economies will therefore be characterised by differences in productivity in different production lines, what I call "structural heterogeneity". Structural heterogeneity leads to inflexibility of the economy. If the cost of labour—as measured in international currency—is not fixed at the level corresponding to the productivity lag in the most advanced branch but instead at a lower level, then the differences in backwardness of productivity in relation to advanced industrial countries in different production lines allow the appropriation of rent.

Rent appropriation provides the financial basis for increased state interventionism. A low degree of flexibility in the economy provides important incentives for planning and hence increasing state interventionism. Increasing state interventionism as a result of rent appropriation and structural heterogeneity, however, will not necessarily lead to overcoming underdevelopment.

The social structure connected with rent appropriation and increasing state interventionism is characterised by a dominant state class (Elsenhans 1976e, 1996b [1981].[2] This state-class appropriates and allocates financial means through "administrative" procedures (as opposed to market mechanisms). The internal dynamics of state classes and the relations between state classes and other social forces may deepen underdevelopment to a considerable extent but can also contribute to development. The social and economic conditions for autonomous technical development are especially neglected. Hence appropriation of rent and the exchange of such income for imported technology will continue. Increased state interventionism, therefore, does not exclude that overall growth continues to depend on increasing foreign exchange earnings. Moreover, increasing state interventionism is primarily oriented to increasing rent-appropriation in external economic relations.

In my contribution, therefore, increasing state interventionism in Third World countries is not considered a transitional phase nor is it a support for capitalism. In the American economic literature regarding capital, capital is defined as equipment regardless of the social connections of production. Capitalism, though, is connected to a specific mode of appropriation and allocation of value; this is Marx's so-called "law of value". However, the capitalist centre has a limited capacity to enact capitalist transformation on the non-capitalist, less-developed countries. This failure to implement capitalist change then results in increasing state interventionism in Third World countries.

Underdevelopment and structural heterogeneity provoke the formation of centralised classes. This is achieved through rent-appropriation and by the possibility of channelling internal surplus to productive investment that otherwise would not have even been produced.

These state classes dominate within the new type of production, the so-called bureaucratic development societies. When non-capitalist economies interact with developed capitalist countries, the result is structural heterogeneity. Additionally, bureaucratic development societies which are dominated by state classes cannot be explained without considering their position within the international economic system. Furthermore, the international division of labour remains an important aspect of this international economic system.

All depends on the use of the rent, which can be—but is not necessarily–used for overcoming underdevelopment. Therefore, it is excessive to judge a state only based on its subordinate status in its external economic relations with the capitalist centre. Instead, states should be judged by the quality of their rent redirection and rechannelling. Rent-financed state classes exhibit important tendencies towards lopsided limited development. They are nevertheless the only classes capable of promoting projects of development. After surmounting important contradictions, these projects of development possibly will lead to self-sustained growth and political mass participation in the underdeveloped world.

Simplistic advocacy for pure solutions—for example asserting that only the market, or only planning, or that only labour-intensive, or only the most modern technology should be applied—are hence rejected. It is shown that getting rid of rent-financed investment based on imported technology is possible only under severe strains. If rent continues to be an important source of income and if inflexibility of the economies of the Third World will continue to impede overcoming underdevelopment, the process of development will continue to be complex. The direction in which it should be steered can be simply articulated: develop mass consumption by social reform. Additionally, mass consumption should be developed by investment in rather labour-intensive production lines for mass consumption goods based on local inputs and locally produced equipment, which may be capital-intensive. But there is a wide variety of solutions for these particular problems (Elsenhans 1975, 1982c).

The importance of rent determines the integration of structurally heterogeneous economies into the world system. They must export to be able to defend export earnings. They must find non-market mechanisms for the allocation of rent. This state interventionism leads to a rather nationalistic view of the international system and a tendency to claim increased resource transfers from the developed capitalist economies, which are blamed for their past colonial and imperialistic wrongdoings. Through this process, the inefficient use of resources in the underdeveloped countries is therefore concealed.

2. Capitalist growth is not characterised by capital-deepening, hence comparative advantages do not follow from factor proportions

I draw attention to the characteristics of the capitalist growth process in order to support the argument that comparative advantage of Third World economies is not shaped by factor endowment. Instead, it is shaped by differential degrees of backwardness in labour productivity within different production lines as compared to developed capitalist countries. This argument is the basis of my contention that rent is an important income in Third World economies. Marxist, Keynesian and liberal economics have normally explained economic growth by capital accumulation. Obviously, technical progress is related to investment in new machinery. Even the value of fixed capital per worker has risen so much that it seems evident that increased productivity and technical progress is due to the use of more and more expensive and higher and higher-performing equipment. In Marxist economics, this tendency is described as rising organic composition of capital. In conventional economics, it is labelled capital deepening or increasing capital-intensity of production.

In order to analyse the relative contribution of capital (labour-power engaged in previous periods of production) and labour (labour-power engaged in actual production of the period to be analysed), a comparison between hours worked and costs of equipment is misleading. In order to compare the stock of fixed capital to hours worked, this stock must be expressed in terms of the numbers of hours which must be worked for the replacement. This will result in a decrease of its value as productivity in equipment construction has increased over time. In order to compare the cost of fixed capital to labour, hours worked must also be expressed in costs of hours worked. The payments of salaries and wages are a convenient indicator. The capital output ratio, which compares the stock of fixed capital to the value of total production, provides a more straightforward measure of capital's relative contribution to production.

The organic composition of capital measures the relation between labour value as embodied in fixed constant capital and to the labour value directly engaged in production. At a stable relation between the value of labour and surplus, the organic composition of capital is a linear function of the relation between fixed capital and total product. If the "transformation problem" of labour values into production prices is neglected, the capital output ratio remains a convenient indicator of the organic composition of capital (Robinson 1978: 13). An increase in the organic composition of capital will be accompanied by an increase of productivity. Marx's contention is that productivity increases are primarily related to capital accumulation and thus to an increasing organic composition of capital.

As will be shown, however,the organic composition of capital does not rise in the capitalistic growth process. Overall increase in productivity is due to higher-performing,and not to more costly (in terms of labour value) equipment. Additionally, it is attributable to better skills and management. It can even be capital saving.

However, if productivity would only result in a higher organic composition of capital, then the share of equipment production in total production would have to rise. This is only the case for some developed capitalist countries as a result of an increased export share in total production and equipment goods orientation of their exports. Increasing the share of national spending on equipment would indicate a rise in the capital output ratio.

If capitalistic growth processes were related to a rise in the organic composition of capital or capital-deepening, then the capital output ratio would historically have risen. For the last century, at least, such a rise cannot be observed. Many like Solow (1957: 316), Fabricant (1959: 27), Kendrick (1961: 166 f.), Domar (1961)and Helmstädter (1969: 48-91) have produced convincing evidence that the value of fixed capital in relation to the value of production has not risen. Pasinetti has provided a theoretical explanation of this fact (1974: 138).

High and rising capital output ratios are not to be found in capitalist developed countries, but rather in socialist industrialised and underdeveloped Third World countries. This is for obvious reasons: In the socialist countries, the growth process is not based on rising mass consumption but on planned investment. Capital accumulation can outstrip final demand and is intended to do so. In Third World countries, however, high-cost imported technology is often more productive than domestically produced technology, which would create domestic wage incomes. Hence equipment—which embodies labour-time at high cost—is combined with direct labour paid at a low wage rate. Because the prices of labour-time are so different between the capitalist and the socialist and Third World economies, the capital output ratio rises. This ratio rises in technically dependent economies in the socialist and the underdeveloped countries because the total value of production under competitive conditions is equivalent to the cost of capital, the cost of labour and the average rate of profit. Such high-cost technology imports can be financed from rent.

The relative stability of the capital output ratio in developed capitalist countries is the direct result of the conditions of profitable investment in such economies. I have shown in another contribution (Elsenhans 1983c: 3-5) that:

- new technologies are profitable only if they cut unit costs (the condition is equivalent to the conditions that is raises the profit rate if real wages are constant),
- new technologies reduce global demands if wages are constant,
- a process of continued technical innovation in capitalist economies will avoid diminishing global demand only if real wages rise.

In commenting on my argument, Emmanuel (1982: 167-169) contends that the introduction of fixed capital could invalidate my argument. Suppose, however, that we have fixed capital representing labour quantities employed (V) in previous periods of production. A more capital-intensive technology is characterised by a higher, equal or lower quantity of (V) per unit of output and necessarily a lower quantity of direct labour (v) per unit of output. The cost of capital is $V(1 + \pi)$, because the capitalist has to earn profit at the ordinary profit rate (π) if he is to be induced to engage his resources in the new production line. The new technology will be profitable if it reduces the costs of production in relation to the quantity produced (Q). A more capital-intensive technology (2) is more profitable than a less capital-intensive technology (1) if the unit costs at the average profit rate (π) decrease for an identical quantity of products.

(1) $$\frac{V_1(1+\pi)+v_1}{Q} > \frac{V_2(1+\pi)+v_2}{Q}$$

By the simple transformation we obtain:

(2) $$(1 + \pi)(V_2 - V_1) < v_1 - v_2$$

Any profitable technology requires by definition a positive profit rate, hence $(1 + \pi)$ greater than 1 and hence

(3) $$V_2 - V_1 < v_1 - v_2$$

$V_2 - V_1$ is the increase of labour engaged in previous periods (in equipment production); $v_1 - v_2$ is the decrease of labour directly engaged in production.

Inequalities (2) and (3) show that, at constant wages, a more capital-intensive technology is profitable only—if the possible increase in labour employed for equipment production is more than outweighed by a decrease in labour directly employed in production. Total labour requirements diminish by a factor $(1 + \pi)$; this is dependent on the average rate of profit. When the varying lengths of service of equipment are taken into consideration, an extension of the life of service of a piece of equipment will require an even greater reduction of directly employed labour in relation to the increase of labour in equipment production as the multiplier $(1 + \pi)^{t_1}$ for technology (1) increases for technology (2) to $(1 + \pi)^{t_2}$ with $t_2 > t_1$.

If the introduction of new technologies at constant wages reduces overall labour requirements, Emmanuel contends that the labour displacement effect could be outweighed by increasing capital accumulation in new production lines, the produce of which is designated for capital accumulation. Emmanuel has in mind an economic upswing fuelled by the demand for equipment goods. I have formalised his arithmetical model (Elsenhans 1986: 269-272). If YG = total (gross) product; C = stock of fixed capital; β = capital productivity (YG/C); c = constant percentage of total product consumed in production (productive consumption in Emmanuel's arithmetical example is 0.1); g = constant percentage of fixed capital consumed in production (amortisation in Emmanuel's arithmetical example is 0.2); π = rate of profit and the rate of accumulation of fixed capital (as all profits are reinvested); t = period after starting the accumulation process; index $_0$ = value of variable at the period of starting the accumulation process; and v = constant sum of salaries for a constant labour force, then we can write:

(4) $$YG = cCG + gC + P + v$$

(5) $$(1 + y)^t\, YG_0 = (1 + \pi)^t (c)\, \beta C_0 + (1 + \pi)^t g C_0 + (1 + \pi)^t\, \pi C_0 + v$$

Total production is also a function of β

(6) $\beta(1 + \pi)^t C_0 = (1 + y)^t YG_0$

The model supposes all profits reinvested and all labour income consumed.

Suppose the profit rate and the rate of accumulation is constant and higher than the growth rate of the real product. Then from (5),

(7) $$\beta_t = \frac{\frac{v}{C_0}\left(\frac{1}{1+\pi}\right)^t + g + \pi}{1 - c}$$

with the limit $\frac{g+\pi}{1-c}$, and $g + \pi$, in case of considering only net production, with $(g + \pi) > 0$ and $(1 - c) > 0$ and < 1, so that both these elements are greater than zero and from (6)

(8) $$\beta_t = \left(\frac{1 + y}{1 + \pi}\right)^t \frac{Y_o}{C_o}$$

with limit 0.

After some period, the surplus is no longer sufficient to pay for capital replacement and profit. This is not the result of wages being too high but rather too low, which leads to capital accumulation outstripping technical progress.[3]

Let be Y net income. If capital productivity is kept constant, the full employment solution requires increasing rates of growth for total product (Y) and fixed capital. This is because when capital productivity is constant, the increase of total production is a function of the increase of fixed capital in the previous period. This increase of fixed capital from the previous period is equal to the rate of profit of that period (because all profits are invested).

(9) $$\frac{Y_t}{Y_{t-1}} = \frac{C_{t-1} - C_{t-2}}{C_{t-2}} = \pi_{t-2} = y_t$$

Formal definitions of the reaction of y to π may lead to $y = \pi_{-1}$.

Full employment at constant wages and constant capital productivity is only possible if the rate of capital accumulation and the rate of growth of production increase from period to period. Formally, in this perspective an equilibrium will be achieved when the share of wages in total demand is decreasing to an unrealistic near zero-level.

Suppose real wages and capital productivity are constant, and if Emmanuel's arithmetic example starts from realistic values for wage shares, capital productivity, and profit rates. Then full employment solutions—according to Emmanuel's example—require annual increases of the profit and accumulation rates no less than 16% and maximum profit rates no less than 55%.[4] These exercises, formalistic as they may appear, however, allow some interesting observations. First, in case of declining capital productivity,the profit rate may decline if the rate of accumulation outstrips the rate of growth of production. This occurs because profits are too high in relation to consumption from wages. Second, an investment-based boom will lead to an increase in global demand for equipment goods. As entrepreneurs consider this demand element to be instable, the investment boom will come to an end because of the expectations of entrepreneurs (Hicks 1982). If entrepreneurs' expectations do not end the boom, then it will end due to a decline in the marginal efficiency of capital (capital productivity) if the growth rate of the capital stock exceeds the growth rate of innovation and production (Harrod 1972).

Having explored the implications of a growth process based on the expansion of the demand for equipment, we can reasonably conclude that the organic composition of capital in a capitalist system can rise only within rather limited ranges. This is a theoretical support for the empirically observed relative stability of the capital output ratio. Therefore, capitalist growth is not capital-intensifying—although capital-intensifying and capital-saving innovations in different lines of production may be introduced simultaneously at any period in different production lines (Stürmer 1968). Because technical progress must be cost-saving at constant wages, the interaction of capital-saving and capital-deepening investment can only occur if real wages rise. Higher consumption and additional capital-intensive investment do not provide any natural economic mechanism which pushes up real wages to the level necessary to maintain a sufficient rate of growth of effective demand.

The main threat to capitalist growth processes is the lack of working class bargaining power which is necessary to balance consumption and production capacity. In other words, capitalism is threatened by underconsumptionist tendencies which may temporarily be compensated by overaccumulation, a process which will result inevitably in crisis. Even the types of overaccumulation described above have their bases in the absence of increases of real wages.

For the purpose of my argument, the following findings from the discussion of Emmanuel's model are most important: If we exclude unrealistic spikes in the increases of the rates of capital accumulation and in the rates of growth, the relative stability of the capital output ratio can only be achieved if increases in consumption push down the rate of accumulation to the rate of growth of production, hence productivity growth at constant labour input. As wages and salaries are the main element of consumption, full employment and the maintenance of the rate of profit require wage and salary increases at roughly the same rate as the rate of growth of total product. Hence, more expensive equipment produced by more expensive labour does not necessarily imply a high labour-value. The capital output ratio is stable if the capital stock increases in line with production. If wages and salaries increase in line with production, then increases of capital in line with real wages represent identical labour values in relation to previous periods.

In this case, the increase in productivity is not due to an increase of equipment's share of total production, hence to more saving in relation to consumption. Instead, increased productivity results simply from technical innovation—or more precisely, to disembodied technical progress (Denison 1967). Disembodied technical progress is the increase of performance of equipment that is achieved by innovation to the difference of embodied technical progress. This is achieved by better labour inputs in the production of equipment. Disembodied technical progress does not increase the labour cost of equipment production but only performance. In capitalist societies with high levels of employment, increasing productivity caused by technical progress causes redistribution. This redistribution takes the form of nominal wage increases instead of falling prices. However, this process obscures the fact that capital accumulation simply does not take place in a capitalist society—at least if capitalist accumulation is defined as ever-rising labour value incorporated in the stock of fixed capital.

Suppose nominal wages remain constant and productivity increases are translated into falling unit prices. According to this supposition, technical progress in equipment goods production will result in falling prices for less-performant equipment of the type produced in previous periods. The accumulated stock of capital would be devalued. The so-called struggle of capitalists for accumulation is less a struggle for more capital. Rather, it is more a struggle to maintain their share of total productive capital by increasing the performance of their equipment through profit-financed and profit-increasing new investment. Hence, it is a struggle against the constantly threatening devaluation of capital goods through obsolescence due to the introduction of higher-performing equipment goods (Sinn 1975).

As a result, the capitalist growth process has had little effect on factor endowment. Capitalist countries do not possess more capital in relation to labour than non-developed economies, but they are able to produce more performant equipment goods than non-developed countries because of widespread skills in technology. There is, however, a change in factor endowment if skills are considered. The development process is a process of skill acquisition. Specialisation according to static comparative advantage does not necessarily lead to skill acquisition in less advanced countries (Amsden 1983:336). It may even lead to the loss of skills in less advanced countries, if imported technology crowds out local tools and machinery production.

Comparative advantage for less-developed countries hence emerges according to differences in the skill increase in various production lines and differences in the skill transfer costs. It is most improbable that skills attached to personal work experience are more easily transferred to Third World countries than skills embodied in ready-made machinery. Hence there is a strong argument for more advanced countries specializing in high-skill, labour-intensive products and for less advanced countries in capital-intensive products; this is described in the so-called Leontief paradox (Leontief 1954). Conventional economics has resorted to the term "human capital" to refer to abilities. It can be hoped that this way of rescuing conventional foreign trade theory will be abandoned because it is a strong basis for Third World countries' claim to compensation for the cost of brain drain (UNCTAD 1982: 5; Logan 1987: 605).

3. Technical progress, the system of relative prices and structural heterogeneity in underdeveloped economies

My next contention is that the character of technical progress necessarily leads to a reshuffling of the relative prices of goods. This reshuffling creates a system of relative prices where factor productivities in any production line in capitalist countries tend to be equal, despite differential rates of growth of productivity. Suppose the transfer of technical innovation to non-developed countries can be realised only at very different costs for different technologies. Suppose also that the rate of technical progress is uneven in different production lines in the developed capitalist countries. If these are true, then the transfer of the system of relative prices from the developed industrial countries to Third World countries must necessarily create "structural heterogeneity".

Structural heterogeneity (Aydalot 1968: 42; Clague 1967: 492) in underdeveloped countries designates the coexistence of production lines with extremely different factor productivities. Structural heterogeneity has two important consequences. First, changes in demand will not lead to easy adaptation of the productive structure but instead to inflationary pressures and rising imports. Structurally heterogeneous economies are not capable of achieving the necessary flexibility to changes in demand or to changes in their own export earnings. An example: In the case of falling export earnings,structurally heterogenous economies would struggle to or would not be able to replace imports with local production. Secondly, structural heterogeneity creates the possibility of appropriating rent. Both consequences—the lack of flexibility and hence the limited possibility of steering production by market mechanisms, as well as the availability of rent—highly favour state interventionism.

Let me start with the trivial observation that the rate of technical progress varies in different production lines. Additionally,the different rates of technical progress are not linked to different rates of capital accumulation. Very often, high rates of capital accumulation in some industries are achieved in order to defend profit margins against rising labour costs, albeit without achieving substantial productivity growth. Branches with rapidly rising physical productivity may be less capital intensive (like office machinery or machine construction).[5]

Differential rates of technical progress in different industries will, however, lead to a reshuffling of the price structure. Branches with high productivity growth will attract labour and capital. Under competitive conditions, an expansion of production will lead to lower prices—or at least to lower price rises compared to the average price increase. On the other end, industries with below-average productivity increases will be forced to shift increases in their costs (for example through rising real wages) to their customers. This reshuffling will stop only when marginal product per marginal spending on additional equipment and labour is equal in any production line. This process will even take place if industries with high barriers to entry are the most profitable ones. These industries must invest their own profits into the expansion of their own productive capacity because other investment opportunities would be less profitable.

Through the process of equalisation of marginal product per marginal money spent on equipment and labour, capitalist economies acquire and maintain their flexibility. An increase in demand for a particular product will lead to higher profitability of funds employed in the respective plants and will more easily attract labour and equipment. This process is possible because capitalist industrial economies possess the capacity to produce the essential equipment by themselves at a reasonable cost. This self-sufficiency remains true even if they import large quantities of equipment. Additionally, this self-sufficiency is reinforced because they possess sufficient qualified workers to staff their new or expanding plants, albeit with reasonable delays. These delays are deemed reasonable because of the gradualist character of technical innovation compared to already acquired skills.

Unlike in developed capitalist economies, all these mechanisms do not exist in an underdeveloped economy to a degree that would provide flexibility. Because technical innovation raises productivity in an uneven manner in capitalist countries, the productivity lag in underdeveloped countries—in relation to the productivity level achieved in industrialised countries –varies from production line to production line. It is small in industries where the developed industrialised countries have achieved only small productivity increases, and it is large where such increases are high. Additionally, the cost of transfer of technology varies from industry to industry.

The theory of the product cycles (Vernon 1966) has described the process of standardisation of technology. After some time, many technologies may become so manageable that they can be transferred relatively easily to economic environments that do not possess the skills required to develop this technology.

Thus, different rates of technical progress in the developed capitalist countries and different possibilities of technology transfer lead to varying degrees of backwardness within underdeveloped countries, according to production lines in Third World economies. If total factor productivity is measured by a product's prevailing price on the international market, then total factor productivity and the ratio between marginal product and marginal cost cannot be uniform nor tend to be uniform in underdeveloped countries. In developed capitalist countries, devaluation will trigger off rising exports of already internationally competitive products, new exports of not yet exported products, and rising production in import-competing industries. Devaluation in underdeveloped countries will to some extent lead to similar reactions. However, essential imports cannot be substituted even at high rates of devaluation, whereas exports of already competitive and previously not yet exportable products will possibly not rise to a level high enough to equilibrate the balance of trade.

Structural heterogeneity is not possible without the coexistence of more developed industrial countries with underdeveloped countries.

Without industrial world, the underdeveloped world would either have to fore go the industrial world's products or make equivalents with its own limited skills and at its own expense. Additionally, if the industrial capitalist world did not exist, essential export products of the Third World could not be exported and would not procure high revenues—revenues which then are used to pay for imports. The price relation between imports and exports would have to be adjusted to the production costs and to the demand conditions in the respective underdeveloped economies.

The characteristics of the process of technical innovation result in a comparative disadvantage for underdeveloped countries in the production of equipment, especially machinery. Conversely, they lead to comparative advantages in production lines based on unskilled labour in traditional production processes or in assembly line-type production processes using imported machinery. This observation is based on the following argument: Every innovation—be it new product or new materials, and of course process innovation—can only be introduced if machinery is constructed which provides possibilities for industrial application. Machinery production, therefore, can be considered the main, perhaps only, source of technical progress in the economy. This is because the transformation of invention into technical innovation requires new machinery. Machinery production in any country is rather labour intensive, if outdated machinery is left out of consideration. This is quite obvious, because the design and construction of new machinery is done by skilled labour in mostly small quantities.

New machinery will be introduced only if its cost is below the sum of the cost of older machinery plus savings in labour and material cost and additional earnings from larger or better products it allows to produce. If this condition is met, the new machinery is more performant than the older one. Machinery for new products is performant if cost is below expected earnings.

If there is a monopoly, new machinery can be competitive at a price slightly lower than this sum. But if there is competition, the price will be pushed down to the level of the cost of production, including research and development for the continued competitiveness of the machinery-producing firm. This decline of the price in relation to performance is the basis of disembodied technical progress mentioned earlier. If performance would rise only in line with the cost of machinery, then the rise of total product would be due only to the rising value of fixed capital. Through the decline of the price of new machinery in relation to its performance, factor productivity increases in those production lines which employ this new machinery. Technical progress is achieved in the production of machinery, but it is transferred to production lines which use this machinery.

Machinery production is impacted differently than other industries by the trend toward increased productivity through economies of scale. On one hand,machinery-using industries that produce raw materials, intermediate goods, and consumption goods try to standardise production and profit from large series. On the other hand, machinery producers will be less oriented towards increasing the quantities of identical machinery but rather towards designing more specialised machinery that increases performance.

If machinery can be sold and applied at the same or an "acceptable" level of performance in Third World countries—a lower level of performance can be offset by lower labour costs—the productivity-increasing effect of the new machinery is also transferred to the respective country.

However, the machinery-importing country has not participated in the learning process connected with the designing and the surmounting of production difficulties. Hence, there is a lack of skill formation in the machinery-producing industry. Very often, the import of machinery contributes to a decline of existing capabilities in mechanical construction and metal working. Perfect specialisation increases via imports of machinery, therefore, enlarges the lag between underdeveloped countries' competitive position in machinery application (due to low labour costs) and local production of machinery. Local production of machinery, consequently, suffers an increasing comparative disadvantage. If the physical aspect of the flexibility of capitalist industrial economies is to be seen in the capacity to produce new equipment in order to satisfy new demands, then the systematic discouragement of machinery production in underdeveloped countries contributes to their inflexibility already mentioned.

The comparative advantage of underdeveloped countries is highest where their relative backwardness is lowest. Let us mention agricultural products (food, beverages, and raw materials) that depend on climate; raw mineral materials, the rich deposits of which are already depleted in the industrialised countries; low skill manufactures produced with a low degree of mechanisation; and low skill manufactures produced in highly mechanised industries, although using a standardised assembly-line type of technology. These products all have limited impact on skill formation. It should be noted that these products are produced by labour-intensive and capital-intensive technologies. It is critical to consider relative backwardness—and not factor proportions.

4. Structural heterogeneity, the exchange rate and rent

The following part of my argument will show that structural heterogeneity would disappear if underdeveloped economies would accept perfect specialisation. Perfect specialisation would, however, lead to decreasing export earnings. This is because of low price and income elasticities for most of the relatively less backwards products of underdeveloped countries.

Suppose relative backwardness is indeed low in certain agricultural export production lines, mineral production, the non-mechanised production of labour-intensive consumption goods, or the capital-intensive assembly-line type production. Suppose that there was perfect competition in an export industry, e.g. oil extraction. Oil exporting countries would increase exported quantities by lowering the price until earnings decrease to the level at which alternative uses of the required factors of production become competitive. The expansion of this production would be pursued until the price is equivalent to the opportunity costs of alternative non-export-oriented productions. If coffee and cocoa markets were not regulated, the prices of these crops would be pushed down to the level of earnings possible from the manufacture of other items using the same resources of production.

Structural heterogeneity implies, therefore, that complete specialisation is avoided. The reasons for this limitation of capitalist production relations in the underdeveloped countries are to be seen in the structure of demand for the products in which Third World countries specialise

Underdeveloped countries are specialised in products with low price elasticities and low income elasticities of demand. Shares of tropical agricultural products decrease in Western consumers' budgets. Raw material consumption in relation to total product decreases because the saving of raw materials is a major source of productivity increase through technical progress. Additionally, the shares of simple low-skill, labour-intensively-produced manufactures in Western consumers' budgets are also decreasing. Capital-intensive technologies for low-skill mass production are designed at a late phase of the product cycle where price-elasticity of demand is at least low or decreasing.

Rising quantities of exports will be realised only at rapidly declining prices. Hence, if price elasticity of demand is low, for a wide range of the demand-price curve, a restriction of production can be used for rising export earnings.[6]

Limited opportunities to diversify exports with increasing earnings constitute a second incentive for maintaining structural heterogeneity. Suppose that productivity diverges considerably between different production lines. Empirical investigations show that productivity differences of 1:10 exist, even if very remunerative mineral production is excluded.[7] If there are such productivity differences, diversification of exports through the establishment of production lines in which productivity is lower will be possible only if the value of the local labour is lowered in international currency. This can be achieved through devaluation. If the exchange rate is too low, exports increase and imports decrease. This results in enhanced competition for labour; in case of full employment, it results in nominal wage increases. If the exchange rate is too high, there is an inverse movement. Without state intervention, the exchange rate must be identical for all products imported or exported.

Hence the international value of equally skilled labour is identical for a given economy. In relation to labour in more advanced economies, productivities of labour in underdeveloped economies, however, differ. In order to employ lower productivity labour, cost at the prevailing exchange rate is too expensive. In order to diversify exports in a structurally heterogeneous economy, the exchange rate must be lowered in line with decreasing additional international value of product. This can be produced by labour that is engaged in less productive export-oriented production lines.

Under competitive conditions, the cheapening of the national labour force through devaluation will lead to lower prices for already competitive products. Suppose that net export earnings are constituted only by payments to labour; that 10% of the total labour force can be gainfully employed at a given exchange rate; and that the decrease in productivity of additional labour (measured in % of the total labour force) can be specified by the function $x = 1/y$ where x is the percentage of labour employed and y the marginal productivity compared to the developed industrialised countries. In this case, full employment will be possible at a devaluation of the currency, and hence of the international value of the local force to 10 % of the initial value. While full employment is achieved, net total export earnings will remain constant at the set parameters. If, however, the government establishes export controls with price fixing power, total earnings could be increased through devaluation. This increase could be achieved by taxing the products where competitiveness is achieved at higher international values of local labour compared to the marginal values.

The specialisation on products with a low price, a low income-elasticity, and highly divergent productivities in different production lines has the following important consequences for Third World governments. Complete free trade will decrease export earnings; however, trade regulations which tax remunerative products may increase total export-earnings. Such additional income is the simplest form of rent.

Rent has been introduced in economics as income from natural resources. From my argument about structural heterogeneity, however, it follows that rent will emerge if there are long-term productivity differences between various possibilities of employment for factors of production. Rent in underdeveloped countries is linked to structural heterogeneity. Structural heterogeneity is connected to the coexistence between developed and underdeveloped countries. Rent emerges as result of different degrees of backwardness. Furthermore, rent only becomes visible if governments reject devaluation on the level of marginal productivity at full employment. The emergence of rent as an important source of income in underdeveloped countries, therefore, is to be explained by uneven economic development and uneven political development between the so-called "Centre"—the capitalist industrial countries –and the so-called "Periphery," also known as the underdeveloped world.

There are various forms of rent appropriation. Rents can be appropriated as differential rents if resource endowment in one region is better than in another one. The actual differences in resource endowment between capitalist industrial countries and some underdeveloped countries have, however, been shaped by diachronic industrialisation. Rich deposits have been depleted first in industrialised countries. After this depletion, rich deposits have been discovered in underdeveloped countries; by this time, mining and transport technology had already been improved. The appropriation of mineral rent presupposes that the respective raw materials are useful as inputs for production in industrialised countries. Such usefulness presupposes the growth of markets. This in turn requires the growth of productivity in the raw material importing countries. The existence of widespread taxation of minerals (Goode/Lent/Ohja 1966) as well as high incomes or a high degree of managerial inefficiency in state mining companies of underdeveloped countries largely prove the existence of differential rents in mineral exports.

Rents from the export of tropical products with no direct substitute appear as an income from monopoly pricing by export restrictions (marketing boards, marketing agreements) (Abbott 1967: 707). The possibility of selling at higher than equilibrium price is due to consumer rents. Consumers are prepared to pay higher prices that lead to higher earnings of the producers if consumer incomes have reached levels at which the increase of prices is not outweighed by a decrease of quantities consumed. Low price- and income-elasticities of demand for tropical products in the industrial capitalist countries are the economic basis for this type of rent appropriation. They are the result of the growth of mass incomes and productivity in the importing countries. Export taxes and state monopoly trading organisations, which provide considerable incomes either to the state, or at least to those in control of such organisations, prove the existence of appropriated consumer rents.

Rent is appropriated in a most ineffective way for development if foreign exchange rates are "overvalued". The argument that foreign exchange rates are overvalued certainly does not apply to all export products of an underdeveloped country. The actually exported products are competitive. The exchange rate is, however, too high for the competitiveness of to be built-up production lines in import-competing industries, and possibly also in potential new export industries. Rent emerges immediately if the respective country devalues its natural currency and taxes the already internationally competitive products. The additional income of the state would have its physical counterpart in increased production in import-competing and possibly emerging new export-oriented activities. Rent appropriated as a result of excessive exchange rates is what I refer to as "hidden" rent.[8] It leads to a high purchasing power of those in control of the export sector and to simultaneous unemployment.

High productivity levels achieved in the capitalist industrialised countries allow underdeveloped countries to import a basket of consumer and investment goods for their exports, which is considerably greater than the basket of goods available if worktime allocated to export products were to be reoriented towards import-competing production.

Hidden rent is the basis of the oft-criticised overpriced labour costs in Third World countries. Without such rent incomes, currency would have to be devalued. Additionally, labour incomes would have to be pushed to the level of productivity in activities in which the productivity lag is larger in relation to the capitalist industrial countries. Labour costs are too high because productivity in some areas–the internationally competitive activities—is sufficiently high to provide foreign exchange for imports.

Labour costs also are excessive because import restrictions protect less competitive production lines. Their high costs are shifted to consumers; this is normally paid from the earnings in the export sectors. The too high wages in the less competitive production lines are therefore financed by a transfer of rent from the export sector to the protected production line; this is a very widespread mechanism of financing inefficient import substitution.

Rent also emerges in the pet activities of the proponents of export-led growth, of the world market-oriented labour-intensive, or of capital-intensive industries. Singapore, South Korea, Hong Kong, and Taiwan[9] have all subsidised industrial diversification through a variety of techniques, including special taxation of already competitive manufactured exports. Hong Kong (Morkre1979: 211)auctions export licences and hence pushes up export prices above the cost of production. Singapore (Holtgrave 1987: 78 ff.) taxes low-wage industries,hence, raising its prices. From this additional income, it finances skill formation in more sophisticated industries. This tendency may be increasing under the pressure of non-tariff barriers in the capitalist industrial countries. This is because in that case, the competitiveness of Third World manufactured exports does not depend on price, as selling prices are set by higher cost producers in capitalist industrial countries.

One objection to my explanation of the importance of rent in underdeveloped countries should not be left undiscussed. Differences in productivity exist between capitalist industrial countries. Countries specialise in products where they have a comparative advantage, thereby raising marginal unit costs. Correspondingly, they reduce production where they have comparative disadvantage, thereby lowering marginal unit costs. Equilibrium may be achieved even if there are great differences in average productivity between two countries because the range of differences within various production lines in each country spans a rather narrow range, but especially because exchange rates adjustments are in the area of triggering the expected adjustments of raising export earnings and decreasing imports spending of the devaluing economy with the expected impact on the labour market, rising demand for local labour. If differences in degrees of backwardness in production lines are great, however, it is improbable that this mechanism of adjustment works

In such a configuration, a decline in export demand cannot be matched by new export production or new import-competing production at the given exchange rate. The ultimate limit for lowering the exchange rate is the productivity in "wage-goods" (Lewis 1978: 19; Bardhan 1982: 169).The neglect of agriculture as an important source of wage goods hence considerably increases underdeveloped countries' vulnerability to fluctuations of the world market. The same principle applies to the neglect of mass consumption industries and the machinery that such industries and agriculture require. Additionally, a highly skewed income distribution whereby the wealthy consume sophisticated items that must be imported or manufactured using imported gear, exacerbates this susceptibility. In addition, demographic increase out-stripping agricultural production puts Third World countries at the mercy of world market fluctuations. The tandem effects of relatively high physical productivity of agriculture in the United States and an artificially low price of agricultural exports of the European community result in the Third World countries being even more dependent on the world market.

5. Rent and the expansion of the state

In the next part of my argument, I will show that rent-creating uneven development on a world scale leads to different modes of production in the West and the South. I will also show that the South will develop a bureaucratic type of regulation of the economy with a centralised ruling class. Both of these forces will contribute to economic development in a contradictory manner. This question is more important than the controversy about the relative autonomy or dependence of the Third World state from international capital (Elsenhans 1996b[1981]:152). The capacity to implement mechanisms for rent appropriation is an indisputable characteristic of autonomy, whereas the appropriation of rent from other economies unquestionably requires economic intercourse with these very economies.

The appropriation of rent that emerges on the basis of world market-induced structural heterogeneity requires the limitation of competition. The penetration of capitalism into Third World economies has created some highly productive branches without "revolutionizing" the production methods across the entire economy. The penetration of capitalism into Third World societies has therefore not created a dominant, dynamic entrepreneurial class, nor has capitalism's penetration transformed existing ruling classes into competing capitalists. On the contrary, old dominant classes (*latifundistas*, oligarchies, state classes in tributary modes of production) and newly emerging classes (the "new middle classes") have been transformed into centralised classes, which I call state classes. They dominate a new mode of production, the bureaucratic development society (Elsenhans 1996b[1981]: 173-185).

I shall digress shortly to the reasons for the resulting limited and deformation creating capitalist penetration. Berrill (1960:356) and a wide literature on the Argentina/Australia paradox (Ehrensaft/Armstrong 1978: 355) have noted that a profitable raw material export sector may promote economic and social development if income earned in this production is distributed equally. This argument is correct for a limited range of cases. A more equal distribution creates a more homogeneous demand, as well as an internal market for locally produced equipment, etc. If productivity differences are high, however, labour cost—even in case of redistribution—may be too high for profitable production outside therent-earning sector. To some extent, this is already shown by the Australian and Canadian cases, where relative equality was linked with strong protections (Coghlan 1918: 1137; Parker 1949: 5).

It is clear, however, that the absence of relatively egalitarian distribution in underdeveloped countries further enhances the tendencies towards lop-sided development through rent appropriation. Most pre-capitalist societies in the "periphery" were characterised by a high degree of political, social, and economic inequality in the so-called tributary modes of production. Societies that were very egalitarian, particularly in some parts of Africa, were characterised by low levels of commercialisation.[10] The breaking-up of pre-capitalist solidarity structures was normally linked to rapid processes of social and economic differentiation.

Therefore, if markets for local technology-produced mass consumption goods were limited, the growth prospects of local entrepreneurs in manufacturing would be dim. In a Keynesian world, total profit for the capitalist class cannot exceed total investment, so long as government and workers do not get indebted (Kalecki 1942). If there are only limited markets for products manufactured with machinery, there are only limited investment opportunities because there is no demand for the physical counterpart of investment, i.e. equipment. There are no mechanisms for transforming actual or potential surplus (which is simply not produced, although labour is available)into investment. Capital becomes shy (Bagchi 1972: 20; Baran 1952: 74) not because of risk-aversion but because of market structure. If mass markets do not exist, the profit-earning class of capitalists will be economically and politically weak in relation to already more centralised politicised classes whose power is based in rent appropriation.

Rent appropriation requires and strengthens centralised classes, which in previous times were oligarchies (centralised by family connections and political ties) but today emerge as state classes. This shows uneven political development on a world scale, which is a result of uneven economic development. State classes are non-capitalists precisely because they emerge from the possibility of pre-empting surplus as rent. They may symbiotically coexist with other surplus-extracting classes, international capital or local capital. But the basis of their economic reproduction is not capitalistic.

Given the limited possibilities for inward-looking profitable investment, rent appropriation through economic relations with the developed industrial countries is the main form through which less developed countries, especially their ruling classes, participate in the (uneven) increase in productivity in the West. The struggle for maintaining and providing new bases of rent appropriation is the struggle of the dominant classes in the underdeveloped world for enlarging their financial bases. Certainly, such classes are dependent on capitalism in the centre, but this does not imply that they are not distinct dominant classes within their distinct modes of production. They are autonomous from capitalists or agents of capitalism. They are just as dependent and as autonomous as the working classes are in capitalist developed countries. These working classes also depend on capitalists, although they oppose capitalists in their social struggles.

The reasons normally put forward in conventional development writing for increased state interventionism simply concern the potential objectives the state can pursue with rent as a financial source. Rent may fuel the import or production of sophisticated goods for high-income classes, a form of new oriental despotism (Wittfogel 1957). The state may promote import-substituting industrialisation, export-led growth or eliminate deeply felt (by whom?) deficiencies in the productive structures. The state may satisfy mass interests and indulge in limited welfarism or populism. None of these objectives can be achieved, however, without resources appropriated by the state. If investment was profitable, private enterprise would emerge. The state fails to emerge as an important economic actor not because there is a culturally determined lack of entrepreneurship but rather because there are not markets where products produced with local equipment can be sold profitably. The informal sector's dynamism in the majority of Third World countries demonstrates this, all the more so when demand is fuelled by an egalitarian income distribution from state enterprises that distribute more money more income than the value added during their production (Elsenhans 1982b: 67). By definition, the state engages in or subsidises production that is not lucrative in the short term. In order to do so, the state has to dispose of resources that are not earned in these not very productive production lines.

This type of state interventionism in today's bureaucratic development societies should be distinguished from other sorts of state interventionism. The most common means of social stratification is the erection of "bureaucratic" structures. These "bureaucratic" structures provide ruling classes with the instruments of forcing dominated classes to produce surplus. A good proof of this is the emergence of tributary modes of production in any region where technical conditions—i.e. the mastery of nature-allowed the production of surplus. European absolutism has to be interpreted as the last attempt of European ruling classes to establish such a mode of production (Elliott 1963: 94; Kantorowicz 1963: 177), which their intellectuals in the 18th century highly admired (Lehmann 1980:153; Clark 1961: XCIV). Under privileged classes very often prefer statist control rather than the hazards of the market. The statist tradition of peasant movements (Mukhia 1985: 246), which strive for the acceptance of certain rules by those in control of the state, as well as the statist tendencies of popular movements during the European "bourgeois" revolutions are further examples (Shapiro/ Markoff/Weitman 1974: 189). The relative stability of the modes of production in Eastern Europe, the so-called "really existing socialism" may be explained by this preference for stability rather than growth, as well as the limit to growth.

In one respect, however, all these cases fundamentally differ from the expanding state in the underdeveloped economies. The resources necessary to finance state interventionism are exclusively appropriated from internal resources and necessarily affect other groups, groups whose production is necessary in order to create a surplus. Development strategies based on increased state interventionism in the Third World today, however, are financed to a large degree by external resources which would not be available without state interventionism. These developmental strategies are also based on internal resources which, because of structural heterogeneity, would not be invested—hence productively used—without state interventionism. This does not exclude the possibility that state classes will use their rent-financed advantages to gain advantage in power relations with competing local classes; this then allows state classes to increase their share of locally produced surplus. This may even result in stifling local entrepreneurship and in increased exploitation of labour and peasants.

The difference between actual Third World state interventionism and other forms of state interventionism, once more, is structural heterogeneity. Let us investigate the conditions of erecting developed countries' growth mechanisms in underdeveloped countries. I have characterised this as creating profitability for investment through rising mass incomes and induced production of improved equipment. A redistribution of income in Third World economies would have the following growth-inducing effects. A smaller variety of modern products would be produced in higher production runs. In addition, increased amounts of simple products—the share of which lower income groups highly demand—would be manufactured.[11] A more limited number of technologies would have to be imported. The possible use of economies of scale would lead to lower costs in assimilating and operating foreign exchange-absorbing technology. Low-quality products could be manufactured with low quality local technology in medium and small-scale industries.

The problem, however, is how to reorient economies already characterised by lop-sided development towards such a growth-inducing structure. High differences of factor productivities in various existing production lines—and more so in production lines to be installed in order to catch-up with more advanced countries—preclude reliance on simple measures of redistribution of income. In an exemplary manner, the Allende experience in Chile has shown that in order to create mass markets in underdeveloped countries, redistribution of income must be linked to previous restructuring of the productive apparatus (Landsberger/MacDaniel 1976: 524 f.; Nohlen 1974: 59). In underdeveloped countries, there are limited idle productive capacities—such as underutilised plants and equipment—that can be put into operation in case of increased demand.[12] Increasing mass demand as a result of local investment goods production would lead to balance of trade deficits. Furtado even argues that the Brazilian miracle was characterised by an adaptation of final demand to the production structure, which resulted in increased inequality of distribution (Furtado 1973: 301). Plants in this sector are often highly dependent on imported raw materials and other inputs; therefore, they cannot easily be adapted to mass needs. In the Tanzanian public sector, import dependence on foreign raw materials is 45%, compared to only 28% in the private sector (W. E. Clark 1978: 127). Idle capacity, however, does exist in underdeveloped economies, but in a "crude" form unused labour-power (Raup 1967: 275). If this normally unproductive time is to be put in operation for productive purposes, the productive apparatus must be reorganised.

For creating the productive capacity necessary to satisfy the rising demand created from rising mass incomes, first the establishment of plants is necessary in which the locally available labour can produce those types of goods (finished goods, intermediate goods, and equipment) which will be demanded when mass incomes rise. In societies with both marked differences regarding the types of products consumed by different income groups and inflexibilities within the economy, policies of income distribution must first aim at changing supply. In order to restructure structurally heterogeneous economies to mass markets, state interventionism is necessary. There is therefore no basis for refuting planning just because the results of actual cases of planning are deplorable. Failures in planning call for better planning or reduced planning but not for unmitigated market relations, as the liberal critics of the developing countries pretend (Bauer 1981: 202).

Once more, the lack of local machinery production creates an important bottleneck and impedes flexible adjustments to new demand structures.

If income is initially distributed highly unevenly, and if rent-generating export sectors tend to worsen this uneven distribution, then the productive apparatus has little possibilities of rapidly responding to a more equal distribution of income—a process that would result in the creation of greater massmarkets (Halbach 1983: 35).

The contradictions of import-substituting industrialisation are the main illustration of the problems that the state must face if industrial development in structurally heterogeneous economies is to be promoted (Venkatasubiah 1958: 199; Baer/Hervé 1966: 90). Import-substituting industrialisation is defined as a process of industrial development in which industries are promoted for which markets already exist. In economies characterised by unequal income distribution, these markets are heavily made up of the upper income strata. Industrial plants are erected with imported equipment in suboptimal size. Growth of capacity depends on additional imports in equipment. Employment growth lags behind the growth of output and does not absorb the vast mass of unskilled labour. The emerging industries produce at high costs. They have to be protected. Their customers have to pay higher prices in relation to possible imports. Revenue from these sectors hence is transferred to the import-substituting industries.

These plants are not internationally competitive and do not earn foreign exchange. Import requirements have to be financed from other sources, such as capital imports, increasing debt,and raising prices of already competitive products, such as raw materials. Import-substituting industrialisation thus depends on rent resources, a process which inevitably must be channelled by some sort of planning agency. This type of import-substituting industrialisation would therefore not be possible if there were no sectors in the economy which were able to provide earnings in addition to their own costs (including profits at the going rate of return). Import-substituting industrialisation is hence a result of the capacity of Third World states to appropriate rent. Import-substituting industrialisation was hence linked to increasing state interventionism. Its most pronounced form is the establishment of public enterprises which, however, has often proceeded in a rather uncoordinated manner.

State-owned enterprises in Third World countries are increasingly considered inefficient. This view is trivial, because they have to be so at a microeconomic level, as they have to perform additional tasks to production. They must provide essential inputs at low prices; remedy deficiencies in the productive structure; create employment in addition to their need of labour; and transform their economic environment. These necessary cost-burdens allow, however, feather bedding for management, which often lacks innovation, relies on foreign technology imports, enhances regional imbalances, and increases income disparities in the working class. Additional costs of economically desired additional effects can be hardly separated from inefficiencies. Furthermore, control of financial resources is often negotiated between such state-owned enterprises and central rent-administrating agencies. Increased emphasis on microeconomic profitability will result in neglecting the assigned additional tasks: in increased use of imported technology (Boutaleb 1981: 31), in monopoly pricing if possible, and high incremental capital output ratios. This factor may even be justified by arguments related to the special difficulties of assimilating complicated technology into production lines where learning costs are important.

The increasing inefficiency of import-substituting industrialisation has led to two alternative proposals. Some authors would like to dismantle the public sector in order to increase market mechanisms and export-orientation. However, as already mentioned, the successful export-oriented economies are characterised by a high degree of state interventionism and normally have started exporting manufactured products only after import substitution (Donges 1971: 54).

Others believe multinational enterprises should be accorded greater weight. Multinational corporations are, however, an element of state-promoted industrialisation. In the dependency development theory,[13] the view is held that multinational enterprises forms a firm alliance with both state capital and local capital. In a structurally heterogeneous economy,profitable investment opportunities depend on state action. These state actions compensate for the lack of growth-inducing incentives in local markets. This is not to say that such a state is capitalist, as predetermined goals may continue to take precedence (Elsenhans 1996b [1981]: 152-163).The controversy about the positive or negative contribution of foreign direct investment becomes trivial if it is clear that accumulation by multinationals in the Third World depends on the economic environment in which they operate. It is clear, however, that multinational corporations are interesting partners for rent-maximizing state classes. The technical efficiency of multinational enterprises and their oligopolistic enterprise-specific comparative advantage result in rent income (Hymer 1976: 25, 91; Vernon 1974: 276-282). This income can be taxed by the state and creates a financial linkage (Elsenhans 1976d:171 f.). This can be spent, in one scenario, via investment obligations. The other scenario is to implement local content rules on new productive capacity that is not competitive compared to imports but which is erected as there exists no other way of using profits (Reza/Mahbubul Alam/Rashid 1987: 73; Gillis 1980: 258).

Until the 1980s, one form of appropriating resources for state class promoted investment has been to increase the capacity of Third World states to go into debt.[14] Insufficient production increases and the erection of protectionist measures, as well as falling raw material prices in the West, have severely hampered the possibilities of servicing this external debt. But even if these obstacles were removed,the contradictions of import-substituting industrialisation already mentioned would still make repayment difficult. The better performance of imported technology in relation to locally produced technology—especially for products consumed by high income groups—has led to the illusion that development could be bought as long as rent and other external sources were available.

In conclusion,we can demonstrate that the rise of state interventionism in developing economies would not have been conceivable without the emergence of rent as a significant source of revenue. Rent‘s growing importance is a result of global market-induced structural variability.

6. The mode of functioning of state classes of bureaucratic development societies with special regard to the integration and diversification of the productive apparatus

It has been shown that the basis of the rising state interventionism in Third World economies is rent and the absence of a price structure consistent with development aims if mass needs were taken into consideration. Rent fuels a process of concentration of funds in the hands of the state and various institutions related to the state.

A mode of production is defined by the division of labour, the mechanisms of appropriating and allocating internal and external surplus, and the mechanisms of creating stability of the system. With respect to those criteria, the rent-financed state-dominated societies of underdeveloped countries have to be defined as particular modes or production. I call these bureaucratic development societies (Elsenhans 1996b [1981]: 173-178). There is a sharp division of labour in which peasantries, urban and rural working classes, and producers in the so-called informal sector are reduced to the status of exploited masses with little rights. Surplus is appropriated and allocated via administrative means and not as reward for competitiveness on markets (the Marxian law of value does not operate). The profitability of private and foreign enterprise depends on public-sector decisions in day-to-day operations.

The leading personnel of government, administration, state-owned enterprises and political support-building organisations (dominant or state parties, "official" unions etc.) constitute a class which is based on office holding. It is divided into more or less formal segments; these segments have fluctuating boundaries and compete for influence, prestige and resources. Some authors have described these rivalries as personal rule (Grindle 1977: 423; Gorlin 1985: 359). Segments form clientelist relationships with social forces outside the state class. State classes, even in their military wings, are not monolithic. There may be typical configurations of conflict: populists versus technocratic developmentalists, industrialists versus agriculturalists, etc. There may also be diverging degrees of authoritarianism and repressiveness.[15] But the state class plays the predominant role in appropriating and allocating surplus, as well as in the political decision-making process.

Bureaucratic development societies are not characterised by strong party organisation with firm ideological commitments as do societies calling themselves "really existing socialism".[16] Instead, they are defined by rather fluid nationalistic ideologies and a predominance—when compared to the ideological apparatuses of mass parties—of the administrative agencies. To the extent that state classes differ from ancient tributary modes of production,[17] state classes of bureaucratic development societies are not committed to the maintenance of a static order based on religious belief. Instead, these state classes seek the transformation of the economy and the society, whatever the direction of this transformation may be. As to their differentiation from the oligarchies that have preceded them in many Third World countries, state classes of bureaucratic development societies do not eat up rents but rather invest them to considerable degrees, even if for dubious projects.

The transformation of already existing centralised ruling classes into state classes has taken various forms. Ruling classes who pre-dated the European penetration were co-opted into the dominant local political system established by the European powers. There has already been an extension of the colonial state. Anticolonial resistance has led to the victory of "middle class" dominated liberation movements for whom—at least verbally—economic development has been and continues to be an important aim in order to catch up with the leading industrialised countries. Limited processes of "modernisation" and the tremendous increase of worldwide communication have eroded any legitimacy of ruling classes who do not integrate rhetoric of their commitment to economic development and social revolution. Certainly, political discourse can be far removed from political praxis, but never completely. This is probably less due to the audience imposing conformity between discourse and praxis. Rather it is because in any dominant class, there are believers in the stated discourse who try to impose some conformity, especially if this promotes their own position in the power hierarchy.

Such state classes constitute a historical opportunity in relation to the requirements of overcoming underdevelopment. Because of their internal dynamics, however, they constitute a danger to this outcome as well.

The historical opportunity is visible in the capacity of state classes to extract and allocate surplus for investment into production lines that are essential for overcoming underdevelopment. Members of state classes maintain their status not through investing in short-term profitable undertakings. In contrast to capitalists, they can channel funds to production lines whose economic usefulness is only guaranteed if complementary measures in investment, technical development and income redistribution are realised. They consequently have the capacity to continue reshaping the economy in the direction of mass manufacturing for mass consumption by expanding the share of locally made equipment. Because of the lack of control by other social forces, however, state classes are not forced to follow such strategies. Their relative openness (Alavi 1972: 62; Saul 1974: 349), their bonapartist position,[18] and their zigzag behaviour often described in the relevant writings provide them a relatively large degree of freedom.

The general dynamics of intra-state class rivalry of segments have been described elsewhere (Elsenhans1996b [1981]: 296-310). Conflict management between competing segments normally tends to increase the number of members of each state class and their privileges; at some level, however, the surplus is exhausted by consumption. Supplementary external resources become necessary. But there are specific inefficiencies in the domain of the regulation of the economy. Normally, state classes opt for technological solutions that are inappropriate in the long-term, overestimate financial aspects of the investment process, disintegrate the economic network, overexpand external debt, divert political conflict into scapegoat-finding in the international arena and refrain from effectively imposing labour mobilisation.

It is unnecessary to restate the general criticisms voiced against administrative regulation of economies. These problems are certainly found in most Third World countries. The specific problem of state classes is that the rivalling segments try to promote their interests in power, income and prestige by controlling economic assets. Any investment plan reflects not only economic rationality, therefore, but also power interests of segments of the state class. The problem is less an absence of a commitment to development but rather the oft interested and biased definition of the requirements for such a development orientation. Redirecting investment from heavy to light industry, necessarily hurts those segments that depend on control of the Ministry of Heavy Industry. The opposite redirection arouses the jealousy of segments opposed to that ministry. The introduction of market regulation necessarily reduces the job possibilities (and therefore the clientele-building capacities) of the segments, who depend on the Ministry of Planning, etc.

Moreover, because any development strategy in an underdeveloped country must confront scarcity of resources, the distribution of such resources—often raw materials, semi-finished products, imported machinery, etc.—among different firms becomes an issue of intersegment rivalry. The timely delivery of inputs largely determines the economic results of production units. Since the interpretation of economic success is one of the assets in intersegment rivalries, the managers of public and private enterprises try to build up personal relations with those members of the state class who eventually decide on the respective deliveries and who engage into segment building. Decision-makers on deliveries have to pay attention to the impact of their decision on the position of their segment. It is not important to provide strategic inputs to an enterprise where no management member has to be strengthened, even if the output of this enterprise is of strategic value. The fact that these scarce inputs can be useful to a management that is affiliated to the respective decision-makers' segment will be more decisive. Such necessarily political behaviour multiplies the already-existing bottlenecks.

The choice of technology by state classes is influenced first by their socialisation process. Members are recruited at least in the second generation from formally educated population strata (even if diplomas are only a necessity but not a sufficient condition). They tend therefore to have a preference that is scientifically biased towards the most modern technology, albeit with little regard towards the problems of implementation (Baer/Figueroa 1982: 68). Production results which are lower than projections invariably occur. This is often attributed to the foreign partner's misdeeds, yet it can also be a result of the deficient economic and social environment.

Even if foreign contractors often push for imported technology in an inconsiderate manner, short-term interests of the state classes also encourage such imports. If rent is appropriated by taxing production lines with high cost advantages, the state disposes of foreign exchange for investment good imports. It is self-evident that when scarce resources are invested, they are directed towards the most productive technology. The analysis of the conditions of technical innovation has shown that more modern machinery—especially of the capital-intensive type employing low-skilled labour—is often more performing than more old-fashioned machinery even at low, but still too high exchange rates (Boatler 1975: 506). However, the more sophisticated the machinery, the greater the loss of learning possibilities of using local subcontractors and local maintenance—who could have imitated and further developed the imported machinery (Röpke 1978: 259). Equipment maintenance does not become an important outlet for a local machine-producing industry, nor does such an industry find an outlet in machinery replacement in such foreign-equipped basic industries. In order to avoid such a segregation of imported and local technical levels, state classes should be prepared to buy old-fashioned or adapted machinery. But this is irrational in a short-term perspective because the output-cost relation is below the output-cost relation of sophisticated equipment. This is because local machinery production in the short-term has the highest comparative disadvantage. In case balance of payment problems emerge as rent diminishes or import requirement rise, devaluation will occur and possibly make profitable production processes based on technology with higher local content.

A well-considered technology policy seems irrational in the short-term because it sacrifices production targets for the benefits of learning-by-doing in a possibly growing machinery-building sector. However, the formidable economic advantage of experienced metal workers for the development process is frequently overlooked.

It is clear that the more an economy disposes of rent, the less it is inclined to produce equipment. Even the South and East Asian newly industrialising countries continue to depend on equipment imports. This differs from most Latin American systems of equipment imports because these Asian NICs are able to use the exports' profits to finance the import of machinery necessary in plants. A closer inspection, however, reveals considerable differences in autonomy between more dependent South Korea and less dependent Taiwan, although normally these are discussed as fairly identical (Yi 1988: 137 f.).

Even politically, the import of foreign technology is advantageous. In relying on locally produced machinery, the state classes become dependent on their own working classes, which at least in some segments (e.g.,metal-working) would improve the bargaining position of the workers. Probably, such dependence would impose restrictions on the state class' conspicuous consumption and make it more vulnerable to local political conflict. In relying on imports of ready-made technology, the state classes become dependent not only on technology[19] but more so even on the readiness of the foreign partner to cooperate.[20] Failures can be exploited by presenting them as wilful harms inflicted on the country's economy by imperialism. National solidarity can be mobilised. If foreign machinery is more productive, then particular enterprises tend to opt for imports. This is because imports strengthen their competitive position in the market and allows other cost-increasing problems in the plant to be coped with. Unpopular measures in the plant itself can be avoided. Machinery imports can be contracted allowing the plant concerned to resolve problems associated with scarcity of certain imports. Foreign exchange that officially paid for such machinery may be put aside and kept on foreign accounts under the cover of unofficial arrangements.

State classes steer the development process by allocating investable funds. Plans may contain production targets, but the operative variable is "investment", and this involves spending money (MPAT 1980: X). Attempts to raise production are made by raising investment spending as long as money is available. The state enterprises exceed credit limits in the state banks, and austerity can only be imposed if the central bank's foreign exchange reserves and international credit are dried up. Investment projects are pushed through the decision-making process by virtue of their systematically overoptimistic evaluations (in order to edge out other projects). Production targets are not met, and, in order to avoid the loss of already invested resources, this necessarily gives leverage to the respective managements for obtaining further financial and foreign exchange resources. In rent-appropriating economies, foreign exchange—even if scarce—is not as scarce as skilled labour.

The difference between bureaucratic development societies and a socialist plan in an economy of the Soviet type is obvious. If production targets are not met with planned inputs, a socialist manager can redress the situation only by mobilizing additional unpaid labour. The manager in a rent-receiving society may prefer to have his shortcomings accepted as inevitable learning costs, which are paid out from rent.

Two factors should be noted. First, production targets are already manipulated during the process of lobbying for investment projects. Second, in the deficient economic and social environment of underdeveloped countries, production targets are difficult to achieve anyway. Therefore, management must consider that planned or promised volumes of production in upstream and downstream plants will probably not be met. There are two solutions: either an increased integration of the particular enterprise by creating in-house suboptimal production facilities for inputs or an increased reliance on imports (Boutaleb 1981: 31). The characteristics of the political rivalry between segments of the state classes lead to an over-integration of the enterprises. These rivalries also lead to an overdependence on foreign inputs (even if such inputs could be produced locally)—instead of the improved interconnectedness of the national economy, as was intended and verbally called for (MPAT 1980: 336-340).

Hence, the main problem of state classes is their relative richness. The resources they dispose of, especially through external financial inflows and rent, are too plentiful. Therefore, they dispense with mobilizing local forces of production to a sufficient degree. They reproduce the contradiction already noted by Singer (1950: 482).Singer deplored that if terms of trade are favourable, there is no interest in diversifying production and in increasing inter-industry linkages. Conversely, if terms of trade are unfavourable, there is no money available to diversify production and increase inter-industry linkages. This is a perverse economic mechanism: decision-makers are induced to waste resources in times when they have good opportunities to finance economic development, and they lack such finance when economic incentives in favour of economic development prevail.

The most important criterion for judging the characteristics of state classes is their capacity to use rent productively in periods of good financial situation. There is a vast literature, even in Third World countries, denouncing the ambiguity of favourable terms of trade and rent appropriation (Mahajan 1960: 360) which comes to the same conclusions as literature on Dutch disease, i.e. rent-induced underdevelopment (Sid Ahmed 1987: 904).

Rent is a dangerously ambivalent source of income. State classes are confronted with the task of transforming rent into overcoming underdevelopment, all while facing a problematic incentive structure which pushes them in the opposite direction.

7. Rent and the emergence of growth-impeding social relations in bureaucratic development societies dominated by the state class

The tendency to waste financial resources from rent is considerably enhanced by the types of social relations and of political discourse introduced by the disposal of rent. The main features are: a high degree of verticality of social relations; a lack of horizontal interest articulation; a wide variety of individual economic situations that preclude the formation of class solidarity; the persistence of forms of clientele and clan-building as opposed to the formation of bourgeois individuals; and a high degree of inaccuracy of information.

Reliance on rent-financed machinery imports for industrialisation has important consequences for the political dynamics of state class dominated bureaucratic development societies. Since the process of investment depends on imported machinery, defending export receipts is of strategic importance for state classes. Any arguments that focus on internal inefficiencies as the root of continuous underdevelopment erode the state classes' leverage over foreign agents and diminish their ability to extract financial resources from industrialised countries. Nationalism as an integrative ideology serves the state classes, together with Third Worldism, anti-imperialism and *antidependencia*.

In its relation to the other classes within their own societies, patronage and clientelist networks dominated by segments of state classes have been largely discussed in the "corporativist" explanation of Third World social structures (Lamb 1977: 45; Lucchini 1969: 46). Medard (1982) provides useful distinctions between clientelism, nepotism and corruption. These aspects of pre-emptive organisation of conflicting interests, as well as the associated constraints on interest expression and political engagement for underprivileged groups, are unquestionably significant. Official unions, compulsory peasant organisations linked to marketing boards, compulsory youth organisations, etc., can also be mentioned. All these networks assure stability, but they ultimately create a soft state (Myrdal 1970: 234 f.; Hyden 1983: 63).This soft state is accessible not so much to the demands of large publics but rather to the demands of well-placed manipulators of such publics. These manipulators, in turn, tend to reproduce clientelist structures with their constituencies. Lack of control over state classes by other classes does not inevitably enhance their wastefulness; rather, limited abuse of power demands moral norms that are unlikely to be met.[21] This is especially true, as Riggs (1960) has pointed out, because in such types of societies, family connections are difficult to repudiate. Often, the soft state turns to violence (Falola/Ihonvbere 1985: 194 f.). Ekeh's (1975) theory of the two publics in Africa gives further insight in the socio-cultural difficulties in implementing "Weberian" bureaucratic rationality. But also, the necessity of stabilizing regimes via retraditionalising (Hyden 1973: 211; Fatton 1985: 3) and "syncretistic" rule (Mawhood 1982: 232; Rivière 1985) explains the maintenance of informal channels of influence. To this, I add that within a mode of production where the appropriation and allocation of surplus is governed by the "political realm", the mode of functioning of this "political realm" is relatively more important than in a capitalist society. In establishing the importance of rent as income and the relative freedom connected to it, I draw attention to the importance of psychological, cultural, social and political factors that govern the use of this income.

In order to avoid overexpanding my argument, I will focus my subsequent argument on these political, cultural, social, and psychological aspects that are linked directly to rent. Financing investment with rent always provides opportunities for benefitting from market imperfections, such as monopolies, throughout the economy. This is already true if foreign exchange at the official exchange rate is cheap in relation to black market rates. If the exchange rate is overvalued, a liberalisation of foreign exchange would lead to rapid increase in imports. Therefore, the state has to control access to foreign exchange and hence investment, which requires foreign exchange. The capacity to invest at the official rate will depend on the decision of state planning agencies, to inscribe projects of these agencies into the national, regional or local development plans. If raw materials have to be imported, the daily running of the plants depends on state decisions. Profitability depends on good relations with the competent authorities. This applies to public, private, national, and international firms. If a private investor imports machinery, he will transform local national currency into international purchasing power and will hence appropriate part of the rent embodied in the overvalued exchange rate. There must be some entrepreneurs who get import allowances and others who do not. The ones who receive this privilege will therefore have monopolistic advantages.

Equipment imports for raising industrial production create comparatively productive plants in relation to the rest of the economy, at least in two ways. Some plants add capacity to production lines already in operation. Productivity in the more modern plants will normally be higher. However, it is impossible for governing boards or planning ministries to determine precisely how much higher productivity is compared to an existing plant. Management will try to raise calculated learning costs in order to be able to buy its workers discipline and support. Workers in the respective plant will then benefit from a monopoly rent. Technology import may also take place in new production lines. As learning costs must be admitted and as skilled labour is scarce, management will ask for high protection (which will in turn provide the basis for monopoly rent). The oft-voiced criticism put forward against multinationals (ILO 1973: 74)—that they worsen the income distribution—also applies to the state enterprises, and it stands on the same basis: rent. Diverse earning capacities as a result of technological advancements based on imported technology, market control and varying income elasticities of demand would result in divergent economic and social conditions of the labour force. The economic and social conditions of workers will not depend on the general power relation between labour and those in control of the means of production. Instead, it will rely on the particular situation of their enterprise.

Instead of horizontal patterns of organisation along class-lines, vertical relations prevail between those in command. Additionally, segments of the working class are associated with firms and maybe with branches. This is in stark contrast to the social ties prevalent during the early period of developing capitalism (Thompson 1975: 213; Prothero 1971: 204 ff.).

Capitalism has grown by expanding mass markets. This was possible because the struggles of the working people largely concerned wage rates (Steglich 1960: 204 ff.; Dobson 1980: 29). Probably even working classes in the West never wanted to fight only for material advantages in the social struggles on the entrepreneurs-labour level, as is shown in the struggle for franchise and social recognition in the political arena. However, against atomistically competing enterprises, only easily quantifiable benefits, such as income and hours worked, and possibly break times and minimal health and safety requirements, could be imposed.

In enterprises with monopolistic market positions, the bargaining process will concern non-wage problems to a greater degree for at least two reasons. First, central planning authorities often try to limit differences in pay due to monopoly rent through general prescriptions, such as nation-wide maximum payment levels according to skill. Management with monopolistic advantages will try to attract and to discipline scarce skilled—and even unskilled—labour through non-wage benefits. This tendency is enhanced because labour itself may prefer non-wage advantages for reason of self-respect. Labour also may prefer it simply because there are too few wage goods on the market in relation to possible deliveries in kind (transport to the workplace through means of the enterprise, housing, social facilities, etc.) or to more extensive work (workers may prefer less hours worked, greater acceptance of absenteeism). If the only thing negotiated is wage rates and hours of work, the atomistic capitalist entrepreneur must increase production through a maximum use of available labour-power. This incentive to raise productivity does not work if non-wage benefits are negotiated. In a typical capitalist enterprise, the trained workers with long-term employment in the plant achieve normally higher output than newly hired workers. In Algeria, there are cases were non-trained workers employed during vacation periods achieved higher output compared to their colleagues with permanent status. Absenteeism is used as an instrument of resistance by labour (Safir 1980: 50, 80).

The availability of rent creates social relations in the workplaces that limit the distributionist and productivity-increasing effect of the class struggle. Increased labour expenses must be offset by increased productivity in this class struggle process; increased production results in increased demand. Additionally, rent disincentivizes management from enforcing productivity increases against labour practises.

A state class bias towards the working class will possibly increase these constraints on productivity. A state class inclined to make real concessions to the workers will certainly want to link concessions to mechanisms capable of enhancing social integration, given the turnover costs of labour, the scarcity of skilled labour, and the advantages to be derived from skill formation on the job. Therefore, general ameliorations for the working people will come in the form of specific ameliorations at highly productive plants. These highly productive plants can absorb these ameliorations due to their strong earning capacity. The argument can be put into even more precise wording: state classes which comply to underprivileged classes' interests will destroy class solidarity among workers—perhaps in an even more efficient manner than state classes which do not or cannot proceed to this type of channelling a portion of the rent to the underprivileged classes (Fitch/Oppenheimer 1966: 104).

Suppose the following argument is correct: Class struggle over the distribution and production of surplus is the most important mechanism to force the parsimonious—and therefore efficient—use of surplus.[22] According to my first supposition, a disheartening picture for bureaucratic development societies emerges: class solidarity of underprivileged classes will be undermined by means of rent-financed vertical clientship-building that divides and pacifies the underprivileged classes.

Certainly, capitalism is not merely an economic system that mechanistically regulates the allocation of labour and surplus. I have argued myself that capitalism requires a social structure in which productivity increases lead to rising mass incomes (Elsenhans 1983c, chap. 2 in this volume). But there is a certain autonomy of the economic realm and there exists a separation of civil society and political realm. This implies that in society—as opposed to community in Tönnies' (1935: 40) old definition—the bourgeois individual comes into being by the destruction of traditional solidarity groups. The destruction of solidarity structures in small groups through capitalism may be deplored. However, this destruction established the circumstances for equality through equal opportunity. Additionally, it is possible that the end of scarcity in the industrialised West will result in the emergence of new such group relationships as economic supremacy recedes (Elsenhans 2001a: 78-85).

In a rent-financed bureaucratic development society, privileged economic positions do not depend solely—and often not even primarily—on economic efficiency. Rather, privileged economic positions depend on personal connections. Additionally, the economic condition of the common man does not depend on the nation-wide outcome of class struggle. Hence, in such societies there is a continual process of rebuilding vertical and horizontal small group solidarity links. Modernisation theory's expected tendency from industrialisation to a differentiation of the economic, social, and political realm is thus counteracted. Also, the individual continues to be tied to small group dependence in its political, economic, and social activities. The kinship ties, obligations to relatives which penalise economically successful individuals, importance of social connections, and even regional and ethnic solidarities have often been described as remnants of preindustrial social structures in Third World countries (Leff 1964: 9; Scott/Kerkvliet 1973: 522). They are, however, very modern forms of adaptation by individuals to the importance of rent in structurally heterogeneous economies. These styles of behaviour may certainly have pre-modern roots. However, they are perpetuated even during the modernisation process because the characteristics of this process make them function so effectively in the struggle of individuals for participation in rent. Industrialisation may certainly emerge without creating a bourgeois society (Kerr/Dunlop/Harbison 1973: 59; Abdel-Malek 1971: 19). Bourgeois rationality has been a condition of industrial development in the West. Its absence may create obstacles to such development in the South, but as long as technology can be imported, this absence will not preclude industrialisation.

The predominance of technology, the deficient growth of mass markets and employment, and the absence of local machinery production have all been considered in my argument as obstacles to overcoming structural heterogeneity. I conclude therefore that the prevalent use of rent for such inefficient development strategies will continue to support social structures in which vertical clientelist relations and limited autonomy of the individual will prevail. This will negatively sanction self-responsible behaviour, especially innovative behaviour in the economic realm.

8. Rent, communication, realism

Another obstacle to overcoming underdevelopment is the structure of communication in a rent-financed bureaucratic development society. In Western industrial countries, people meet each other with relative openness in their social and economic transactions. The basis for this human contact is normalised towards accepting behaviour oriented towards: profit maximising; the rating of individual success through income; and the relative independence of the social and economic situation when rating an individual's human qualities by other people (at least insofar as the rules of regard, honesty, and discretion are observed). Every person encounters some form of failure as a result of competition in numerous realms of social and economic life, every person experiences unsuccess of some kind. Many objectives are not achieved; others are. As a result, a generally accepted view emerges in which individual cases of unsuccess are not interpreted as definite failure of that person's life plan. In acompetitive society, modes of behaviour are reinforced in which individuals accept that others are superior to them in some areas without losing self-esteem.

If the distribution of resources in a society depends on personal connections, such open communication becomes more difficult. As knowledge about alliances and rivalries within state classes provides advantages in power, the only information which is communicated is that which increases one's own power position. Manipulation of information becomes an important part of the political process. Conjecturing and guesswork increase. A rarely existing free press does not look for news. In addition, in order to disinform the dominated part of the population, mystery-mongering expands. To prevent further demands, information about investment, reserves in productive capacities, and the stock and financial situation of enterprises are often withheld—even from central planning agencies.

The viscosity and the verticality of the information flows which results from excessively hierarchical structures (Elsenhans 1987: 83-86) and excessive compartmentalisation of decision-making is further enhanced by typical behaviour in state-dominated bureaucratic development societies. Any contact with an unknown part of the society constitutes a risk, for one does not know the means of influence of the person one is addressing. A reasonable strategy is to communicate as little concrete information as possible; to colour one's own situation; and to cautiously explore the wishes and situation of the addressee. Secrecy abounds in the political process and the alliances in state classes. Additionally, informal relations are highly important, but such status cannot be derived from the official position of the addressee. As a result, a substantial proportion of contact occurs with addressees who are difficult to rate and who deliberately conceal important information. In communication processes, therefore, the aim of communicating facts becomes secondary to the aim of avoiding hurting the addressee's feelings. The result is a decrease in clarity, completeness and accuracy of information.

The individual's economic circumstances are determined by their employer's specific conditions, their personal ties in a variety of forms, and their personal links with friends and relatives. Consequently, an individual's entire economic and social situation must be concealed even from persons of the same social and economic standing. Association on the basis of identical economic and social situations is difficult to develop due to the difficulty of communicating about these circumstances.

As good connections are important for achieving one's own objectives, communication about the various cases of profiteering is subdued. Others will view the disclosure of such information as evidence of unreliability and a lack of discretion. This is a disadvantage anytime the potential to profiteer to one's own gain arises. The amounts of money and privileges which can be appropriated through rent and connections largely exceed ordinary incomes from economic performance or even from property. Conspicuous consumption for maintaining connections becomes paramount. The respect for the susceptibility of partners in communication becomes the most important rule of behaviour. Individuals receive minimal information yet communicate their regard for one another.

In accepting this lack of precision, the feat of avoiding losing face is cultivated. Everyone strives to avoid putting another person in a position of humiliation. As a result, few people encounter failure. The psychological ability to overcome unsuccess is not learnt. Consequently, there is a great aversion to risk. Criticizing the existing state of things—if possible on the basis of holistic theories, which blame foreign forces for unsuccess—brings about less risk than actually acting themselves. This predisposition contributes significantly to the enormous excitement for theorising about imperialism and dependency that influences the intellectual climate in many Third World countries. In the Arab world, Hammad Ammar defines this as a "fahlawi" personality: "This personality is characterised by a constant search for short cuts in place of hard work to reach the desired goal. Sudden enthusiasm, foolhardiness and underestimating obstacles are features of the fahlawi personality as they are corollaries: quickly receding interest, discouragement before obstacle and lack of consistent and organised effort. Another is the burning preoccupation with surface impressions; thus, the fahlawi worries more about getting things done than about how they are done; he is interested not in true accomplishment that comes only through hard and sustained work, but rather in avoiding the impression that he is incapable of accomplishing things. He would not admit failure and would always look for some excuse or scapegoat to cover up for his lack of accomplishment" (Ammar 1954 quoted from Dessouki 1973: 190).

Westerners tired of civilisation espouse admiration for the prudent manners of interaction in Third World societies. This is contrasted with the Western emphasis on clarity, completeness, and correctness of information. However, these traits are achieved only at a price, namely a multitude of smaller and greater psychological injuries. Human beings are only prepared to expose themselves to these psychological injuries under the constraints of competition. If commercial contacts become less competitive as a result of other forms of interactions, then respect for the other becomes more important than information about hard facts. Pre-capitalist and non-capitalist modes of production are normally characterised by relations of reciprocity, esteem, solidarity, and rivalry. Even by the early periods of their history, such societies had developed rituals for avoiding injuries. They are really the result of a civilizing "process". Western civilisation appears to be inferior, if not uncivilised, in this aspect. It is no accident that the English gentry of the 17th and 18th centuries who behaved commercially were considered as uncivilised by the European nobility. Furthermore, it is no accident that the efficiency-orientation of American business is often considered in Third World countries as uncivilised and unsophisticated. The respectful communication in bureaucratic development societies is, however, an obstacle to development. Innovative behaviour hurts the interest of some; these segments become anxious and attempt to apply sanctions. Innovative individuals and workers who may wish to have their rights recognised are criticised for not abiding to the rules of "suum cuique" and of respectful behaviour vis-à-vis others. These ideas are still extensively adhered to by a sizable portion of the population across all social strata in many Third World countries.

Therefore, it can be concluded that there will be no catching up of state class dominated bureaucratic development societies to the level of technical capacities of developed capitalist countries. This implies that the international economic basis for structural heterogeneity in the

Third World will continue to exist for a very long time. Bureaucratic development societies, therefore, cannot be considered as forms in the transition to capitalism.

9. The demand for a New International Economic Order, as an expression of the contradictions of state class dominated economic development in structurally heterogeneous economies

The basic contradiction of state class dominated economic development is the continued dependence on imported technology. The result of this dependency is very often an increase of foreign exchange requirements if the investment process is accelerated. The excesses of import-substituting industrialisation (in reality import substitution without adequate social restructuring), the increase in foreign debt, the reliance on multinational corporations, and hence the tendency to blame these companies as scapegoats, are all aspects of this dependence on imported technology. The savings gap and the foreign exchange gap in import-substituting industrialisation can already only appear if further growth in production depends on further growth in imports. A country that can simultaneously produce equipment and export products will easily shift factors of production from exports to import-competing equipment industries in the case of balance of payments problems.

Continued dependence on foreign technology leads to foreign exchange shortage and worldwide conflict over the distribution of resources.

The New International Economic Order that Third World governments call for is certainly a heterogeneous shopping list (Laszlo/Baker/Eisenberg 1978). The majority of demands, however, are for more government revenues. If there is no effective mechanism in place to ensure that resources are directed to the truly impoverished, increasing help will instead result in increased government revenue. Debt restructuring benefits governments' budgets because the majority of the Third World debtors are public enterprises, central banks, and governments. The controversial clauses of the proposed code of conduct for transnational enterprises reflect the attempt of Third World governments to assure technology transfer below the cost that oligopolistic technology owners can charge (UNCTAD 1978). Rules concerning the relation of foreign enterprise to fiscal authorities and to local public or private big industry ultimately influence the foreign exchange reserves. Stabilisation of raw material prices will immediately support government revenue if the raw materials concerned are already taxed. Government revenue will rise if a sellers' monopoly is established.

At a first glance, it may be trivial to state that the relations between developed capitalist societies and state class dominated bureaucratic development societies primarily concern the distribution of financial resources. In the realm of scarcity—the economy—actors are typically assumed to be seeking to increase their financial resources. However, a closer examination of the link between developed capitalist countries, however, contradicts this view. When a developed capitalist country's foreign exchange earning potential is reduced, it is unlikely that it will confront its consumers and request increased export prices or financing arrangements. It will devalue in order to increase its competitive position. The state may intervene especially if crisis looms large, but its intervention will hardly be oriented to rent appropriation. In addition to the possible protection of the national market, the overriding aim of state intervention in capitalist countries when interacting with a developed capitalist country is the cheapening of its products in international currency through devaluation and subsidy. Declining terms of trade may even be an important instrument for promoting growth in developed capitalist countries.[23] State class dominated bureaucratic development societies, however, need rising terms of trade in order to maintain their import capacity. This difference most clearly illustrates the differences in the growth paths of both types of society.

We can view equipment and final goods production in a capitalist economy as a result of a process of joint production, even if some of its investment goods are imported. Demand is increased in line with average productivity. Productivity increase is due to rising performance of machinery. As long as real wages do not rise more rapidly than productivity, this sort of expansion of demand through real wage increases has no negative consequences on unit costs. Balance of payment difficulties can be easily resolved through devaluation because devaluation pushes down the prices of export goods and the prices of the local part of inputs and equipment. Capitalist economies can therefore expand demand through internal measures and protect this expansion through devaluation. Rising real wages improve the relationship between the value of labour time and the value of commodities produced domestically. Devaluation decreases the value of local labour power in relation to foreign goods. The combination of both mechanisms is possible because the costs of production are only marginally influenced by the cost of imports. Capitalist countries can dispense with competing for financial resources because the basis of their richness is the productivity and innovativeness of their labour. Capitalist developed countries depend on the world market less for value than for growth incentives.

Capitalist developed societies tend to overproduce and can accept decreasing net international earnings in the form of declining terms of trade. Bureaucratic development societies, just like the old precapitalist societies of the ancient civilisations, tend to overconsume and are thriving when terms of trade rise and when external financial resources increase. There seems to exist a pre-established harmony between both the First and Third Worlds. This harmony is actually breaking down; indeed, joint action in the West and in the South is necessary if a liberal world economy shall be preserved.

10. The perspectives of the system

Rent appropriation by Third World governments will no longer be a sufficient mechanism to balance world production and world consumption. Low-wage labour in Third World countries will therefore compete against high-wage labour in developed industrialised countries. This creates the danger of a worldwide underconsumptionist crisis. It can be avoided if there is a New Deal between the West and the South. The West would have to accept increased resource transfers to the South, and the South would have to implement social reforms that will allow financial resources to be invested towards overcoming underdevelopment.

Just as a capitalist system on a national level can survive only if consumptive capacity matches productive capacity, so too on a world levels capitalism is only possible if total demand rises with total productive capacity.

The limited efficiency of state classes in promoting productive investment may be considered as a contribution to the solution of this dilemma. Certainly, in the 1970s the preparedness of some Third World countries to run huge balance of payment deficits and finance them through debts maintained effective world demand (Anell 1981: 77). However, the 1980s have convincingly demonstrated the limits to an increase in indebtedness.

OPEC has shown that there is considerable leverage for rent appropriation. Mineral fuels exports from Third World countries (OPEC exports) rose in value from a 1972 value of 30 (26) billion US$ to a 1981 peak of 272 (269) billion US$. Certainly, oil is not an exceptional commodity, as has been often declared by the court scribes of Western raw material interests where supply management is not possible.[24]

Rent and high export taxes are also to be found in the export of other raw materials. But even before the oil price rise of 1973, oil was already a very important export item for Third World countries. Raw materials exports from the Third World may be used for increased rent appropriation but even a quadrupling in price of the non-oil raw material exports to some 400 billion US$ (1980 89 billion US$ in US$ of 1978, Elsenhans/Köpf 1981: 241) would be equivalent only to a 4% production increase in the industrialised world (GDP 1980 8.8 trillion US$). A first conclusion can be avoided: Within the existing international system of coexistence between capitalist industrial countries and state class dominated Third World bureaucratic development societies, the latter do not have the "extractive capacity" necessary to make world production meet world consumption capacity, as productivity in the West continues to grow. Hence, rising mass incomes in the West continue to be required.

Rising mass incomes in the West are not problematic if there are parallel increases of labour costs in the economies with comparable level of productivity.

Profitable relocation of productive capacity is made possible by the transfer of technology and/or the difference in real wages between the production sites in the West and in the South. While this is important for total employment in the West, the labour movement in the West is caught in the following dilemma. Due to the prospect of technological transfer, the process of relocation is hastened if the labour movement in the West continues to raise real wages in line with rising average productivity. It leads to the substituting of high-wage jobs for low-wage jobs as long as there is no absorption of the whole labour force in the Third World into modern sector productive employment. It is not excluded that the increase of the number of low-wage jobs in the South ultimately could lead to rising real wages as well as better working and living conditions for workers in the South.

Only in this case will adjustment to the conditions of the workers in the West take place. Hager (1982), Cline (1982), Pfaller (1983) and myself (Elsenhans 1981c) have shown that the possible impact of relocation of industries on the labour markets in Third World countries, even in the case of a most optimistic evaluation of backward and forward linkages, will only marginally contribute to the absorption of under- and unemployment in the Third World.

If, on the other hand, labour in the West restricts pay rises in order to slow the runaway of industries, it will further exacerbate under consumptionist tendencies in the West.

There are a number of objections to this scenario. It is argued that the loss of jobs in the West due to Third World manufacturing imports is small compared to other job-killing processes, such as productivity increases (Mukherjee 1978: 79; Hsieh 1973). However, the current impact of desired inclinations is not indicative of future repercussions. Productivity increases do not eliminate jobs if they are accompanied by real wage increases. We observe, however, real wages lagging behind productivity growth in many countries of the West (Balassa 1987: 292).

Others argue that relocation can be coupled successfully with industrial restructuring in the West (Biggs 1980; Giersch 1978: 27). Indeed, some more technologically advanced countries have effectively succeeded in such endeavours. The less advanced industrial countries find themselves, therefore, between the anvil of Third World low-wage competition for their traditional exports and the hammer of high-technology exports invading their markets (Ikonicoff/Sigal 1978: 696; Vellas 1981). They feel forced to adopt wage restraints and protectionism in order to manage their balance of payment problems. In Italy, the domestic system of production has become an important element (*Le Monde*, 15 March 1979: 36). It is those countries who initiate the race for cost reduction through wage restraint and even wage reduction which induces other industrial countries to follow. This race for cost reduction—which closely resembles the race for devaluation in the 1930s—will necessarily lead to underconsumptionist crisis.

Some commentators argue that the microelectronic revolution will recreate comparative advantage for the industrial countries of the West (Bluestone/Harrison 1982: 94). Certainly, there will be a rearrangement of comparative advantage. But productivity increase which is the result of the introduction of microelectronics will have to be matched in the developed industrial countries by real wage increases (or fewer hours worked, which has the same effect on unit costs of production). This, in turn, will endanger the competitiveness of production lines with less than average productivity increase. Trade is not determined by absolute advantage but by comparative advantage. Additionally, the introduction of microelectronics will alleviate major shortages of skilled workers in Third World countries and strengthen the cost-competitiveness of Third World productions (Ernst 1983: 142). The assumption that increased exports of manufactured goods from Third World nations will result in increased exports from industrial capitalist countries (Balassa 1987: 302; Lydall 1975: 112) does not take into account that additional exports from the Third World are low-wage products. As a result, the overall cash generated by their manufacture is frequently less than total income paid previously in the West. Also, additional exports from the West are smaller than the value of the displaced production. In order to maintain total demand, real incomes in the West would still have to rise by the element of improved terms of trade of the remaining branches in relation to the running-away production line. Finally, some authors argue that the Third World still runs high balance of trade deficits with the West especially in the manufactured goods trade (OECD 1979: 11 f.). Most of these deficits come from the oil exporting countries. The possibility of permanently exporting vast amounts of manufactured goods to those countries depends on rent appropriation. Until the 1980s, the newly industrialising countries were a vast market for manufactured goods of the West, and they were prepared to incur massive indebtedness. Increases in global demand caused by high oil prices and high financing have a cyclical nature. Falling oil prices and debt issues have highlighted the fleeting nature of demand growth.

There is now a paradoxical coexistence between developed capitalist countries and bureaucratic development societies. Capitalist countries' high wage levels (necessary for consumption) render underdeveloped countries competitive in an increasing number of production lines. Simultaneously, bureaucratic development societies need to appropriate rent in order to finance economic diversification. These two factors produce a new challenge for the maintenance of a liberal world economy and fairly peaceful West-South relations.

Export-led growth cannot be generalised for each and every low-wage country in the Third World. Only when structural reforms within such countries result in large multipliers and the expansion of local markets through rising mass demand will export-led strategies not be a threat to the bargaining power of the workers' organisations of the West. In the absence of such policies, structural heterogeneity can only be overcome by aggressive policies of devaluation. Prices for already competitive products would fall. Increased supply of cheaper old and competitive new products would "benefit" the Western consumers; however, they simultaneously hurt the Western producers and lead to real wage deflation and stagnation. This is the well-known underconsumptionist trap of productivity increases outrunning production increases;

this leads to realised production being below the full employment level.

A complete liberalisation of the external economic relations of the bulk of Third World countries is not probable because of structural heterogeneity and because of the massive rates of devaluation required for full employment. It has been shown that in order to avoid foreign exchange losses, Third World governments combine rent appropriation with export subsidizing. On closer inspection, the liberal model of adjusting trade to factor proportions is only partially followed even by those Third World countries which are considered to be most liberal. Vernon is right in warning that the state-ification of manufactured export production may lead to aggressive dumping strategies (Vernon 1973: 107). The factual evidence—as well as the consequences to be expected from a possible pursuit of the liberal model—constitute arguments in favour of rent appropriation by Third World governments.

In spite of Western governments' opposition to resource transfers of the type the Third World proposes in its claim for a New International Economic Order, even Western governments are actively engaged in creating the conditions of rent appropriation via import restrictions (Jeanneney 1978: 84; OECD 1985: 11-18). If a completely free international economy hurts important Western interests, then rent appropriation through Third World governments is considered by the same Western governments as an acceptable second-best solution.

The perspective of a completely liberalised world economy cannot be realised because it would aggravate the employment problem in the West without solving it in the South. Structurally heterogeneous economies which provide the possibility of rent appropriation will continue to prevail in the South. State classes will continue to be the ruling classes of bureaucratic development societies which will appropriate rent and diversify in non-traditional exports, which they will even subsidise.

Such a world system is extremely unstable for two reasons, in the short run and the long term. In the short run, rent appropriation is linked to highly nationalistic attitudes in the South. There is a tendency to blame for any shortcoming on the West and the colonial or imperialist wrongs attributed to the capitalist industrial countries. The possibility of playing off one superpower in the North against the other creates highly instable situations because the threat of one Third World country to change the privileged partner among the superpowers and their allies may be viewed by the other superpower as critical to its overall strategic position. This danger is mitigated by the fact that the economic deficiencies of the Soviet Union and its allies make it difficult for them to offer the required economic resources.[25] This danger becomes, however more threatening by the same fact, as Soviet influence is greatly enhanced when violent conflict makes partners attractive in the North. The Soviet Union provides fewer financial resources than the West, instead sending arms for internal or external war.

In the longer run, this system is instable because rent-financed development strategies will not lead to overcoming underdevelopment except under very special conditions. Although political conflict is not necessarily a result of misery, it cannot be excluded that various anti-Western ideologies will be adopted by the masses in the South if underdevelopment continues. This will probably be less trade-union type reformist ideologies aiming at material improvement and rather will be chiliastic ideologies of millenarianism such as Islamic revivalism. Probably the only way of avoiding this alternative would be the channelling of rent for purposes of overcoming underdevelopment.

11. Rent, state classes and the West-South cooperation

Appropriation of rent is a natural consequence of structural heterogeneity. It is uncontroversial that state classes in the Third World appropriate rent to varying degrees. The reluctance of Western governments to discuss the principles of a New International Economic Order with the governments of the Third World leaves, however, important decisions to the governments of the South. The following are the reasons:

- Raw material prices can be raised as long as price elasticity of demand is low and opportunity costs of substitutes are high. Currently, a plethora of Western literature has persuaded Third

World governments of the contrary. However, this does not preclude the possibility that new Third World scholarship will, instead of simply bemoaning exploitation, try to replace its defeatist Marxist *dependencia* forerunners by calculating possible rents on the basis of empirical investigation of the relevant data.

- As long as the great power rivalry in the Northern hemisphere continues, the capacity of Third World governments to appropriate resources under various pretexts remains important. As long as Western governments continue to believe that mobilizing mass support for mass-directed new development strategies will benefit "communists", state classes can ask for new transfers in order to avoid this threat.
- The profitability of foreign plants in Third World countries depends on Third World government regulations. As long as ordinary rates of return are received, transnational enterprises will continue to invest or to co-operate. Transnational enterprises will certainly oppose counter-monopoly actions by Third world governments. TNEs will also oppose regulations which push down exceptional profit rates to ordinary ones. However, they will oppose these developments only if and as long as their opposition appears promising.

Under such conditions, rising Third World government incomes can certainly be delayed—but not avoided. Rent may accrue to state classes which simply perpetuate underdevelopment because, at least for a while, they have sufficient money. In that case, the only hope would be that by accident productive forces will be developed too.

There is a possible alternative scenario. State classes are not composed merely of hypocrites. A class cannot stabilise its power if all its members pay only lip service to its creed. If everybody disbelieves, the hypocrites would not be able to discipline the cynics who want to tell the truth. In the state classes, the number of segments competing for power, prestige and income is large. Some segments are not privileged enough to be forced to become disbelievers or hypocrites. They are social bases for alternative development strategies. These bases will become more powerful if alternative development strategies appear less unrealistic.

If foreign exchange is available, alternative development strategies are economically even more feasible. Perhaps more foreign exchange than actually appropriated by Third World governments is needed for making them appear realistic to segments of state classes—who are prepared to push such strategies or to accept such strategies if pushed by others. But since such strategies mobilise local factors of production, they are certainly less costly in the long run than the situation the West will incur by neglecting the necessity of overcoming underdevelopment in the Third World: without alternative strategies of development, the state classes can only resort all the more to rent appropriating and rent wasting.

The characteristics of alternate tactics have been discussed previously. The key idea is that greater income equality will stimulate domestic equipment manufacturing and create more effective pathways for integrating modern imported technology (Elsenhans 1982c).

We should thus base a long-term strategy of the West vis-à-vis the South on the following considerations: state classes will be capable of appropriating rents, at least in the long-term. Social crisis in the South will impose upon state classes strategies of maximizing foreign exchange earnings. Such strategies become more and more costly for the West if the discrepancy between needs and productive capacity for mass needs increases in the South. Therefore, we should now use financial transfers to the Third World for creating productive capacities. These productive capacities can be the base for an increased local production for mass needs, with at least some local supply of machinery. In economies operating near full-employment—even at a still low level of real income—the liberal project proposed for the world economy would work. It would work because rising exports will raise internal employment, real wages and imports. In this situation, the limits will be established in such a way that growing involvement in the international division of labour does not disrupt global demand or result in ongoing South unemployment.

The demand of the state classes of the Third World for a NIEO presents a historic opportunity that can be circumscribed as follows:

- The Third World remains still divided enough that rapid unilateral increases in rent appropriation are improbable.

- Western governments can still demand concessions in return for accepting convenient aspects of the NIEO.
- Segments of state classes in all countries concerned can be found for alternative development strategies—if Western commitment to such strategies is clearly stated and if financial resources are allocated to such strategies.
- Western governments can strengthen segments of state classes in the Third World by linking financial transfers in the context of the NIEO to concomitant internal reforms in Third World countries.
- In the capitalist West, the spontaneous tendencies of the international division of labour create employment problems by export-led manufacturing and the erosion of the bargaining power of the working classes' organisations.

The problem of the state and the concept of the NIEO is not a problem of mere forms of regulating the world economy. It is a problem of relations between social classes in the international system. Underdevelopment as structural heterogeneity has created productivity differentials that allow for increasing rent appropriation. In order to be successful, the dominant classes have to address themselves to the Western industrialised countries. The power relation depends on their solidarity. If the Western industrialised countries were to consider it useful to oppose counter-monopoly, they would probably be forced to import some, probably many of the elements, of the monopolistic structures of the underdeveloped countries.

The scenarios described offer three outcomes. First, a parallel race into deflation. Second, a generalised power play for rent and monopolistic bargaining between an increasingly state-dominated West and an increasingly nationalistic, already state-dominated South. Lastly, a cooperative relationship linking at first some, then eventually more Third World countries and the West in a process of overcoming underdevelopment by some sort (but not by any type) of state-directed development policy. The distinctive characteristics of alternative development strategies, as well as the political ramifications of their implementation country by country, appear to be the most critical areas for empirical inquiry. Rather than examining the acceptability and feasibility of the New International Economic Order. The question of whether the processes identified in such alternative growth plans are of capitalist or socialist character probably misses the point. In this historic juncture, the alternative of socialism is not available to the Third World.

12. Concluding remarks and summary

The long-term controversy about the character of the state in the Third World has primarily suffered from two problems:

- The state has been explained from its purposes.
- The state has been judged according to its behaviour vis-à-vis international capital, which was considered the primary reason of underdevelopment.

Intellectuals' pronounced aversion against markets has coloured their analysis and identification of capitalism and underdevelopment in the Third World. From this, a negative view of those states was deduced which co-operated with capital. Intellectuals looked down on it not for lack of growth, but rather for the so-called dependent character of that growth.

In my argument about the conditions of capitalist growth, however, it has been shown that even if foreign economic relations may facilitate growth, the basic mutually reinforcing mechanism of growth resides in the internal economic and social structure.

This is also the case for underdeveloped countries. They will not overcome underdevelopment if they do not create—in their economies and in their societies—the conditions of growth by increasing mass incomes and local equipment production. The notion of dependency appears hence not only as inaccurate but as delusional. Dependency suggests that there is no way out from underdevelopment (which does not exclude some growth) without breaking the "system". The observable facts, however, are difficult to deny. In some underdeveloped countries foreign direct investment is still confined to some enclaves. However, in other countries, affiliates of multinational enterprises are able to accumulate, create jobs, and broaden and deepen production programmes. Export-led growth has brought considerable increases of mass incomes in some countries; in others it has not. Import substitution has allowed in few countries—such as Japan, but also Canada or Australia—to catch up with the developed capitalist countries. In a greater number of still underdeveloped countries, import substitution has at least led to appreciable—though cost-inefficient, if compared to world standards—industrialisation. It would be absurd, given the Soviet and Chinese examples, to pretend that planned industrialisation is impossible. The emphasis put on the mechanisms of regulation (market versus plan) and on the external economic relations inevitably leads to eclectic theorizing.

In this contribution, I have started with the argument that capitalist development is not the result of blind market forces but rather requires a relatively egalitarian income distribution. In today's developed capitalist countries of the West and Japan, this relatively egalitarian precondition has been achieved through various forms of social struggles that cannot be discussed here. However, the critical point is that these egalitarian arrangements facilitated an overarching pattern of self-centred capitalist development. The important implication is that capitalist growth is not characterised by a rising organic composition of capital or capital-deepening, or a rising capital intensity of production—rather it is characterised by the upgrading of skills. Hence factor endowment (as far as capital and labour are considered) will not explain foreign trade. Even comparative advantage will be a bad guide for overcoming underdevelopment. This is because the most important production line for skill formation is simultaneously the production line where comparative disadvantage for technically less advanced countries is greatest.

Capitalism exhibits an expansionary tendency. A key component is the search of individual capitalists for cheaper labour and cheaper and new resources. They are driven to do so when labour cost rise in the centre—which is as a necessary condition of the stability of the capitalist growth process—and also when cheap resources are depleted in the centre. This expansionary tendency cannot transform non-capitalist economies on its own. The penetration of capitalism into societies where there is no countervailing power of forcible redistribution leads to only partial modernisation of the economy. The dynamics of competition between capitalists simply does not lead to the necessary structure and required level of final demand that provokes and promotes overall capitalist growth.

I have shown that partial "modernisation" of the economies of the periphery leads to the emergence of rent as an important source of income and structural heterogeneity. Regardless of the historical structures—be it remnants of tributary modes of production or of the bureaucratic colonial states or of other forms of political organisation—upon on which Third World states could be built, the main economic sources which fuel the expansion of the Third World state are rent appropriation and the appropriation of internal surplus which otherwise would not have been produced.

On the other hand, structural heterogeneity is the description of relative prices which do not provide flexibility to an underdeveloped economy. Structural heterogeneity also, as a result of comparative disadvantages, discourages the local production of equipment. Ultimately, it encourages the destruction of local skills in equipment production if complete specialisation is accepted.

Inflexibility of the economy precludes the establishment of the capitalist growth mechanism by simple income redistribution. In that case, any horizontal organisation along class lines of the underprivileged classes is made difficult. This is because economic results will not be achieved by the means available to such organisations, namely changes in the price of labour and changes in the price of the goods of non-capitalist commodity producers (market-oriented peasants and informal sector producers). There is the possibility of appropriation of otherwise unused resources as well as the necessity of planning—even if plans are incoherent. Both of these are the two aspects of the potential appropriation of resources by administrative means, as well as the necessity of allocating resources by administrative means. This is the point at which the exact Third World state can be deduced.

These bureaucratic development societies and their state classes exhibit certain tendencies towards the inefficient use of resources and to growth-impeding social and political structures. I have underlined the tendency to neglect—within the economic system—the role that local equipment manufacture might play in eliminating rigidity that makes responding to new demands impossible. Hence, the obstacles in the economic structure to social reform and income redistribution will not be removed easily. In the political system, there is a low degree of participation. Interest organization along class lines continues to be hampered. There is a high degree of verticality. In the social system, solidarity relations in small groups are continually rebuilt and hamper a clear articulation of social conflicts. Communication is characterised by lacks in completeness, clarity and correctness. These factors contribute to inefficient resource use in the economy.

State classes accustomed to solving problems of scarcity through rent appropriation will tend to react to economic inefficiencies by asking for more external resources. They have been successful in this method to some degree, supported by growing nationalism in the South, the relative solidarity of the Third World countries in their claim for more resources from the North, and the global bipolar structure of the superpower system.

If the inefficient use of available resources by the state classes only precluded the abolition of poverty in the Third World, then a rational strategy for the developed capitalist countries in defending their interests in their relations with the South would be limited to restraining the financial claims of the South. The current state of West-South relations, however, is characterised by focusing on relative changes in productivity and wage levels. Western countries are still more productive than Southern countries. Western countries also have higher real wages than the South. However, in relevant branches of production the relative gap between West-South productivity levels is much slimmer than the relative West-South real wage gap. If the state classes in the South do not succeed in creating the social and economic conditions of full employment at rising real incomes for the mass of their population, then a nearly inexhaustible source of cheap labour will compete on the World labour market attracting productive potential to the South. The bargaining power of the labour movements in the West will be continuously eroded as this process will not lead to full employment in the South. From that point of view, the inefficiencies or efficiencies of state classes in the bureaucratic development societies must become a major concern for the Western labour movement. Indeed, it must become a major concern even for all those who are interested in the maintenance of a fairly free world economy and fairly peaceful relations between the West and the South.

I have described the state classes of the South as constituting a historic opportunity for overcoming underdevelopment. However, the realisation of this potential is perpetually jeopardised by state classes' internal economic inefficiencies. This possibility is also jeopardised by the social structures that evolve as a result of rent's widespread use. The dangers of failing to create the conditions of self-sustained growth in the South threaten the global economy. The remedy, however, is not the simple abolition of the public sectors and state interventionism in the Third World. Rather, the solution will involve strengthening the reformist segments of the state classes by giving concessions in the West-South negotiations regarding resource transfer, and it will also involve privileging appropriate development projects.

Notes

1. Ianni 1965; Caputo/Pizarro 1970: 69; Shivji 1980.
2. This notion has been widely accepted in German development writing; see for example: Hanisch/Tetzlaff 1980: 38; Jacoby 1985; Berg-Schlosser 1979; Hein 1985; Kasch 1984: 86; Ziemer 1984.
3. Of course, there is a solution to the problem if the rate of growth of product changes at the moment at which $\beta_t = \frac{(g+\pi)}{1-c} + \frac{\frac{v}{C_0}(1+\pi)^t}{1-c} = \frac{(1+y)^t}{(1+\pi)^t} \cdot \frac{Y_0}{C_0}$

   That the development of capitalism is linked to erratic movements of parameters may be true. However, that they occur exactly the way Emmanuel's arithmetic requires seems less probable.
4. c = 0,05—0,2 (5% to 20% intermediate consumption)

   g = 0,05—0,25 (capital replacement between 20 and 4 years)

β = 0,25—0,8 (capital output ratio between 4 and 1.25)

v/C_0 = 4—1,25 (capital per worker from 4 to 1.25 times wage sum in period of starting production).

5. Data on growth rates and capital output ratios in various issue of DIW, here Krengel/Baumgart/Boneß 1974.
6. The theory of immiserising growth is connected to these problems, cf. Bhagwati 1958: 201 205.
7. Amin 1973: 188; Squire 1981: 53; Bruton 1968: 322; Nelson 1968: 1243. This relation is not generally understood, cf. Lydall 1977: 24: "In European early industrialization, differences between 'modern' and traditional sector were less than in today's Third World." Obviously, because there was no existence of foreign countries which transferred their system of relative prices onto the early industrializers.
8. "For example, why not tax the export sector, subsidize the new industries and do away with the overvalued exchange rate so that industrial exports are encouraged." Hirschman 1968: 27.
9. Mytelka 1986b: 258; Haggard 1983: 83; Shih 1968: 121 f.
10. Despite important external trade relations, internal structures were determined by lineages, Meillassoux 1978: 327.
11. Chinn 1977: 79; Elshorst 1986: 7; Oshima 1971: 170.
12. Robinson 1979: 32; Ardant 1975: 239; Vakil/Brahmananda 1956: 219.
13. Newfarmer/Mueller 1975: 12; Gereffi/Evans 1981: 43; Bresser Pereira 1978: 326.
14. Matter 1976: 43; Tandon 1986: 194 f.; Fitzgerald 1978: 274.
15. "No debe argumentarse en este caso que se trata de 'un meno cambio de forma', pues las diferencias entre un regimen autocratico-represivo y una 'democracia restringida' incieden sobre la propria forma y las posibilidades de lucha entre clases y, por lo tanto, afectan las posibilidades historicas del Estado capitalista dependiente." (One should not argue that this is only a change of form, because the differences between an authoritarian repressive regime and a, restricted democracy' have a direct impact on the very form and possibilities of the class struggle and, in this way, impact the historical possibilities of the dependent capitalist state.) Cardoso/Falctto 1977: 384.
16. Chabal 1986: 93; Adamolekun 1986: 70; Mamdani 1976: 273; Scott 1980: 155.
17. The Tunisian nationalist Ahmed ben Salah argued in an interview (Nerfin 1974: 76): "On parle d'étatisation, de capitalisme d'Etat. Ce n'est pas vrai; l'Etat, pendant la décennie, a été un promoteur d'actions, qui a pris en réalité une place vide, ... l'Etat a

joué le rôle qui lui était impartie par la volonté des masses populaires de changement de structures." (One speaks of stateisation, state capitalism. This is not true: in the last decade, the state has promoted activities, taking an empty seat in reality... The state has taken the role which was due to it on the basis of the will of the popular masses to change the structures).

18. As a result of not yet formed classes or rising classes which not yet have become dominant O'Donnell 1977: 60; Murray 1967: 30.
19. MPAT 1980: 325; and also the discussion on the Code of Conduct negotiated during the confrontation over a New International Economic Order, UNCTAD 1978.
20. A rent can be appropriated in exports only if the trade partner accepts to pay the rent. If the oil-importing countries raised a tax on oil of the amount of the difference in production costs between OPEC and the oil importing countries, the rent would disappear, cf. also Chinweizu 1987: 547.
21. Cf. Benot 1966: 52: "Au fonds il faudrait un ordre de moines, intransigeants et inaccessibles aux faiblesses du monde." (One would need a monastic order, intransigent against and inaccessible to the weaknesses of the world.).
22. This class struggle is different from the class struggle over the distribution of surplus appropriated from external sources or simple lack of class struggles.
23. "Low prices for primary materials relative to imported manufactured goods normally are or should be an added incentive towards industrialization: on the other hand, they diminish the resources available for financing economic development. In this report, stress has been laid on the second, unfavorable aspect of deteriorating terms of trade. How far this factor has been offset or mitigated by the added incentive towards industrialization is a question which requires separate exploration," United Nations 1949: 127.
24. Initially, it was claimed that oil prices could not be increased, to the difference of coffee prices, Petroleum Press Service, 27, 10 (October 1960): 357. Later on, in order to promote the rejection of parallel price monopolies for other raw materials as promised by some leftist OPEC countries, oil was promoted by mainstream Western academia to the status of a special commodity so that higher prices could only be imposed for oil (since it was a special commodity). A nice example is Krasner 1974: 73.
25. Machowski/Schultz 1985: 415; Kühne 1980: 330; Kridl-Valkenier 1985.

4

Ultra-imperialism, Ultra-reaction and Ultra-Stability

The Political Economy of the International System in the 21st Century: The Demise of National Liberation Movements and the Global Decline of Social Democracy*

The International System is changing. New powers emerge. New political forces emerge. I call the new political movements which rise in Asia and Africa cultural identitarian (Elsenhans 1994a). Others may call them fundamentalist[1] and associate with them an increased probability of the clash of civilisations (Huntington 1993). Their rise may indeed imply a greater likelihood of interstate and internal violence. This does not necessarily have to be the case, however. I will distinguish between two scenarios in the current discussion.

In the first scenario I envision a more peaceful world as cosmopolitan political forces with an internationalist outlook increasingly influence national governments. This scenario resembles the one shared by the peace movement of the late nineteenth century, particularly its two main components: the liberals and the social democrats. These two forces were also present in the second half of the twentieth century. They found a further ally, the national liberation movements of the decolonisation

* Text written around 2005 and abandoned for private reasons.

period, which had been considered to be a cosmopolitan and ultimately peace-promoting force. All these forces are associated nowadays with the label "civil society". Although they comprise the most divergent entities, they normally exclude the really existing civil societies in culturally non-western countries where civil society is increasingly dominated by cultural-identitarian movements (Kaviraj 1989: 15).

In the second scenario I expect increased violence directed at members of other cultural or religious communities as a result of the emergence of nationalism—and even racism or cultural-identitarian exclusivism. In this instance, forces which analytically have to be considered parts of civil society become prone to violence.

The opposition between these two scenarios is consistent only under two assumptions:

- The tendency towards a peaceful international system is based on the assumptions of the institutionalist and idealist approaches in international relations theory. In these approaches, cosmopolitan internationalist forces on the left and the centre-left (in the Western classification of political ideologies) are more peace-loving and oriented towards the respect of legal norms and institutions based on such norms other than nationalist, conservative and right-wing forces. Because the realist school in international relations theory focuses on the necessity of violence and the threat of violence in order to maintain the balance of power, this view can gain hegemony in the camp considering itself to be the centre of the peace movement.
- Nationalist forces such as the New Cultural-Identitarian Political Movements (NCIPM) of the South have their bases in the rather privileged social strata. The latter create such movements in order to avoid re-distributive economic and social measures by forces representing the poor or committed to the promotion of the poor sections of society. They use the projection of internal or external enemies to keep these poorer segments of society from gaining political influence and transforming their force of numbers into political power.

My contribution argues that there is a decline of social democracy in the industrialised West and of the secular nationalists, in combination with cosmopolitan Third World forces that emerged from the national liberation movements of the de-colonisation period. This will not lead to a greater instability of the international system because the structure of the balance of power imposes also on such newly emerging movements' peaceful behaviour. Moreover, these NCIPM must meet challenges within society if they want to become majorities, and these majorities depend on moderately thriving middle segments of society.

1. Some remarks on "realist peace"

There is an interesting split in the motivations characterizing the peace movement of the late 19th century. This movement was based partly on an antimilitarist interest of the working poor in their economic and physical well-being. This movement also rested on the interest of well- to-do liberals who supported free trade and the "globalisation" of economic activities basically through the market. The social democratic parties of the West and the secular forces of the South have been relatively statist, however. Hence the democratic state, still a state, was the source of the tendency for peace. The present New Cultural-Identitarian Political Movements (NCIPM) of the South and the new centrist forces of the West are relatively anti-statist. They also once again privilege the market as an instrument for co-ordination. The decline of social-democratic and secular nationalist forces implies a decline of the state as an arena of interest aggregation. The state will be substituted by the market, hence the decline of one peace-promoting mechanism and the simultaneous rise of the other.

Idealist and so-called institutionalist interpretations of international relations do not oppose realist interpretations on empirical grounds alone. They imply a theory of action in which they argue that several assumptions about the definition of interests and aims to be pursued by foreign-policy decision-makers are too simplistic and too narrowly state-centred in the realist approach of international relations. In light of sociological and political theory outside the field of international relations, the critiques proposed by the large variety of non-realist approaches seem banal. Indeed, interests and goals are always defined according to interpretations based on perceptions, ideas, norms, etc. Hence interests are defined by the intellectual construction of reality by relevant actors.

The theoretical importance acquired by constructivism in international relations theory cannot be interpreted as a theoretical innovation. Instead, it should be seen merely as catching-up with the standard level of social-science theory. The entire decades-long debate over the working class voting for conservative parties and the conflict between white-collar and blue-collar workers is predicated on assumptions and arguments central to constructivist theories of international relations. The ordering of society into mentality groups by Geiger (1932: 78) dates from the early 1930s and was designed in order to explain the rise of fascism. The classical topos of Marxist theory—i.e. the transformation of a class in itself to a class for itself (Marx 1972 [1847]: 181)—is isomorphic with Anderson's (1983: 15) concept of nations as invented communities. Incidentally that position was already developed in Renan's (1996 [1882]) famous Sorbonne address. Foreign policy analysts, e.g. Ziebura (1955) and later Kiersch (1972), were focused on the problem of why actors in the same states were led to define national interest in different terms. My own work on the French war in Algeria (Elsenhans 2014 [1974]: 373-426) dealt with the changes in interest perception of major French political parties. France's failure in Algeria to implement an intermediate solution between assimilation and outright independence was not pursued with commitment. France could therefore not reach its goal of accepting equality of rights for the Muslim Arab-Berbers (the majority in Algeria) and rejecting the Arab-Berber claim to majority rule against the minority interests of French citizens in that country.

That interests are defined not only through a power distribution in the wake of a configuration of the state system is evident to all those who do not have to free themselves from the fetters of a simplistic North American diplomatic history that leans towards the traditional state centred lens. Neither Treitschke (1953: 21) nor Ranke (1957: 3) ever rejected the importance of *Zeitgeist* and perception in the definition of interests by individuals.

But there is also an empirical aspect of the opposition between realist and non-realist theories. The critics of the realist approach have often taken the interest of realist authors in military power and threats/deterrence as proof of their approval of the use of violence. But the appropriate and timely evocation of negative consequences of certain ways of behaviour may contribute much more to maintaining peace than simple appeasement. The toleration of the occupation of the Rhineland by Nazi Germany is an often-quoted case. Against the backdrop of the breakdown of peace and of the Versailles system, realist authors like Niebuhr (1949: 187 ff.) or Carr (1966: 63) have argued that a certain pattern of defining interests is preferable to others because it contributes to peace.

To some extent, the realist school of international relations can be interpreted as a transposition of the theory of democratic representative government to the level of international relations. It therefore certainly has an ethical dimension (Giesen 1992). A world state would inevitably lead to an unchecked Leviathan. A Leviathan cannot be controlled by the moral quality of its citizens, because human freedom is only the freedom of the dissenter, as Rosa Luxemburg (1963 [1918]: 73) assumed. It is also the freedom of a dissenter to follow patterns of behaviour that are morally abject. Freedom is the freedom to be vile within the limits of legal norms. Checks on the behaviour of governments are based on institutional arrangements that allow citizens to withdraw support from a government, not only to exercise free speech (Hirschman 1970: 9). It is most likely that among the two forms of expressing dissent, first voice—the right to protest—and then exit—the right to refuse cooperation and compliance—the availability of exit limits the danger of the iron law of oligarchy as described by Michels (1925: Chap. VI.2). Only the withdrawal of support by its citizens makes a government vulnerable to other governments. The rivalry between states makes governments—even dictatorial ones—dependent on the support of their citizenry.

The Kantian perspective of reduced violence between republics has a basis in the lower transaction costs of citizens of republics withdrawing support from their government. Peaceful citizens can increase their leverage on an executive to which they have delegated authority, if the executive needs their support. Therefore, any republic that depends on representation and not on plebiscitary decision-making will enjoy more democratic freedom because citizens can refuse support more easily. The republic's defence depends on the commitment of citizens more than any dictatorial regime. With respect to the ancient empires of Asia and the Latin American 19th century republics, the absence of democratic freedom has been explained by the absence of external threats necessitating the mobilisation of local mass military power (Andrzejewski 1954: 29 ff.).

The liberal counter argument says that an increase in the power position of a state depends on it becoming authoritarian in its dealings with its own public, especially with its own minorities (Kant 1963: 26; Krell 2004: 197-198). This argument must be qualified. The democratic peace argument is frequently linked to the empirical reality that democracies are far more effective than non-democratic regimes at mobilising their populations for war efforts (Kehr 1970). The capacity of Britain to mobilise female labour in war production much earlier than Nazi Germany during World War II is proof of this argument (Klein 1959: 205).Non-democratic procedures are not a guarantee for better performance in the application of external violence.

Realist authors in international relations theory insist, implicitly or explicitly, on the role of maintaining the balance of power between states. They regard it as a tool for preserving governments' vulnerability to external and internal challenges, so preventing them from becoming Leviathans.[2] This is the basis for their concentration on the argument that the pursuit of power by all states is morally legitimate. But the pursuit of power also implies the parsimonious use of power. It is no accident that political leaders inspired by the tenets of realism put an end to conflicts like the French war in Algeria (de Gaulle) and the American war in Vietnam (Nixon). Leaders in both cases pretended to act in the name of national interest; that is, preserving their respective states' positions in the balance of power. These wars had been undertaken by political leaders who were convinced that their enemies had to be defeated in the name of civilisation. They referred to those bases of the global order, which are normally valued by idealist and institutionalist approaches.

Not only do realist methods acknowledge that the use of power is occasionally essential, but they also acknowledge the converse: the use of power is not justifiable when it does not promote the aim of a favourable position in the balance of power. Their pragmatic advice to governments to increase power is based on the theory of limited government. This explains their empirical concentration on the ways governments seek to maximise their power vis-à-vis other governments at the international level in order to optimise it.

Realist positions can accept a diversity of values. The rogue state is harmless so long as it is rational. Because the rogue state is rational, it will not follow its bad intentions, provided that dissuasion works. The necessity to learn from discussions is the result of a credible balance of power.

The idealist and liberal approaches locate the rule of law more in the moral qualities of its citizens and less in their intellectual capabilities to realise that an ultimate punishment has to occur in case of deviant behaviour. Any collective endeavour towards moral improvement—from Savonarola to the Baptists' republics in early bourgeois Germany to the "terreur" during the French Revolution and the Cultural Revolution in Maoist China—was directed against diversity in the name of moral conformity. A realist-based international system, whether constructionist or not, will almost certainly accept diversity better than an idealist-based one.

Non-realist positions of an institutionalist or idealist orientation often reject the realist position because of the transaction costs involved in the pursuit of power. The argument has a status comparable to the critique of commercial advertising. Regulated advertising, such as the prohibition in Germany against comparing one's own and competitor products, may help reduce costs. In the same vein, realist positions do not exclude mutually agreed-upon limitations in the pursuit of power. There is no fundamental difference between the German peace movement of the 1980s and the Vienna Congress of 1815. The German peace movement of the 1980s pursued the goal of establishing a security partnership between NATO and the Warsaw Pact countries by mutually refraining from the build-up of offensive capabilities and concentrating on defensive arguments (Bredow/Brocke 1987: 161 f.). Similarly, the Vienna Congress attempted to establish European security by retreating from and geographically separating the majority of powers, at least in critical regions. All major powers had to withdraw from the Rhine and the central passes of the Alps. At the time, these had been the most developed and richest regions of Europe. Austria withdrew to the east of Lake Constance; France was present in only a small section of the Upper Rhine; and the weakest of the great powers in Europe at that time, Prussia, was established on the middle course of the Rhine, a region without any previous connections to this predominantly Protestant state.

Thus, in international relations theory, there is therefore no fundamental objection between arrangements following realist prescriptions and institution-building based on idealist or institutionalist arrangements. It is clear that if Kant's republics have a better democratic control of national governments, then they improve the mechanisms of maintaining peace. These republics, however, cannot do away with the necessity of maintaining an appropriate balance of power, especially given the fact that even democratic republics can be persuaded to engage in war provided the costs are low enough. The colonial wars of the late nineteenth century are sufficient proof of this, having appeared to be nearly free of cost after the invention of the machine gun.[3]

The contention between realist and idealist or institutionalist positions is therefore based on the following empirical question: to what extent can the transaction costs in the pursuit of power be reduced by appropriate internal arrangements within states. Should the goal be to increase the vulnerability of the governments and, in states with limited government, to promote the education of the public so that the pressure of forces favouring non-violent conflict resolution and the maintenance of an appropriate balance of power increases?

In order to establish my optimistic perspective of maintaining peaceful international relations for the twenty-first century, I will make the following five arguments. By discussing them, I want to substantiate the core proposal that a functioning balance of power with great powers whose governments represent the political centre will tend to produce non-violent international relations. This is more likely if the middle strata of society finds an appropriate environment for pursuing their aim of relatively moderate enrichment from markets allowing limited government intervention into the economy:

- The Vienna system was characterised by peaceful international relations in its core, despite the lack of any substantial political influence of "peace-oriented" political movements. The emergence of powerful middle classes added to the stability of the balance of power. This did not, however, constitute a sine-qua-non condition for a relatively low degree of violence in the core of the international system. The peaceful character broke down because of the weakness of states in the periphery of the international system. This happened when the system's geographical periphery was expanded via technical improvements in transport and communication. In that context, maintaining a functioning balance of power became impossible due to the ideological orientations that cemented the political coalitions emerging from the dynamics of social change in some core regions.
- The forces that claimed to be anti-nationalist and pro-peace—normally called cosmopolitan—declined at the end of the twentieth century for reasons which had nothing to do with their orientation regarding the mechanisms of interstate intercourse. Hence, the rise of new political movements can only indirectly imply a greater propensity of the international system for violent conflict resolution.
- The rising New Cultural-Identitarian Political Movements (NCIPM) are less cosmopolitan in outlook, but they are not necessarily peace-averse. Their capacity to deal with internal conflict without recourse to expansionist threats is rather large: They may disproportionately draw legitimacy from limiting the re-distributive mechanisms of their predecessors in favour of the poor. The cement that holds

these internal political coalitions together in the newly emerging greater powers, e.g. India or China, is less exclusivist than European nationalism of the nineteenth century. This will therefore tend less to promote violent conflict over territorial boundaries. The conflict between ethnic groups is always more clear-cut than the conflict between what Huntington called civilisations.

- The state structure is dominated by saturated powers with relatively minimal conflict areas. These conflict zones also find place in very few areas with a highly symbolic dimension. The emerging international system comprises only limited areas known as weak bellies. Despite the monopoly of the United States in technically sophisticated weaponry, this international system is multi-polar in structure.
- The emerging interstate system and the internal structures of the states will limit social change and create incentives for small terrorist organisations. However, it will also limit the emergence of large-scale mass movements or guerrilla organisations that could spread anomie and the politically unproductive violence this engenders.

2. Peace in the nineteenth century through the Vienna system and the limits of a Vienna System

In its core, the Vienna system comprised only powers that were determined to keep a lasting balance of power by establishing an appropriate set-up of boundaries and spheres of influence as well as a consensus on what was legitimate government.

This balance of power was characterised by a territorial reorganisation of Europe, which put all weak bellies, with the exception of the Rhine region and Italy, under the control of great powers. The plan for the Rhine region has already been outlined in comparison to the 1980s shared security arrangement and the Vienna arrangement. The middle powers on the Rhine were thought to be strong enough to resist minor encroachments of neighbouring greater powers and weak enough so as not to use their geopolitical situation in the centre of Europe in a new attempt at hegemony. For the same reason, the political organisation of Germany was characterised by a regulated balance between decentralisation and the influence of great powers. This gave Prussia and Austria a primordial responsibility but did not prevent the middle powers from enjoying the support of France and Russia in order to maintain autonomy vis-à-vis the leading powers in Germany, Austria, and Prussia. In particular, the very weak states that had emerged from the breakdown of the Holy Roman Empire were kept from regaining their independence in order to reduce the possibility of the greater powers within Germany building clientelist networks, as had been the case with the ecclesiastical princes before 1803. The arrangement in Italy was of a similar type, although that country was less exposed to great power rivalry due to Austria's relatively strong position.

In Western Europe, this system was compatible with the transition from pre-capitalist modes of production to capitalism, with its rapidly increasing economic trans-border interactions. This coincided with the liberal vision where the political power of governments is curtailed in order to facilitate free trade. In Western Europe, therefore, transborder movements of capital and technology rose already in the middle of the 19th century. This was quite compatible with the major elements of the liberal political order.

Peaceful adaptation was possible where the expansionist tendencies of capitalism faced obstacles in the political arrangements of the Vienna Congress. The sub-optimal size of the German middle states was complemented by their economic integration into the *Zollverein*. It should be noted that the *Zollverein* was a basically liberal enterprise that was not meant to erect high barriers to entry for British products but only to provide modest infant-industry protection (Hahn 1984: 47). A movement towards freer trade also occurred with an already weak infant-industry protection becoming even weaker. The event normally cited here is the French-British commercial treaty of 1860 (Dunham 1930).

The Vienna System left Western Europe with nation-states but allowed neither a united Germany nor a united Italy. Fifty years ago, this observation may have been trivial. That the decision makers of Vienna did not want nation-states is obvious, as the concept of nation was considered one of the sources of the revolutionary upheavals of 1789-1815. The nation was a concept of the left and was opposed by the political right because it implied a certain degree of equality between the lower and upper strata of society (Haupt 1974). It was instrumentalised by the right when the extension of universal suffrage required mass politics. In contrast to Britain (Ostrogorski 1903: 233) and the US (Keil 1986), the still-weak working classes of continental Europe had used internationalism as an expression for a lack of integration in their national political systems (Linden 1988: 323). The established parties, through a nationalism based on shared racial origin (Fitch 1992), opposed such a nationalism of the *"plebiscite de tous les jours"* (Renan 1996 [1882]: 240 ff.).

From today's perspective, the lack of foresight concerning the rise of the nation as an invented community is less worthy of criticism. Nation-states based on common languages comprise a minority of today's world. China's linguistic unity seems to take the form of a common interpretation of icons with a wide variety of pronunciations from region to region. India's multilingual character, at least with respect to its Northern region, is due to a social process quite similar to church reforms in Western Europe in the 16th century (diffusion of religion in vernacular).

Jaspers' (1949: 20 ff.) axial period was conditioned in India by the existence of a high degree of urban development. Newly emerging religions like Jainism and Buddhism, which opposed the alliance of divinities with the mortal ruling classes, had to contend with already existing stratified social structures. The character of these new religions as vehicles of social progress meant that believers could pray in any language, not only in secret languages such as Sanskrit, known only by elitist priests. Vernacular languages no different from each other than Chinese dialects became standardised through scripturalisation. Linguistic differences exist within Latin American republics and less so between them. However, the linguistic diversity of Africa is well known. In Africa, state building would not have been possible in most cases if the colonial languages had not been used. With a few exceptions, such as Vietnam, Korea, Bangladesh, Turkey or Iran, it is highly improbable that the European nation-state based on the common language of a given citizenry has any chances of developing in Asia and Africa.

State formation is based on a variety of distinct strategies of political integration throughout history. The West European situation of states being identified with their populations' shared language was a lengthy process that began with Engels (1972 [1884]: 395). The emergence of nations had something to do with the egalitarian character of European societies. As a certain commonality existed between the higher and lower ranks of society, the higher ranks had to adopt the language of the lower ones. The higher ranks had to be kept from developing idioms that openly defied the unified character of the domain of feudal rulers. The creation of unified languages could be the result of violent processes such as the destruction of the Languedoc in France during the Albigensian crusades (Strayer 1992; Sumption 2000) and the destruction of linguistic similarities between North-western Italy, French Provence, and Catalonia which existed at the time of the troubadours (Ceriello 1950: 6). It could also be the result of diffusion processes, such as the generalisation of one German dialect of the colonised territories of the East to the rest of the country (Berger 1954). Like all colonial languages, this was more homogeneous than the root language it drew upon (cf. from Italianto Spanish: the number of irregular verbs can be quoted as an indicator). In the case of Germany this included, at the level of the written language, Switzerland (already independent from Germany), but not the Netherlands, which both gained their political independence in the sixteenth century.

The regional set-up created by linguistic unification through the absolutist state was large enough in Western Europe, Germany, and Italy—hence ultimately West of the Slavic-German border—to create units within which the construction of capitalist societies could take place. In this respect, the equation between state and linguistic group seems to have been linked to very specific, even accidental, historical conditions.

The construction of capitalist societies was based on class struggles. The rise of capitalism implied rising mass incomes, not increased exploitation (Elsenhans 1983c, 1997). The precise configuration of a modern European state is nothing but a result of the relics of past class struggles. Anyone who has attempted to explain the European party system's structure to students in India must be aware of this method.

The first opposition against the followers of the crowns were the liberals (Whigs). They fought for property rights against the royal prerogative. With industrialisation, working class parties emerged. These labour parties fought for the concretisation of work contracts. What type of regulations can be imposed on the weaker contracting part? Shylock raises that question of what can be stipulated in a contract giving him the right to a pound of flesh. The struggle of the working class for the ten-hour day concretises the limitations that must be respected by labour contracts (Marx 1965 [1867]: 184 ff.). Any longer definition of the workday was illegal without the rest of the contract being illegal. This tendency of limiting the freedom of the stronger party in defining dispositions in contracts that were unfavourable to labour has been essential since the early nineteenth century for the establishment of the continental European welfare state. Such struggles take place on the basis of organisation and communication and are largely influenced by the techniques of communications that are available. In the nineteenth century, the technique for communication that was available was basically the printed word, with audio-visual means nearly non-existent.

Written language became an essential vehicle for organizing the force of numbers against the powers that be. The process of the constitution of a bourgeois society has been associated by some with communication (Habermas 1965: 43 ff.), including coffee shop frequentation (Hadwiger/Hippier/Lotz 1983: 12 ff.). This becomes obvious in considering that international trademarks travelled to various linguistic areas in the nineteenth century in their written form and are pronounced differently in different linguistic set-ups. Take the example of Singer sewing machines and compare it to the twenty-first century. Nowadays international trademarks, such as Exxon, travel in their spoken form, and are even chosen for their capacity to travel in this manner.

India would collapse if state politics, an important part of Indian political life, had to be conducted in Hindi throughout the country.

Whereas the European ruling classes usually communicated in national languages, in the postcolonial state formation of Asia and Africa large class coalitions opposed an external enemy yet interacted with him in his language. Those in command of this language were the first to be considered partners for negotiation, once negotiations became inevitable. Indeed, the national liberation movements were not able to oust the colonial powers by military conquest, whereas the colonial powers could only crush the liberation movements with unacceptable humanitarian costs. The Algerian war of liberation as well as the decade-long struggle of the Indian Congress party may be cited here as examples.

Belonging to a group of speakers of the same language is an easy criterion for defining social groups. Yet worshipping Shiva or Krishna, or both, or other gods along with them, or a multitude of gods within the framework of a caste-based organisation, will create a great variety of specific identities, even if respondents may still consider themselves Indians. The same game can be played with all other cultures. States in Africa or Asia could not be built on linguistic homogeneity. State building in Africa and Asia was based on a multiplicity of criteria. Very often the accidental existence of a colonial territory created by the colonial power was the first common element for a state to be created by a liberation movement. The pure existence of a state structure in an administratively defined territory could be the first unifying element. Here the state was a point of reference for identity creation. In addition, common cultural practices could be regarded as a meaningful cultural heritage and linked to the high culture of the clerics as the expression of an identity comprising the lower ranks of society, too.

Vienna could not prevent the class struggle from being organised through common languages in Europe, resulting in the inevitable emergence of a unified Germany and a unified Italy. The unification of Italy and Germany could be digested by the system, although it led to conflict in the Rhine region, where the great powers had intentionally sought to keep a low profile. This was exacerbated by the German annexation of Alsace-Lorraine. The well-known rigidities of the balance-of-power system after 1894 contributed to certain aspects of alliance-building considered to be a cause of World War I (Langer 1936; Singer/Small 1968).

Dynastic absolutist state-building, particularly in Eastern Europe, had not resulted in large linguistically unified territories—just like the state-building process existent in Asia or Africa today. In Eastern Europe a new irredentism involved a contradiction between the extension of the West-European-type nation-state to Eastern Europe and the maintenance of an appropriate balance of power within Europe (Rotfels 1956).

In the 1920s, in East Central Europe—the area between Germany and the Soviet Union known as intermediate Europe—the enlargement of democratic participation through nationally unified communities became impossible.[4] Pre-capitalist state building had created neither a common Polish linguistic community out of Poles, Belarussians, and Western Ukrainians, nor a uniform identity among the Southern Slavs, including Bulgaria. At the crossroads of communication between Britain and its Indian Empire, the Russian advance to the Mediterranean from the Black Sea created a soft belly as early as the 1820s (the Greek question), which even in the late nineteenth century was extremely destabilizing because it comprised mainly Christian populations under Muslim rule. From 1853 onwards, the majority of conflicts between European powers dealt mainly with the Balkans, not with imperialist expansion outside Europe. In 1878, it was already out of the Balkans that the race for control of Africa started. Britain occupied Egypt in 1881 after the creation of Bulgaria. Britain accepted the French occupation of Tunisia as a counterbalance in 1884.

The paddle steamer suddenly made it relatively easy to penetrate the hitherto "dark continents" or inaccessible old kingdoms. In order to preserve the balance of power, each power tried to establish its presence or to occupy the mouths of promising river routes leading inland, some of which, like the Mekong, were later found to be unnavigable because of cataracts (Ganiage 1938: 35). The peaceful character of the Vienna system is demonstrated by the fact that a slew of agreements negotiated under its auspices prevented the use of prospective colonial bridgeheads for occupying large stretches of territory that might have toppled the balance of power. The Berlin Congress of 1884/5 was basically an arrangement about the avoidance of conflicts arising between the dominant powers from the extension of their colonial bridgeheads into the "uncivilised" hinterland (Fieldhouse 1965: 182; Hargreaves 1974: 45).

World War I was fought over issues concerning the balance of power in Europe and not because of colonial rivalries. The demographically and economically most dynamic continental power, Germany, feared being isolated from the other powers. Germany was allied only to Austria, which was on the decline anyway. World War I ended with the defeat of Germany and the dissolution of the Austro-Hungarian state. As a result, the soft belly of intermediate Europe was transformed into a group of weak states plagued by border conflicts. The shift in the balance of power caused by German unification in 1870 was corrected by denying Germans in the former Austro-Hungarian lands the right to self-determination. This meant that Germany could not be integrated as a status-quo power in the modified Vienna system.

The ethnic legitimisation of boundaries, which had replaced the legitimacy principle of the Vienna Congress, was not conducive to a balanced European system. Its denial was perceived as an insult by Germany, where the wish for revenge or a revision of the Versailles treaty became universal. World War II was made possible when, in the economic depression of the 1930s, originally moderate German middle classes opted for fascism, with its clear commitment to war. The political perspective of gaining hegemony offered by fascism had become politically realistic because the major victorious powers neither stuck to the 1919 territorial arrangements nor engaged in peaceful change in the period prior to these new political movements taking power, especially in Germany. What Hitler had been given by October of 1938 would certainly have stabilised the Weimar democracy in Germany. Germany's striving for abolishing the Versailles system did not imply that all elites supported war as an instrument to realise it. In challenging the Versailles system, the fascists had considerable difficulties garnering support from

German elites (the 1937/38 crisis about the Second Four-Year Plan) and the public behind the principle of going to war (Sopade 1980: 583).

Obviously, violent means were applied where they were relatively cost-free, especially in the conquest of Africa and major parts of Asia, but only sporadically in India and not with permanent occupation in China. From the end of the nineteenth century onward, the British *Raj* had to compete with an ever-stronger Congress Party in India, and imperialist powers in China confronted those who seemed capable of modernising the country while maintaining its independence.

The absence of viable states could not be overcome by externally promoted state-building (tried by France in the nineteenth century in the form of the Arabic kingdom in Algeria during the Second Empire, Rey-Goldzeiguer 1977). This existence of "reasonable" states would have allowed maintaining open-door policies in the periphery with local governments powerful enough to resist their countries being taken over by a particular Western power at an advantageous moment. What today can be called state decay was a serious impediment to a proper functioning of the balance of power.

The peace movement existed at both levels: between states within the core and between the core and the periphery. As the debates on the colonial question in the Second (Socialist) International demonstrate, even the forces most committed to peace ideologically became infected by the notion of colonial wars having a civilisational mission (Schorske 1965: 79). Thus, in the fateful crisis of July 1914, their "patriotism" ultimately prevailed over the commitment to a peaceful management of interstate relations. The plans for mass action against an impending war had been debated at so many international conferences; they could simply not be carried out (Schorske 1965: 53 ff.; Koulakssis/Meynier 1985).

Vienna did not organise the conditions of peaceful change while still preserving the balance of power. Ethnic irredentism led to nonviable states and a periphery unable to oppose the encroachments on state sovereignty by local representatives of core powers. These core powers always found ways to invoke the necessity of preserving the honour of the flag. All of this occurred in a social climate marked by a rise in the forces of peace, liberalism, and social democracy to such an extent that Prussia even limited its armaments so as not to have to recruit such "unreliable" elements as officers (Kehr 1970: 155). As well, international financial capital was characterised by high rates of external expansion. This was achieved not so much through international conflict but by transnational business co-operation (Hallgarten 1935: 188 ff.). The Moroccan crisis was certainly a Franco-German issue, but it was also an intra-German business conflict: the second German steel producer, Mannesmann, was part of the French consortium (Poidevin 1970).

3. Peace based on the predominant influence of "peace-loving" political forces

I take it for granted that the two major wars of the twentieth century have led to a considerable strengthening of theoretical approaches which expect peace to result from the movement towards intensified international integration, including on the economic level. Cordell Hull's policy of the most-favoured-nation clauses in all post-1935 US commercial treaties,[5] the creation of the Bretton Woods institutions, and an intensified network of transnational or international institutions were all meant to relieve political pressure in economic relations and intensify solidarities through common economic interests.

Nobody would deny, however, that the existence of the atomic bomb and the convergence of the two blocks in their capabilities of mutual self-destruction were powerful incentives to avoid uncontrolled escalation. The fact that nuclear weapons were not applied even if the enemy was unable to retaliate does not prove that mutual deterrence was not decisive. Leaders of nations were aware that their nations would be judged on past behaviour in not yet foreseen situations,and hence avoided employing such weapons.

The escalation ladder itself became a topic of research (Kahn 1965). Western Allies did not open land routes to West Berlin in 1948 and did not intervene in Hungary in 1956. The Soviet Union refrained from opposing the marginalisation of large communist parties and trade unions in France and Italy between 1947 and 1949 (Fauvet 1959: 115), which had gained considerable influence through their leading role in the resistance during German occupation. All of this reached its climax in the Cuban missile crisis, where ad hoc, elaborate fine-tuning ultimately enabled escalation to be stopped short of armed conflict. The development of a Vienna-type process for defining areas of vital interest took place, complemented by arms control. Although both of these were backed by the peace movement, the peace movement itself was not the motor of this process.

The peace movement failed whenever it attempted to put the balance of power on the back burner through measures such as unilateral nuclear disarmament or the refusal to deploy an anti-missile system against SS-20s in the early 1980s. This does not rule out that the peace movement reinforced the tendency of governments to seek peaceful means in redressing the balance of power. Such a supportive role with regard to maintaining the balance of power is by no means meaningless. It eased the objectives of the balance of power set by the Vienna system. Yet the most committed forces within the peace movement were not necessarily the most supportive in rationalizing the balance of power. The question emerges as to whether there was a link between society's movement to support peaceful interstate relations and a decreasing importance of the realist aspect of peace maintenance via the balance of power. Only in this case can the constructivist, idealist and institutionalist approaches hold their own against the realist approach.

Although there are no quantitative content analyses about the relation between the commitment to non-violence independent of the balance-of-power considerations—and the position of different political currents on a right-left spectrum of political forces, as well as the basis of their position vis-à-vis the capital-labour conflict over the distribution of national income—a rough specification of political currents in Western countries may nevertheless be attempted:

1. There are openly anti-welfare-state forces that support only the market and promote the pursuit of power in international relations with reference to social Darwinist arguments.

2. There are moderate pro-market forces which are cosmopolitan in outlook but do not attach a great importance to mass movements in favour of peace, as they fear that such movements might spill over into the realm of conflict between capital and labour.
3. There are centre-right forces in favour of a moderate welfare state and supportive of national interests in a relatively narrow sense.
4. There are left-centred political forces with a stronger commitment to the welfare state and a normally more cooperative stance in international relations, but which insist on the importance of national interests.
5. There are more radical left-wing forces that give a high priority to redistribution without really questioning the importance of private property, and which normally have a cosmopolitan outlook in international relations based on the conviction that political majorities are not only in favour of more economic and social equality, but also of more peaceful international relations via cooperation.
6. There are forces that view the existence of private property not only as a source of continued social inequality, but which link it with strategies of private property owners to endanger international cooperation, since the interests of private property lead to state behaviour that is liable to support conflicts profitable to private property.

Social democratic forces in Western Europe can be considered as representing position four; Christian democratic forces would correspond to position three; communist forces to position six but on the move towards position five; and Third World secular national liberation movements are located in positions five and six. It is the decline of positions three and four, and possibly also five and two, that gives positions one and six the opportunity to ascend. Positions three and four are reinforced by high levels of employment which serve as the basis of growth for small and medium-scale enterprises. Unemployment and a lack of economic perspectives for small and medium-scale enterprises weaken the centre and open up perspectives for positions one and six, which hope to find support in extremist solutions, one of these being external war, the other internal violence or both. In a market system without the perspective of individual improvement, they tend to breed Utopias, such as the claim to national grandeur against the realities of the existing balance of power. The aim of revenge against the Versailles treaty among German youth (after 1919) and the rejection of the Israeli state by Arab youth would seem to be examples of this.

The rough specification I have drawn up would indicate that a decline of positions four to five, the secular national liberation movements in the South and social democratic forces in the West correspond to a decline of the forces on which constructivist, idealist and institutionalist positions base their hope for an increasingly peaceful world-wide state system, founded on an increasingly globalised and civilised society.

An analysis of the decline of these forces shows, however, that the salient factor was not their relative positions in the field of international relations but the contradiction inherent in their economic and social policies. The decline of positions four to five may have reduced the weight of some peace-loving forces but not the tendency for peaceful conflict regulation as the weight of position three increased. Thus, the shift in relative importance of these six currents might ultimately have an impact that is hardly conducive to a less peaceful international system.

The pattern of decline of social democratic political movements in the West and the secular nationalist liberation forces of the South is due to their more leftist wings, which correspond to positions five and six, and not to the forces which can be classified as position four. Indeed, the social and economic policies this decline can be attributed to are deeply embedded in a view of market failure expressed by positions five and six. Both types of political movement are heirs to the late-nineteenth-century critique of capitalism. They did not opt for embracing capitalism by managing it in order to empower labour.

This has to be contrasted with the Keynesian perspective. There is nothing wrong with free markets, including free labour markets, provided there is full employment. In the case of full employment, the assumptions of neo-classical economics hold that workers are free to negotiate fair conditions for selling their labour time thanks to the scarcity of their labour power. Keynes proposed state deficit spending not to raise productivity but to guarantee this negotiating power of labour vis-à-vis capital by empowering labour even through blatantly unproductive spending. The empowerment of labour on the labour market implies commodity relations. The lean state associated with Tönnies's notion of society as opposed to community (Tönnies 1935: 40 ff.) is one aspect of the principle of commodity relations reducing the necessity of a homogeneous society. An agreement must be reached on the conditions of exchange. Any diversity of preferences or judgement is acceptable, provided that both parties to a contract accept the rules of exchange. They are forced to do so simply by engaging in exchanges on a completely anonymous market. The option of exit provides each player with the possibility to search as long as he desires to do so for a better partner for exchange.

The option of exit exists with respect to all other matters, which become private wherever collective needs are dealt with by civil society. As long as no positive action is required in order to correct the market, no positive agreement on other than formal rules is needed.

Positive agreements are necessary for promoting a not yet profitable activity, which allows technical progress in view of the requirements of an uncertain future, or blocking an (often environmentally) obnoxious activity.

Positions three and four have underrated—whereas five and six have overlooked—the equalizing effects of the market.

The participation of labour in the fruits of technical progress is guaranteed through the scarcity of labour, not through legal stipulations in the work contracts of individual labourers made mandatory by state labour regulations. Scarcity of labour combines rising mass incomes with the regulation of the work process based on participation, as workers are more productive if they are interested in the product of their labour and labour flexibility. The greatest labour flexibility in Germany occurred the 1950s, a period of job-hopping, when labour was always sure to find favourable work contracts due to full employment (Pietsch 1978: 265).

In reaction to the crisis of the 1970s, social democratic parties abandoned full employment macro policies yet maintained older labour laws in the interest of labour, protecting, for example, against "arbitrary" layoffs through stipulations in work contracts. The centre-right (positions three and two) has gained ideological hegemony in social and economic policies not only because of the crisis of Keynesian macroeconomic policies but also, and especially, because of their opposition to the oft-absurd consequences of labour protection laws with respect to the flexibility of labour markets. The effects of such regulations were particularly deleterious for small and medium-scale enterprises, the backbone for employment in typical developed capitalist countries.

The weakening of social democratic movements therefore goes hand in hand with the weakening of segments of the peace movement that are less committed to the maintenance of a stable balance of power. However, this weakening can be found even more within the idealist and institutionalist positions, which expected greater "peace" from morally superior people.

I hence assume that the forces of peace can, at best, help adjust the balance of power in a non-violent manner to the necessities arising out of new social and economic issues, and lead to a reconfiguration of political movements within states (which may eventually become transnational or global). In that case the weakening of political forces of type five and six has little impact on the degree of violence that is likely to emerge in the future international system of the twenty-first century.

The secular national liberation movements of the South likewise were heirs to the statist traditions of anti-capitalism of the nineteenth century. They were convinced long before the world economic depression of the 1930s that there was a link between underdevelopment and exploitation in the form of unfair prices, a substantial element of the "drain of India" theory (Dutt 1970 [1949]: 100 ff.). This theory criticised the transfer of otherwise investible resources from the colonies to the industrial centres. The terms-of-trade explanation of underdevelopment belongs to this tradition. At that time underdevelopment was seen as the consequence of unfair prices for the predominant exports of the Southern raw materials. The so-called Singer-Prebisch (Singer 1950; Prebisch 1962) thesis argued that the raw-material-exporting underdeveloped countries were not earning incomes on the world market that would be sufficient to finance the import of investment goods that could be used for creating import-substituting industries. Underdeveloped countries were thus kept from overcoming underdevelopment through industrial diversification, which would have allowed them to refuse selling raw materials at declining prices. Although the argument has also been used by movements falling under types one through four, it was most strongly proposed by movements of type five and six.

Movements of type four to six heavily engaged in state-led import-substituting industrialisation. The crisis of import-substituting industrialisation has been so extensively commented upon that there is no need for an in-depth treatment here. Empirical evidence shows, however, that import-substituting industrialisation can also lead to prosperous small and medium-scale enterprises, even without state-promotion (Schmitz 1984). This, however, needs raising agrarian productivity on smaller farms together with a fair distribution of rural income in the wake of agrarian reform. Rising mass demand from the rural areas creates the Keynesian conditions for growth: expanding mass markets (Elsenhans 1983c).

The decline of secular nationalist forces in the underdeveloped world is the result of the failure of state-led development strategies, which, because of their distrust of the market, *per se,* focused only on the supply side instead of on the rise in mass incomes (especially rural incomes). They preferred using state subsidies to build-up modern plants behind high walls of protectionism against foreign competition instead of letting small and medium-scale enterprises grow on the basis of an expanding internal demand. This resulted in rent seeking and a low growth of employment. With the exception of the East Asian economies, which had no scarce raw-material resources, underdeveloped countries neglected the possibility of creating demand on the basis of devaluation-driven cheap exports, which was considered "exploitative." Mainstream development theory explicitly rejected this solution in the 1960s. It was considered inefficient and a concession to the West. In the case of devaluation, Western consumers would benefit from higher degrees of exploitation because of cheaper supplies from the South (Berument/Pasaogullari 2003; Buffie 1986).

The Taiwanese and South Korean cases show that a process like this could lead to full employment and overcoming underdevelopment if it is strongly supported by internal reforms, especially agrarian ones.[6] Multiplier effects from the export sector and from increasing internal demand would lead relatively rapidly to full employment, which was achieved in South Korea in the early 1980s (Bai 1982: 135): Full employment, in turn, would lead to democratisation (S. H. Kim 2000) by means of an alliance between small and medium-scale industry and an increasingly reformist labour movement (H. J. Kim 1999), which could be classified as belonging to position four in terms of economic and social policies.

The contemporary globalisation process is largely characterised by a shift from import-substituting industrialisation to export-oriented industrialisation with a strengthening of positions three and four. I do not share the doomsday scenario of globalisation so popular nowadays, but I do assume that the drive towards export-orientation is not strong enough to create full employment without complementary internal reforms, which I have described elsewhere (Elsenhans 2000b: 42-46).

4. The New Cultural-Identitarian Political Movements (NCIPMs) are less cosmopolitan in outlook but not necessarily peace-averse, having a rather large capacity to deal with internal conflicts without recourse to expansionist threats

There are two social groups in the South that withdraw their support from state- interventionist secular nationalist forces when NCIPMs arise and become politically relevant:

- The honourable small businessmen and those who want access to the situation of small businessmen when the capacity of the rent-collecting interventionist state declines following import-substituting industrialisation's failure to create surplus-producing enterprises; and

- The marginalised ones, especially youth, who do not find employment opportunities due to the lack of dynamism of the so-called modern sector, as this sector depends on subsidies, especially for importing sophisticated investment goods.

These two social groups turn to the NCIPMs, which already existed during decolonisation as a current within the national liberation movements. At that time, they were, however, politically marginalised by the success of secular forces. The success of the secular forces was closely linked to their appearance as cosmopolitan forces and the prevailing definitions of modernity in the West at the time. The secular forces were able to help the national liberation movements rise to power against their local cultural-identitarian rivals by obtaining concessions from the colonial powers. The latter considered them to be the preferred and reliable partners for future political and economic relations between the old colonialist metropolises and the newly independent states, and sometimes, such as in Algeria, severely regretted not having seized the opportunity in time to bolster them. These moderate groupings dominated the worldwide coalition of anti-colonialist forces, as exemplified by the movement of non-aligned countries, which greatly promoted the cause of decolonisation through the Afro-Asiatic group in the United Nations General Assembly (Ahmad 2008: 20; Chowdhuri 1976).

NCIPMs are on the rise because state-interventionist secular elitist forces have not supplied what they had promised: jobs and the empowerment of labour. At the start of the development process, skilled labour, especially educated young people, was scarce, whereas the state sector was rapidly expanding. The ruling elite, which I call state classes,[7] was able to constitute an organic clientele in the state-owned or state-supported economic sector and the rapidly expanding administrations. The very success of this strategy in extending education to the masses led to a situation in the 1980s where there was an oversupply of educated young people and a scarcity of resources for further expansion of the state-owned or state-supported modern sector. These youth from the middle strata had no other choice but to use their only available resource—

education—in trying to launch small businesses. That said, markets were limited. And yet these new diploma holders had a unique resource in their struggle for jobs. In contrast to the old "elites", they came from social strata which had not participated in education-based colonialist bridgehead building. They were thus familiar with the local culture and the local language in which they were educated. Opting for cultural nationalism allowed them to fight those who already held the scarce jobs in the public sector, state-owned enterprises and administrations.

Those who had been kept out of the labour market due to a lack of employment and education had been promised a substantial change in their economic situation during the period of decolonisation. Decolonisation was propagated as a means for improving the economic lot to large categories of the colonially oppressed population. Decolonisation was also presented as an instrument for ending exploitation and providing the financial resources to create jobs. Following independence, the rents at the disposal of state classes were used for a number of rather limited social programs, which raised the hope of the poor and marginalised that their economic situation would improve. Illusions about the capacity of state-led industrialisation persisted as long as the theme of imperialist exploitation remained credible. At the very latest with the oil-price crisis of 1973, it became clear that job creation did not depend on the availability of external rents. Indeed, the oil countries were quite able to attract considerable financial surpluses without creating full employment, as exemplified by the showcase for the social-reformist state-led industrialisation process in Algeria (Elsenhans 1982b).

The honourable small businessmen realised that their growth potential was curtailed by the existence of a protected and modern, state-owned or state-subsidised sector and by over-regulation of the economy by the state class. Without the continuing financial support of the state, which had run out of rents, the state increasingly appeared to them as a rapacious collector of resources. The state had to be opposed because it endangered the growth potential of the small and medium-scale sector (Rudolph/Hoeber Rudolph 1987: 42; Gould 1993: 316). With dwindling resources, the organisations of the state classes distributing the rent became more selective in choosing their clients. The exchange of services became nearly inevitable. Anti-corruption campaigns[8] have been a welcome instrument for the NCIPMs to enlarge their audience, not only at the state-business level but, especially, at the mass level, where over-bureaucratisation, for example, even just obtaining simple papers in due time, is endemic. The ideological heritage of the secular national liberation forces could not help but to erode, resulting in a decline in their capacity to bind the marginalised to the project of economic and social transformation.

Both new attitudes could be exploited by the rivals to secular nationalist forces, which opposed the cosmopolitan—basically Western—and economical orientation of the so-called socialist state classes. The NCIPMs have proposed alternative solutions based on moral economy (Müller 2002; Upadhyaya 1968), implying more market regulation (Elsenhans 2006b [2004]).

There is no denying that an essential element of these alternative solutions is the revalorisation of an ancient past, hence a nationalist and ethnicist reaction. With the exception of the Muslim world and the rather unique circumstances of the Palestine conflict, the NCIPMs have been able to gain ascendancy only by extending their bases from ideologically nationalist youth to honourable businessmen. To this end, the predominantly nationalist and often xenophobic discourse had to be replaced with a more economic-oriented discourse about strengthening the nation through the development of national industries (Diwan 1995: 13; Keyman/Koyuncu 2005: 124). Given the structure of available industries, this meant the expansion of small and medium-scale enterprises.

There is no need to elaborate on the much lower degree of cosmopolitanism in the NCIPMs. But they follow identities based on ethnic boundaries even less than national liberation movements do. The national liberation movements had created certain solidarity between Third World countries, allowing imperialism to be considered the external enemy, and one that had to be countered by a mobilisation of all available political resources. This Third World solidarity has broken down through the rise of the NCIPMs. Conflicts between regions of the former Third World have increased, despite the continued existence of considerable commonalties in economic terms. The NCIPMs certainly claim some regions as belonging to their cultures, but cultural identities are normally manifold.

An individual can have a personal cultural identity with various dimensions. In contrast to the gradual character of identifying with different dimensions of a given cultural heritage, the number of people considering themselves to be truly bi- or even multilingual is rather limited. The opposition between identity based on culture and identity based on ethnic origin can be nicely illustrated by comparing South Tyrol to Kashmir. In the context of European nation-states with their basis in ethnic criteria, the Italian claim to extend its natural boundaries to the highest range of the Alps could be squared with ethnic realities only by granting a large degree of internal autonomy to the Bolzano region. Italians living in this region sometimes feel like foreigners in their own country. In Kashmir, there are two contending cultures with numerous overlaps. Those in favour of India include Muslims, alongside Buddhists and Hindus. On the pro-Indian side, all refer to a secular state where religion cannot be a factor for state building but would still remain an element of cultural identity. On the pro-independence and pro-Pakistan sides, the goal of secession from India is justified by the argument that the protection of Muslim culture and the possibility of leading a Muslim lifestyle require a Muslim state, a position that other Muslims may not share. Individuals may easily shift between one of the two notions of culture without changing their religion or their ethnic identity, but only their notion of the dimension of the public realm.

Cultural identity is a tenuous link of community. As most of the greater newly emerging powers of Asia, Africa and Latin America are multi-ethnic, belonging to an ethnic community cannot be used as an argument in demanding boundary changes. These multi-ethnic states might be characterised by intensive, even interethnic, conflicts within their own borders. However, the very fact that they are multi-ethnic excludes the possibility of launching irredentist movements based on ethnic links between their own population and populations living in parts of neighbouring countries and which have some ethnic affinity. Normally there is no clear link between an individual's culture and his overarching political identity. Culture is not ascribed. The identities in the multi-ethnic "nation" state of Asia are more modern than in Europe and are probably rather similar to those in the United States. With some plausibility, it can be argued that the focus placed on cultural diversity as a source of conflict in the United States reflects less any real sort of challenge than the difficulty which the United States faces in bridging the gap between belonging to the European family of nation-states and its character as a multi-ethnic state. The idea of a common ancestry would be divisive.

Due to the non-ethnic character of the diversity of cultural identity, it can be doubted that the diversity of communities living in multi-ethnic states of the African and Asian sorts will lead to high levels of internal strife and to aggressive foreign-policy behaviour in order to divert attention from internal conflicts. This manner of reasoning about the transformation of internal conflict into aggressiveness vis-à-vis other states seems to have a rather limited applicability for the majority of regions where NCIPMs are on the rise.

The NCIPMs become stronger by winning the support of middle classes, which no longer expect very much from state-interventionist secular nationalist forces. They are in favour of the market. They are opposed to an overall responsibility of the state, although they do not necessarily correspond to the textbook version of action groups in a state-free civil society so dear to contemporary political theory and its claims to moral superiority of civil society over the state. As a consequence, increasing internal strife is managed by a withdrawal of the state and the simultaneous enlargement of the role of the market and, occasionally, of uncivilised civil society with new middle strata assuming the leadership of these NCIPMs.

It has to be admitted, however, that the origin of NCIPMs is sometimes deeply rooted in the uprooted middle-class youths who have no place in the market[9] and in marginalised populations who,in the 1930s, would have opted for a socialist perspective of more state intervention to help them overcome their economic misery. The current ruling party in India, the BJP, demonstrates rather well how staying in power basically depends on curbing the influence of the more extremist currents representing the marginalised population and the ideologically charged youth. Although these groups may remain the storm troopers for public campaigns, they have to be kept under control by the more moderate elements. It is a well-known argument against the clash of civilisation theory that fundamentalism in the Islamic world comprises a large variety of currents, most of which are not even perceived in the West because they are not violent.[10] The importance of the pious businessman in the rise to hegemony of Islamist movements has been dealt with frequently.[11] The ultimate failure of Islamist movements has been nicely illustrated in the Algerian case: Violence has frightened off such pious businessmen who had temporarily offered them their support.[12]

The foreign policy orientation of these NCIPMs will therefore depend on the economic strength of the middle strata. A world characterised by economic depression must be avoided. The middle classes would finally lose the economic basis for success via competition on markets because demand is simply too low. This will push these middle classes—in a manner quite similar to the 1930s in Europe—into the hands of the ideologically influenced youth and the violence-prone marginalised populations. An expanding world economy which transfers growth impulses to the new emerging powers of the South will, in turn, create incentives for these middle classes to pursue their economic and social goals of enrichment and distinction with respect to the lower classes. They will most likely adhere to the national values of a cultural-identitarian identity but will not turn these identities into violent-prone behaviour. This argument obviously implies that political democratisation contributes to peace—incidentally, not by keeping NCIPMs out of power but by making them dependent on moderate elements in their rise to power.

5. The interest in cooperation

With the decline of state-interventionist import-substituting industrialisation, economic growth increasingly depends on exports.

Export earnings depend more and more on the quantities of manufactured products, since raw-material demand has been declining in the industrialised West in the wake of the "dematerialisation" of production. The prices for raw materials have relatively fallen over the past two decades with the exception of crude oil. This tendency will not be completely reversed through rising demand from newly industrialising countries. The larger countries of the underdeveloped South, like India and China, are extremely raw material-dependent, especially energy-dependent. They will be able to pay high prices according to the development of their own export earnings. Raw material exporters will benefit from productivity increases in these countries as a result of improving terms of trade with economies which are increasing their capacity to supply exports. As this capacity of new exporters will not necessarily reverse the deterioration of the terms of trade with the technologically leading economies, the transformation of raw material rents into real consumption will require increasing orientation of import to the suppliers of the newly industrialised countries.

Entering export-led industrialisation depends on low international prices of local labour. Low prices of local labour in international currency are not achieved in the form of low real wages, however. Rather, they depend on the capacity to devalue the local currency below purchasing-power parity (Elsenhans 2002, 2004a, b). No one could survive in the industrialised countries of the West at one-fiftieth of the wage level there. Real wages in the countries leading the drive to export-led industrialisation are at about one-fifth to one-seventh of the real wages in the West (Strack/Helmschrott/Schönherr: 1997). A Beijing household can buy up to ten times as many goods with its salary at home than if it were converted into Canadian dollars and spent in Canada (Chen/Gordon/Zhiming 1994). In most of the underdeveloped world, GNP per capita at purchasing-power parity is about four times higher than GNP at the going exchange rate. Success in export-led industrialisation depends on the capacity to devalue. This capacity implies that additional labour being employed in export industries and receiving a wage in local currency does not depend on imports of basic wage goods (Rittenberg 1986: 177).

Devaluation would otherwise automatically raise the cost of these wage goods resulting in the decline of already low real wages. Export-led manufacturing growth thus depends on the local economy's capacity to produce a surplus of wage goods. At still low levels of real wages, the capacity of local agriculture to produce a surplus of food is crucial for the success of export-led manufacturing. A thriving small-scale industrial sector (an important segment of the so-called informal sector) is a supplementary condition, which is easily fulfilled given an expanding agricultural production. It is no coincidence that the food-dependent African countries where the Green Revolution has not been particularly effectual have great difficulties entering export-led manufacturing. The rice-growing East Asian and Southeast Asian countries with considerably higher real wages have been particularly successful at this because of their food independence. The shortening of the ripening time for rice has increased the annually available land for food production massively.

Intensifying export-led growth depends on industrial diversification, which requires entering into the manufacturing of more technology-demanding goods.[13] Imports of technology and inputs play an important role here. With an import content of 50%, a devaluation of 50% leads to a reduction in costs of only 25%. With state-supported import-substituting industrialisation for achieving more self-sufficiency also in semi-finished products and investment goods from imports, the previous shares of international costs can be maintained if, after devaluation, necessary inputs to be substituted by local production double in local currency cost. Despite the discourse about export-led industrialisation being dependent on the opening of a given economy, all successful export-led industrialising countries have been characterised by high degrees of state intervention in the creation of new industries and training schemes. The reduction of machinery imports in the textile industry was pursued along similar lines by South Korea and Taiwan.[14]

The newly emerging powers in Asia and Latin America are therefore interested in maintaining access to and good relations with

Western countries and their markets. This enables them to subsidise exports through devaluation (which subsidises their labour costs out of the surplus of their agricultures, Elsenhans 2005: 37 ff.) and industrial policies of diversification.

The industrialised West and emerging nations are drawn together by their shared desire in a limited liberalisation of the world economy. Leading industrialised countries have been defending their export capacity by engaging in industrial policies, including the use of subsidies as described in strategic trade theory. They ultimately aimed at to be first and reap the fruits of a technological monopoly. Catch-up economies want to engage in industrial policies to achieve competitiveness at lower rates of devaluation or, in other words, maintain their export earnings.[15] The West and the South converge by accepting moderate levels of rent mobilisation.

Rent-based political structures emerge in both cases, although the negative effects of efficiency normally associated with the rentier state (Auty 1991; Mahon 1992) manifest themselves mostly in countries which maximise raw material rents because of the close contacts of manufacture exporters with the world market inherent in both strategies (Akyüz/Gore 1994; Khan/Jomo 2000b).

The importance of labour for the production of manufactured goods in catch-up countries (in contrast to raw-material production such as oil) will also help limit the political effects of rent (Elsenhans 1993). However, these effects will be felt nonetheless in the form of an increasing disempowerment of labour. As comparative advantage is at least initially associated with goods produced by unskilled labour, export manufactures may be produced to a large extent by small and medium-scale industry. This was the case of Taiwan, where the state did not explicitly sponsor large-scale conglomerates like in South Korea.[16] The pattern of investment in mainland China shows the predominance of local as well as Chinese-owned overseas businesses in the export sector (Qiu 1999: 99-100). Foreign direct investment from Western countries is concentrated in high-technology sectors, which are not yet prepared to massively engage in exports.

Export-led growth implies cooperation with the West. The latter is ready to accept limitations to the principle of free trade for the sake of political stability in the non-western world. Sources of instability may remain, however. The export-led manufacturing drive is not sufficient in order to overcome marginalisation in most of the larger economies of the South without complementary internal reforms, such as agrarian reforms in favour of redistribution. Marginality may persist, with serious repercussions for the industrialised world. An agricultural surplus resulting from the Green Revolution allows devaluation. Devaluation, in turn, allows undercutting costs in all branches of production where technologically backward economies can transform comparative advantage into cost competitiveness. As long as labour surplus and marginality persist, popular movements cannot be triggered by the traditional instruments of the working class, e.g. strikes, with the result that popular movements are quite difficult to organise. Non-governmental organisations, along with their competitors, the NCIPMs, step into this organisational void.

The West is all the more ready to agree to a limited liberalisation of the world economy that allows rent-seeking if the relevant partners in the South are stable and saturated powers. Most of them are saturated powers. Because of the multi-ethnic character of the majority of greater powers in the South, the principle established after the defeat of Nazi Germany—that ethnic self-determination cannot be achieved through boundary changes but only by means of equal rights as citizens regardless of one's ethnic origin or linguistic affiliation—is fully endorsed by these new powers. Minorities exist just about everywhere, but the territorial status quo established between the end of World War II and the process of decolonisation must be respected. Tibet will remain Chinese, and the solution for the Indo-Chinese conflict over the Himalayan border will not be based on ethnic arguments but on the interpretation of past treaties and their relevance as well as the determination of boundary lines, roughly drawn in pencil on imprecise maps. The Kashmir conflict will not be solved by a plebiscite like the post-Versailles referenda in Eastern Europe. Pakistan has not extended its boundaries in order to include the

Pashtun population of Afghanistan, nor has Iran sought a revision of its boundary with Afghanistan in order to include the Farsi-speaking Herat region. Thailand accepts the independence of Laos, and no one supported Saddam Hussein's claim to annex the Arab-speaking Khuzestan to Iraq. The stability of boundaries in Africa and in Latin America is a major principle undergirding the relations between states on these continents.

Although the denial of statehood for the Kurds (Lusso 1965) is comparable to the injustices done to Poland in the late eighteenth century by its partitioning among the three neighbouring countries, secessionist movements in Kurdistan are not openly supported by any greater power.

Despite widespread frustration in the Muslim world about the repeated failures in revising the partition of Palestine, the great majority of Muslim and Arab countries are willing to accept the existence of Israel as a distinct state. The bone of contention is the delimitation of boundaries, providing Israel with a reasonable strategic depth for coping with Arab threats. Such threats will become irrelevant only if—similar to the idea of structural incapacity for offensive action in the last phase of the NATO-Warsaw Pact confrontation—the Arab side will have become structurally incapable of waging war on Israel. Pledges to recognise Israel are not enough to stop Israel's encroachment on Arab territories because no verbal commitment of the Arab states takes away the threat that some Arab elites can return to aggressive behaviour. Rendering Arab economies and the public incapable of such a return to aggression is the condition for a compromise in the Middle East.

The readiness of the newly emerging powers of Asia to cooperate with the United States, particularly in the war on terror, should not be interpreted as a unipolarity of the international system. There can be no doubt that the United States can intervene militarily anywhere across the globe. Their rivals, China, India, Russia, and perhaps the European Union at a later stage, can project military power only to limited, adjacent areas. The 2003 US-led invasion and occupation of Iraq war teaches an important lesson, however. The United States can destroy the modern army of a small country and may even be able to do so in a conflict with powers like China or India. They are, however, unable to establish an effective regime of occupation. Thus, the experience of the French in Algeria still holds: France had 400,000 French soldiers and 200,000 local auxiliaries in that country for controlling a population of 8 million (Elsenhans 2014 [1974]: 447).

Generalised guerrilla warfare can be defeated only through a labour-intensive ground war and police operations. Even if modern technology should have doubled the effectiveness of infantrymen against guerrilla fighters, the occupation forces would still have to recruit one-twentieth of the local population. If "indigenisation" succeeds and provides half of the required occupation forces, then the permanent defeat of a country numbering more than one billion inhabitants would require an occupation army of 25 million expatriate soldiers—or almost all the able-bodied young men of a nation like the United States. This problem was recognised at an early stage by Nazi planners in Russia; the brutality of German invasion forces in the first phases of Operation Barbarossa was explicitly intended to solve the lack of manpower in effectively controlling occupied territories later on when the bulk of the German armies further advanced (Nolte 2003: 26).

Assuming it does not want to commit downright genocide, the United States must respect the military implications of the sheer size of the populations of the newly emerging great powers. China and India, and probably also Indonesia, Pakistan, Brazil and Bangladesh, are simply indigestible. Thus, no Western state or coalition of Western powers can accomplish victory in the Clausewitzian sense, i.e. imposing one's will on others through violence. In the late nineteenth century, the machine gun allowed the destruction of armies in areas of Africa without the emergence of an all-too-visible genocide. Nowadays, everyone has machine guns and tanks, and many have, as a last resort, the atomic bomb, the use of which would mean worldwide genocide. Moreover, the objects of colonial occupation were either "ancient empires" or small societies with low degrees of social differentiation. The ancient empires (tributary or Asiatic modes of production) had acquired some form of organised statehood but lacked social cohesion. The small, often stateless, societies in remoter parts of Asia, and especially in Africa and Latin America—apart from Mexico and the Inca regions in the sixteenth century—were characterised by social cohesion but lacked the force of numbers.

Regardless of the shortcomings of the post-colonial states in Africa and Asia as well as the post-(populist) dictatorships and newly democratised states in Latin America, a sufficient degree of social cohesion has been achieved there, even in the case of highly fragmented societies. The idea of an occupying power having a civilizing mission may have existed within German and Japanese societies after 1945. In Asia, Latin America and Africa, it is non-existent because of the failures and crimes of Western colonialism.

Nowadays, with the higher levels of firepower at the disposal of technologically advanced—as well as technologically backward countries—the superiority in technical (especially nuclear) capabilities can be used only to secure one's survival. This power cannot be used to guarantee one's ultimately limited interests in other foreign countries. This idea is demonstrated by the shift of French imperialism under the leadership of de Gaulle during the Algerian war from great-power status based on a colonial empire to great-power status based on nuclear force (Elsenhans 2014 [1974]: 344-358).

6. The holy alliance of the saturated powers

My insistence that countries with large populations will use guerrilla tactics to resist the permanent invasion of powers having vastly superior military technology is based on sheer numbers and not on the superiority of guerrilla tactics over modern warfare. The guerrilla is not invincible, large numbers are. The slogan "*el pueblo unido jamás será vencido*"[17] contains some truth. The Kalashnikov machine-gun is wrongly associated with the guerrilla myth—rather, the guerrilla myth lies in the importance of the people, its cohesion, and its size.

After independence, local guerrillas in Asia, Latin America or Africa could only indirectly address the relevant power centres in Western capitals. Those choosing to continue the repression of guerrillas are no longer Western governments, which have the option of withdrawing from their colonies and maintaining some sort of great-power status. Due to their political independence, the political forces opposed to guerrillas are local in nature and therefore unable to withdraw. The latter face the option of winning or losing everything if a compromise cannot be found. Limited democratisation and a sharing of power between guerrillas and repressive apparatuses is the normal outcome of violent liberation movements fighting local governments. The quasi-complete elimination of the power structure is highly unlikely, regardless of how popular the guerrilla may be.

Guerrillas can be defeated, however, if the powers in place use all available resources. This was the argument of the French theoreticians of counter insurgent warfare (Trinquier 1961, 1980). The decade of civil war in Algeria would seem to be the classic example of how the doctrine of counterinsurgency developed by French colonels can be applied. Despite its many horrors, this war did not cause more civil casualties (proportionate to the civil population) than the French war against Algerian independence from 1954 to 1962 (200-300 thousand, Elsenhans 2014 [1974]: 589). The decisive factor was not the higher sophistication of Algerian generals in comparison to the French colonels, but the limited options of the Algerian generals. It was plain to everyone that, in contrast to the European minority in Algeria before 1962 and the French army, the Algerian generals had no other choice but to stay on and win. Thus, the expectation of political victory by the guerrillas was slowly eroded. Villages became weary of the sacrifices and the government was cynical enough to tell them that, as the national government in place, it could not be held responsible as a foreign power and sanctioned for human rights abuses done by local guerrillas. Defections occurred. The guerrilla had to resort to greater violence in order to maintain support. The government manipulated the groups causing this violence and intensified the violence even more. The insecurity became intolerable, and the guerrillas were forced to relinquish important social bases (Samraoui 2003). Similar scenarios are occurring in Kashmir, the Peruvian Andes and probably in many other places around the world, which do not arouse the attention of the Western media.

The limited chances of guerrilla success are perceived locally too. Guerrillas often fail to attract politically experienced leaders. This stands in contrast to the guerrilla movements of the decolonisation period. Politically experienced leaders with an eye for the political impact of carefully dosed violence in order to achieve the strategic goal of any guerrilla—discord in the enemy camp—no longer control the use of violence. The other important component of any guerrilla movement, the mystiques of violence, takes over. In Algiers in 1957, the local FLN command planned to bombard the city's gas facilities, but only at night, when no human casualties were to be expected (Einaudi 1986). The World Trade Center, for instance, could have been attacked at three o'clock in the morning, when it was nearly empty. The result at the level of the world public opinion would have been quite different.

In the local context of the "nation state," the terrorist movement cannot break the will of those in power with the forms of violence at its disposal. The guerrilla therefore has to hit much harder than during the period of decolonisation and must also hit at the centre of power in the West if it wants to attract attention. The level of violence to be used will not polarise Western opinion, which, following political independence, no longer feels accountable for the local authorities in place in the South. Rather than dissension inside the enemy camp, there is unity in fighting terror. There is no fundamental disagreement in the West, or outside the Muslim world for that matter, about the necessity of fighting terrorism, but merely about the best way to go about it. Local allies are expected to do the dirty work as secretly as possible.

The future international system may be characterised by transnational terrorism. However, there will be a large international alliance to fight it. This alliance will comprise all great powers. This alliance will be supported by major smaller powers. This alliance will be so formidable as to discourage elements from joining the anti-status quo groups, which are essential for the achievement of large multi-class alliances. There are no broad social bases for anti-status quo forces.

At the great power level, multi-ethnic empires will prevail. All the states concerned, with the possible exception of Russia, will not consider ethnic irredentism as a means of increasing their power. All other forms of increases in power (and the concomitant compensations which have to be awarded to other competitors) can be negotiated: they do not imply symbols of "national" identity such as territory inhabited by one's own nationals.

Rivalry about relative advantages in power will not lead to war as long as war is relatively expensive. The whole argument about power politics leading to war is based on the link between power politics and the nation state, which has to aim to preserve the national symbols of power. Therefore, the European stakes led to war in 1914, but the colonial stakes during the whole period of the second wave of colonialism did not lead to war between the great powers. Nuclear weapons make war expensive. State rivalry under the condition of nuclear armaments will lead to peaceful competition between predominantly multi-ethnic empires. The extension of that part of the international "civil society" that is linked to Western non-governmental organisations will ultimately discourage any positive appreciation of war and violence, if not openly, in the name of status quo. Consumerism and the decline of bellicose ideologies in the West will support the peaceful behaviour of great power governments. Those among the great power governments that promote peace get a premium of appreciation, even if they support the status quo.

In the economically less advanced world, it will be more difficult to create large identities on the basis of multi-ethnic structures on which war efforts can be based. The probable evolution of the mindset in the great powers will reinforce their "realist" interest in peace.

Because of this stability in the core of international power, smaller states will try to become clients of more powerful ones, especially because economic openness has become a precondition for welfare.

Challengers to the established order may develop in the smaller states as well as in the greater powers. Challengers will be resolutely opposed by the greater powers, especially those with the largest influence in their respective regions. Other large nations are unlikely to back such competitors. The scenario will resemble the 1815-1848 period of cooperation between the greater powers in Europe, when change was extremely limited at both the internal and external levels.

Contrary to that period, there will be no large "anti-order" movements with immediately legitimate values. The nationalist movements in Germany, Italy, Poland and Hungary drew their strength from their character as representing imagined communities of common descent. Cultural origin is certainly a weaker bond. Multi-ethnic empires will depend on weaker links between the state and a more diversified society. They will be more reluctant to engage in external adventures.

Where "anti-order" movements develop, they will face large difficulties in broadening their social bases. Therefore, they will comprise only the most dissatisfied and extremist elements of the currents of opinion they want to represent. As long as the political systems show a minimum of responsiveness, anti-order groups should remain isolated. Due to their isolation, they will tend to remain extremist so that a vicious cycle of their isolation is maintained.

The argument that democracy and human rights are conditions for peaceful behaviour will open the door for great power intervention in favour of existing governments, as challengers will often be accused of violating democratic principles and human rights. I would therefore predict an international system which is "ultra-stable" or "ultra-imperialistic" (Kautsky 1914). No reasonable power puts into question the existing hierarchies. Such a system will be ultra-reactionary in the sense that no new major political movements will emerge.

Notes

1. Ali 2002; Barber 1996; Riesebrodt 2000; Tibi 2001; Dessouki 1973; Keddie 1998.
2. They clearly warn against the state, which can always become criminal, cf. Siedschlag 2001: 14.
3. Uzoigwe 1985: 38; Crowder 1971: 2-9; Oloruntimehin 1971: 95; Gann/Duignan 1978: 138 ff.
4. Mantoux 1938: 3 ff.; Northedge 1966: 399 ff.; Seton-Watson 1937: 157.
5. Gardner 1964: 15 ff., 123 ff.; Feis 1940: 95; Condliffe 1940: 199.

6. Mitchell 1988: 76-79; Birdsall/Ross/Sabot 1995; Ka/Selden 1986: 1298.
7. Cf. in this book above chap. 3, and Elsenhans 1976e, 1982a, 1996b [1981].
8. Carlier 1992: 193; Thakre 1998; Najmabadi 1987: 203.
9. Arjomand 1984: 24; Krämer 1994: 204; Carlier 1992: 187; Lamchichi 1990: 145.
10. Önis 1997: 753 ff.; Jha 2003: 1-2; Varshney 2002: 85.
11. Kepel 2000: 265; Aly/Wenner 1982: 351; Khelladi 1992: 104; Jha 2000: 13.
12. Yacine 1998; Momayezi 2001: 343; Martinez 1998: 328.
13. Smith 1997: 757; Bello 1998: 430; Sun 1996: 11, 23.
14. Mytelka 1985: 259 f.; Haggard 1983: 283; Shih 1968: 121-123; Holtgrave 1987: 58-81.
15. Mayer/Butkevicius/Kadri 2002: 21; Pang/Lim 1989; Ernst 1994: 49-50.
16. Yi 1988: 137-144; Fujita/James 1990: 737-753; Cheng 1990: 150.
17. "The people united will never be defeated", Chilean political song, having become a sort of anthem for the left in Latin America in the 1970s.

5

A Fissured, Not-So-Capitalist World System*

Capitalism is not some kind of naturally occurring phenomenon that emerges spontaneously from a system of market and exchange. Capitalism depends on the countervailing power of the masses against the enrichment of the few. In many societies, this countervailing popular power is weak, because pre-capitalist structures are dominant. Historically, such structures have always been obstacles to the transition to capitalism. It is thus highly doubtful that a capitalist world system can ever be realized through the spontaneous tendencies resulting from market regulation. I argue here that such a system requires high levels of employment on a global scale. But the forces of capitalism are currently too weak for such an "empowerment" of labour to occur. Rents continue to shape social structures in important regions of the world. With their influence on the system of states, rent-based social structures inevitably encroach on the nature of the international system. The much-trumpeted emergence of a global civil society of non-governmental organisations is incapable of compensating for the worldwide weakness of labour. The danger of "turbo capitalism" would have to be met with the regulatory instruments of the state. In my view, however, a far greater danger comes in the form of an intensive worldwide struggle for rents. This is accompanied by an increasing

* Text published in German *Welttrends*, slightly shortened: Elsenhans, Hartmut (2009): Kapitalismus kontrovers. Zerklüftung im nicht so sehr kapitalistischen Weltsystem. *Welttrends Papiere 9*. Potsdam: Universitätsverlag Potsdam.

structurisation of the international system by political power. The solution does not lie in increased governmental intervention, but in increased capitalism. This is the only way to empower labour.

1. Profit depends on mass consumption

Capitalism is not shaped by the limitless striving of entrepreneurs for "surplus". Certainly, entrepreneurs are possessed by this impulse. However, it is constantly checked by pressure emanating from the "lower orders" for higher mass incomes. The limits that this pressure imposes on the enrichment of those at the top of the structure distinguishes capitalism from other class societies. Moreover, this enrichment depends on the capacity to innovate technically in order to meet growing demand (at best, mass demand). Capitalism is a counterpart to a bourgeois revolution; it mercilessly removes all privileges for social estates and state guaranteed monopolies. Wealth is appropriated as profit.

Profit is different from rent. Rent, like profit, is an income which derives from an economic surplus. Profit, however, is earned under conditions of perfect competition on anonymous markets. Rent is earned on the basis of market imperfections, monopolies or political power. Bourgeois revolutions are not necessarily democratic. Such revolutions, however, call for equality before the law, and thus for an impersonal rule of law. A legal contract of equality binds individuals, irrespective of their social origins. And, in the absence of political privileges, the wealthy can only appropriate profit and enhance their riches if they are compelled to play by the rules of capitalism. This means, in practice, selling on competitive markets at higher prices than their costs of production.

Kalecki's (1942) theory of profit holds that producers of consumption goods can sell their products at higher prices than their cost (i.e. wages paid and inputs acquired) if there is additional demand for their products. Under the usual simplified conditions, this demand can originate only from wages paid in investment goods production (cf. chapter 1, section 2, in this volume). Profit in consumption goods production is thus equal to wages paid in net investment goods production. The wealthy of both pre-capitalist and capitalist societies cannot increase their own demand for consumption goods, because they would lose their competitiveness (Luxemburg 1951 [1912]: 104 f.). The state can create demand beyond its tax income only by running government deficits. In the long term, these are socially unsustainable, because they entail redistribution in favour of the wealthy through debt servicing. Permanent export surpluses render foreign economic partners insolvent.

Profit in consumption goods production leads to a positive profit rate in consumption goods production. Investment goods producers know which technologies applied in consumption goods production are the most innovative. They can easily shift to consumption goods production on the basis of their own investment goods production if they do not receive comparable profits. Profit in consumption goods industries equals wage payments in net investment goods production. Consequently, total net profit is equal to net investment goods production, and thus also to net spending on investment goods. It is irrelevant if capitalist entrepreneurs are aware of this link. They are looking for income, irrespective of whether it is generated by market imperfections or innovative investments.

Pre-capitalist forces can block the transition to capitalism if they are able to stall or negate the capitalist mechanism of rising mass incomes creating profit. Socio-cultural explanations of "elite" behaviour are useful only for explaining the demise of precapitalist blockages; they can tell us little about the transition to capitalism. Indeed, subaltern political movements may contribute to the empowerment of labour.

Spending on investment goods production is more than just a characteristic of capitalism (Amin 1973: 61). It is the very basis for capitalist profit (and not primarily of capitalist productivity increases, to which it is also linked). "Peripheral capitalism" is not actually capitalism, despite the presence of market-based interactions between economic actors. Whether or not a state financed industrial development in an underdeveloped country will lead to capitalism is not the result of "harmony", "proportionality", or even decreasing dependency. In fact, it is reliant on income creating spending on investment, and hence local jobs in investment goods production. This triggers scarcity of labour.

Neoliberal economists and Lenin (1960 [1899]: 64-69) contend that capitalist investors always face sufficient effective demand. This is because accumulation creates its own (internal) market. Bortkiewicz (1907: 455-459) and later Okishio (1961) both advanced critiques of the Marxist law of the tendency of the profit rate to fall (Marx 1959 [1894]: 133-186). These two authors showed that, in case of constant real wages, any innovation reduces unit costs of similar or substitute goods, and thus of directly or indirectly paid wages per unit of production. Capitalists cannot increase their consumption if they want to avoid loss of competitiveness. Maintaining demand requires rising mass incomes. New products, which do not replace existing ones, can also be purchased only if real incomes increase. Demand can therefore expand in relation to the increasing production of consumption goods only if real wages increase. If this effect is blocked because of unemployment, then the entrepreneurs of consumption goods production have no incentive to purchase more expensive investment goods in relation to the level of production. This was Rosa Luxemburg's (1951 [1912]: 79-110) argument against Marx. The total amount of net investment decreases, regardless of any attempts at rationalisation. During the world economic crisis of the 1930s, net investment and therefore profits became negative.

In its physical form, net investment has its counterpart in buildings and machinery. Machinery promotes a certain category of technical progress; the production of identical goods. Machinery executes repetitive steps in the production process and saves on costs through economies of scale. Technical progress which is oriented to the special excellence of the product is linked to the artistic proficiency of the craftsman. The higher the share of mass consumption goods in production, the higher the share of machinery in total value formation. Swiss and American clock makers overtook their British competitors due to homogeneous markets, the world market, or an egalitarian internal market. Large production runs allow larger batches in machinery production, as well as the development of special purpose machinery, which increases productivity. Despite similar technical knowledge in the United States and Germany prior to World War I, special purpose machinery could not be applied in Germany.

Declining capital unit costs are a result of mass production. Mass production allows for innovation in process technologies, and it creates knowledge about new production opportunities. Bicycles and sewing machine were massively in demand among poorer and middle-income households at the end of the nineteenth century. But without these technologies, cars would never have been developed.

Capitalism is capital saving. The empirical counterpart to Marx's organic composition of capital is the capital output ratio (Helmstädter 1969: 48-91). This did not increase over the historical timespan for which records exist; there were some oscillations, but no observable trend. The capital output ratio is much lower in developed capitalist countries than it is in typical underdeveloped countries. It is also lower than it was under the socialist economies of the Cold War-era, where managers failed to limit capital costs. This was exploitation by inefficiency (Elsenhans 1996b [1981]: 144), and it comprised one of the key causes for the downfall of the Eastern Bloc (Elsenhans 2000c).

Workers can consume only the consumption goods provided by consumption goods production. They cannot redirect productive capacities in investment goods production to the production of consumption goods. A consumption goods sector working at full capacity utilisation can increase production only through additional net investment. The purchase of these investment goods is easily financed by credit creation from the banking sector.

2. Rising mass incomes as a precondition for capitalism and bourgeois revolution

The "doubly free" proletarian (Marx 1965 [1867]: 120) would never have emerged without the "empowerment" of labour. The expected ability to impose bargaining power on the labour market was crucial for the readiness of European subalterns to take a chance on disassociating themselves from clientelistic dependency. It was partly confidence in the collective power of labour that allowed the rural masses of Europe to liberate themselves from the old or new lords of rent and venture into the cities in search of work.

The precondition of labour's "empowerment" was an increase in production and productivity in agriculture. Rising mass incomes initially lead to (often overproportionate) increases in food demand (more and better food). Yields in north-western Europe have been increasing since the end of the Middle Ages. These yields were later enhanced or supplemented by immigration into "new" settler countries such as the United States. In nineteenth-century Japan, agricultural production and agricultural yields increased, just as they did in England at the same time.

Such increases were sometimes accompanied by rising food prices. Consequently, real wages increased only very slowly, even if industrial prices fell rapidly. Spending among poor households showed an increasing share delegated to food consumption. Despite this, the consumption of industrial products among these households also increased rapidly. This mechanism is often neglected in statistical considerations of the development of real wages during the Industrial Revolution in north-western Europe.

In many social science discourses, we still hear the argument that the Industrial Revolution was linked to intensified exploitation of labour. But this position was disproven some seventy years ago (Habakkuk 1939; Chambers 1946). After a period of decreasing land concentration since the end of the fifteenth century, the enclosure of the "commons" occurred only during the late eighteenth century, when labour was already being employed by industry on a massive scale. The "expulsion" of the rural population did not primarily hit the interests of small landowners. Indeed, until 1851, employment in British agriculture increased, though not as fast as the rapidly rising population. The concentration of land ownership was in fact rather limited in the core areas of the Industrial Revolution (Elsenhans 2007[1976]: 166-194).

In Britain, real wages rose at the end of the eighteenth and the beginning of the nineteenth centuries (with the wars against France causing an anomalous blip in this pattern). Many authors have pointed to the origins of this increase during the mid-eighteenth century. Either way, there is no doubt that the geographical core of the Industrial Revolution was a high wage region. From the eighteenth century on, it attracted migrants from across the British Isles.

The much-decried English poor laws were an instrument for redistributing the land rent to households that were unable to produce their subsistence through agricultural production (Elsenhans 1992a [1980]). In contrast to the marginals of the contemporary Global South, this segment of the population did not generally die of hunger in nineteenth-century Britain.

The creation of an additional industrial job cost less than the earnings of a worker of a limited number of months. This is also a contrast to contemporary capitalism, where the cost of a new job is several yearly earnings of a single worker. Such investment could be financed by middle-income households, perhaps with the support of local bankers. "Previous accumulation" was not necessary. Likewise, colonial exploitation of the rest of the world was not necessary (though, of course, this happened anyway).

Following this new empowerment of labour due to its scarcity, bourgeois politics emerged as a cooperation between legally equal citizens, or "citoyens". Labour ceased to be fragmented and developed into a reasonably homogeneous layer, a class for itself (Marx 1972 [1847]: 181). It could, at least in some periods, develop a shared consciousness. At high levels of employment and wages higher than the cost of subsistence, labour did not need clientelistic links to the powerful or gild-style professional unions. It could thus dispense with communitarian, identity-based "preferences" in religion, sexual behaviour, etc. This created the social basis for the philosophical insights of the Enlightenment.

Incidentally, throughout history, entrepreneurs have endeavoured to prevent precisely such a constellation from emerging. They have tried instead to tie their particular workforces to their enterprises via clientelistic links. The goal, of course, has been to undermine the formation of workers into larger organisations.

3. Structural homogeneity as the result of working-class resistance, not of harmonious technical development

The average skilled worker makes career and educational choices based on anticipated income. Comparably demanding lines of work must be remunerated with comparable wages. In this way, a high degree of uniformity emerges in working conditions. This provides the foundation for a perception among workers that they are all in a similar situation. They are "materialist"; in their struggle for more rights, they value and focus on concrete working conditions such as wages, working time, and security (Steglich 1960: 242; Dobson 1980: 18-29). In the newly industrialising economies of the South, precisely these orientations are dominant, despite a quite radical degree of cultural variance.

The "factor of production" labour enjoys similar incomes because of its scarcity. When this scarcity is combined with converging rates of profit, capitalist economies experience a convergence of productivity, as measured by the relation between factor costs and sales. The theoreticians of dependency have referred to this as structural homogeneity. If demand for a certain product increases, enterprises lure workers with better wages from other productive activities in order to increase production. They cease this practice when prices decrease and market saturation depress their profit rates to the average. Wages thus increase following average productivity, and not in relation to company-specific or branch-related productivity. In a flexible capitalist economy, physical productivity increases vary to a striking degree. That said, monetary productivities are highly homogeneous. This process is realised irrespective of the extent to which the specific economy is open to the global market, provided that high levels of employment and competition are maintained. This leads to the removal of temporary rents, because no enterprise can impose higher profit rates than average without enjoying market imperfections.

Given the differing rates of productivity growth in the economically dominant capitalist economies and homogeneous productivities due to changes in relative prices, the backwardness of underdeveloped countries varies in relation to developed countries. Price increases for those products where the backward country is particularly backward may not suffice to render production profitable. Redistributive measures may therefore simply peter out into inflation. This inflexibility of underdeveloped economies has been called "structural heterogeneity" (Nohlen/Sturm 1982).

Structural homogeneity is the basis for the flexibility of capitalist economies. It also explains their capacity for "self-centred" development. Neither of these factors results from political, socio-cultural, or foreign economic relations-based mechanisms for "organic" or "harmonious" development. They are simply the result of scarcity of labour. A good example is the relatively universal productivity of hairdressers in all types of economics. This has not increased very much since the Middle Ages. Clearly, then, the strikingly variegated price of haircuts across economies reflects differences between countries in average wages—and thus, in average productivities.

4. The disempowerment of labour as the pre-capitalist historical norm

Technical development does not necessarily lead to a rise of the marginal product of labour. Technical development may allow cumulative learning and thus unleash certain civilisational processes. However, it does not necessarily create the conditions for capitalism in the form of "empowerment" of labour.

In the human struggle for improving living conditions, initially egalitarian social structures create inequality. At low levels of the mastery of nature (i.e. of technology), economic activity shows diminishing returns, at least beyond a certain threshold. At some point in the process of demographic growth, a threshold is reached, beyond which additional workers contribute less than their cost of subsistence. The share of this additional labour in total worktime available is higher than its share in total production. Let us suppose that a society or a single worker produces 80% of the required subsistence within 50% of the available working time. In order to satisfy the remaining 20%, they have to engage 50% of the working time. This is because, at the margin, labour productivity decreases to 25% in this example (extensively: Elsenhans 1994b: 394-401, 2021b [1995]: 103-107).

There are no distributional conflicts between those supplying this unproductive labour and those supplying productive labour, provided that land is equally distributed. Re-distribution is realised within the "family".

Human beings are generally lazy. Consequently, they strive to ensure that their labour time falls within the remit of highly productive labour. They might have privileged access to better land. Because they love their children more than other humans, they aim to render hereditary certain privileges and usufructuary rights. Given unequal access to highly productive resources and demographic growth, some families hit the threshold of declining marginal yields earlier than others. These families are not able to achieve the production of their total subsistence needs even by supplying low productivity labour. They are compelled to obtain transfers from the better off. In this way, they accept dependency. Inequality is consolidated.

Communitarian modes of production are characterised by countervailing mechanisms. These include the regular redistribution of usufructuary rights and the periodic destruction of economic surplus. Surplus simply results from the necessity to decide on the extent to which seeds are sown, at a point in time when it is not possible to make predictions about the uncertainties of the weather. Naturally, this decision must account for the possibility of unfavourable weather. The number of seeds sown has to be higher than the average required. In this way, the periodic emergence of an agricultural surplus becomes inevitable.

Those households which are threatened by famine because of low marginal productivity might reject the idea that the surplus be used for religious festivities. Instead, they might incline towards trying to influence this world (rather than the hereafter) by permanently venerating the deceased ancestors of the powerful. This constitutes the basis for a—by no means historically uncommon—partnership between the powerful and those who are threatened by marginality.

Societies which depend on the division of labour and cohabitation must find a mechanism for rendering comparable the burden of toil in different activities. Basic biological differences in physical constitution point to certain, readymade bases for the division of labour. These include military protection by younger men, and conflict arbitration by the elderly. Under capitalism, this problem of reducing concrete to abstract labour is solved by the labour market. In non-capitalist societies, this reduction requires political negotiations. Political alliances and inequality of power are the inevitable result.

Under some historical conditions, differences in social status between the powerful and the poor become extensive and profound. Under such circumstances, we are dealing with what I call a tributary mode of production. In these systems, the powerful create a hierarchically organised apparatus. A centralised class squeezes a predominantly agricultural population, mostly by means of a land tax. The surplus is then distributed by formal hierarchies, according to the discretionary power of the centre—that is, ultimately, the palace court. Social dynamism is limited. The exploited are organized in lineages, tribes, or ethnic groups, but they do not constitute a homogenous social class. We can frequently observe areas of direct administration (in Arab countries: dar es-sultan) and of indirect administration (in Arab countries: dar es-siba) characterised by very different local structures.

The distinctive parts, or segments, of these hierarchical structures are embroiled in rivalries with each other. Military power, prestige and luxury consumption become important. Resplendent prestige building projects mark the apparent "superior unity" of the community (Marx 1973 [1857-1858]: 299). Economic efficiency is of secondary importance. Intra-class conflicts are managed by increasing the rate of exploitation—that is, until society breaks down (Ibn Khaldûn 1967: 570-572). This gives rise to a period of troubles, until new military gangs establish themselves as rulers and bring order to chaos. A new dynastic cycle begins.

In these societies, a vision of equality survives, though it is mostly confined to peasant movements. Their demands are frequently religious in character, such as the struggle for the recognition of ritual equality as children before a universal God; a key feature of Jaspers' (1949: 20 f.) axial period.

Even the most technically advanced area of craft production remains dependent on the powerful. These producers become suppliers to the court. They specialise in luxuries. Cost-reducing processing technologies are immaterial to them, due to the absence of cost competition. Legally independent traders also depend on the courts, because they need secure trading routes and monopolies.

Land rights may be individualised in order to rationalise taxation. Alternatively, collective property may be recognised in order to increase tax revenues. In this way, villages become collectively liable for the payment of all taxes, including the taxes of the poor (such a distinction separated the two Mogul emperors, Akbar and Aurangzeb). Marx popularised the concept of a society defined by solidarity. He drew on reports of servants of the English East India company, who seem to have been interested in reducing the cost of tax collecting by maintaining collective responsibility for their payment.

The rate of exploitation in tributary modes of production was higher than in the core regions of the transition to capitalism. This is demonstrated by the volume of stones in the works of art produced by the tributary modes of production, such as the Taj Mahal in Agra. It becomes more apparent when we contrast the short timeframe required to finish these structures with the much lengthier processes involved in the construction of European cathedrals throughout the Middle Ages.

Anti-colonialist critiques have frequently alleged that India was impoverished under British rule. However, these critiques have been unable to demonstrate that India possessed an industrial, mass market-based production comparable to European industrial production of the early modern era. Indians knew of the lathe; they used it for carving temple columns. Technological and technical superiority was reflected in the work of "artists", not in the application of discoveries for the cheapening of products.

5. Capitalism is expansive, but not contagious

The sixteenth-century European expansion described by Wallerstein (1974) was not capitalist in character. It comprised a kind of trade expansionism. In fact, this is characteristic of all precapitalist modes of production. China did not give up on expansionism just because it ceased engaging in maritime expeditions. Since the fifteenth century, the Chinese state has expanded territorially into what is today southern China (Hostetler 2000).

The theories that deduce imperialism from the internal contradictions of capitalism are unconvincing. Enterprises normally react to additional markets, and thus also to the opening of external markets. Increasing difficulties for investing surplus capital because of the rising organic composition of capital (Lenin 1964 [1916]: 240 f.) are contradicted by the stability of the capital output ratio. Luxemburg insisted on additional demand from the natural economy. This is not necessary if there is an increasing mass demand within capitalism. External demand from the natural economy cannot be higher than the exports of the natural economy. This absorbs capitalist demand from within the imperialist economy. Consequently, Luxemburg is forced to identify foreign loans as a source of finance for additional imports from the natural economy (Luxemburg 1951 [1912]: 401). The limits of such a source of demand were already obvious from the pre-1914 debt crises, and they were only underlined by the great depression of the 1930s and the post-1982 financial crisis.

In fact, capitalist economies expanded into the non-capitalist world for a very different reason. Quite in keeping with the law of comparative advantage, non-capitalist economies became competitive, initially in raw material production. Even if a particular economy produces goods with a higher productivity than any other economy, it nevertheless engages in foreign trade, assuming that its productivity is higher in some products than in others.

Any productive activity results not only in the availability of the intended product, but also in a more skilled producer. The pattern of specialisation influences growth opportunities. Senghaas' (1977) plea for a decoupling here is based on Vernon's (1966) product cycle. According to this, technically leading countries necessarily possess comparative advantage in future, technologically leading products. A catching up economy thus needs a period of learning behind a protectionist wall. But this is not essential. Before World War I Britain earned very well with its textile exports. As a result, Germany was able to position itself on the world market by specialising in the branches of the second Industrial Revolution. By 1938, Germany had overtaken Britain, despite the fact that most innovations in the new industries had been made first or simultaneously in the UK (Aukrust 1964: 32 f.). In a similar vein, the initially superior tributary modes of production of Asia forced Europe to specialise in simple mass consumption goods. This was in conflict with the interests of leading merchants and engineers in Britain who, at the end of the eighteenth century, wanted to open the Chinese market to British luxuries.

Britain's pattern of specialisation supported the development of machinery. It reinforced the orientation to mass consumption products that had already begun as a result of Britain's internal distributional structures. Technical knowledge resulting from that pattern of specialisation launched innovation in new products. These replaced the old luxuries of the tributary modes of production. Economic logic compelled non-European civilisations to export raw materials.

Exclusiveness is the major characteristic of a luxury product. The supplier has a permanent interest in limiting supply in order to increase sales proceeds. By contrast, the purveyors of mass consumption goods base their strategy on increasing the number of customers through falling prices. They accept free competition, as they did in their struggle against the East India Company and monopolies during the eighteenth century.

Europe had been endowed with natural resources for mass consumption goods and machine production. As a relatively well irrigated and still temperate zone north of the semi-arid area of the globe, Europe produced cereals in sufficient quantities and, after the introduction of potatoes, also enough carbohydrates. Europe was poor in "amenities"—that is, "exotic" foods, tropical beverages and fats for (say) soap, such as palm oil. Typical European raw materials, such as wool, did not enjoy much demand in the warmer climes of the tributary modes of production.

When it came to industrial raw materials, especially iron, Europe had good deposits. Technical innovation in mining, however, was counteracted by the exhaustion of the better deposits, such as late nineteenth century nonferrous metals, early twentieth century oil, and, since the middle of the twentieth century, coal and iron ore. New mining methods increased productivity. These aimed at compensating the deterioration of deposits. With higher productivity, however, they could be employed in the mining of untapped deposits outside Europe. This included the underdeveloped world as well as the regions of recent European settlement.

Because of the monotony of European food production, even small increases in mass incomes led to rising demand for tropical agricultural products. These comprised, initially, sugar, then tea, coffee and cocoa, as well as cotton.

These products required only limited quantities of labour. Consequently, they did not lead to "empowerment" of labour in the Global South, despite expanding European demand. Where labour did become scarce, the European colonial ruling classes solved the problem with violence. They legitimised this with racist arguments, as in the case of slavery. This blocked the European configuration that emerged in case of scarcity of labour—that is, rising mass incomes. Surplus was appropriated as rent and monopoly profits. This points to the fact that the "wealthy" have never actually attempted to globalise the politico-economical basis of capitalism.

The limited growth of demand for raw materials is the result of the structure of the capitalist growth process. In capitalism, raw materials are employed economically, because they represent costs. Raw material consumption per unit of output has been decreasing since the Industrial Revolution. If incomes increase, then the consumption of agricultural "amenities" faces saturation. The trickle-down effect of raw materials production to investment goods production has been high in the core regions of industrialisation, such as in the Ruhr valley. But they were low in the rest of the world. In general, new mining regions are insufficiently large to support local manufacturing of mining and transportation technology utilised in the raw materials sector.

A comparative cost advantage in products with low income elasticity of demand will suffer from declining prices. In the late nineteenth century, the Global South initially experienced improvements in the terms of trade. From the mid-1920s onwards, however, these declined. However, raw material prices were too favourable to trigger economic diversification in the South (Singer 1950: 482). They provided exporters with differential rents—that is, additional incomes because of richer deposits and lower production costs, especially in mining. The "elites" of the South appropriated higher shares in these rents through nationalisation and changes in the conditions of concessions (Mexico 1938). They founded OPEC (1960), the most effective raw materials cartel in world history (Elsenhans 1974).

In the latter stages of colonialism, the colonial powers created institutions in order to limit supply and allow for the appropriation of rents, at least in the case of tropical agricultural products. Their goal was to counteract the social crisis originating from underdevelopment.

6. Rent as a structural component of non-capitalist societies: From the state classes to the new cultural-identitarian movements

Despite attempts on the part of the colonial powers to control rents in their colonies, however, surplus in the form of rents remained available. The world economic crisis of the 1930s, decolonisation, and a burgeoning social crisis congealed to produce the state classes of the Global South. I use the term "state class" to refer to a social class that has access to surplus due to its control of the state apparatus (Elsenhans 1996b [1981]: 173-198, also chapter 3 in this volume).

State classes have historical antecedents, such as Muhammad Ali (1805-1848) in Egypt or the Chinese self-strengthening movement of the mid-nineteenth century. The state class of Meiji Japan was largely successful in its attempts at economic modernisation. During the world economic depression of the 1930s, the Soviet Union made an impressive demonstration of its successes in investment, technology transfer and industrialisation. Development, it seemed, was possible without capitalism.

In the decolonising Global South, the state classes were initially supported by broad alliances of peasants, workers and the "new" middle classes; the sociological bases for national liberation movements. In their drive for independence, Western-oriented nationalists frequently invoked 1776 and 1789. The colonial powers thus considered these nationalists to be guarantors for a reasonable power sharing system. Later, these nationalists were credited with aspirations for an orderly retreat under favourable conditions for the West. This alliance allowed the Western-oriented secular nationalists to outflank their culturally particularistic rivals for leadership of national liberation movements.

The colonial rulers had been confronted with societies where marginalisation had been exacerbated by demographic increase. This intensified the breakdown of networks of solidarity and the shedding of important parts of the rural population. The transition to cash crop production or plantation economies entailed declining per capita food production. Deindustrialisation had taken place on the basis of high raw material rents. These economies were unable to respond flexibly to an increase in internal mass demand due to their structural heterogeneity. Higher raw material earnings were sought for financing internal restructuring. Similarly, a planned economic diversification became the instrument for channelling the new resources into productive investment.

According to Rosenstein-Rodan (1943) and Leontief (1951), French development planning in Algeria (1956-1961) consisted of the formulation of production targets for particular branches of production. Concrete investment targets were deduced from these targets. This allowed for the projection of an interlinked future industry (Elsenhans 2014 [1974]: 650).

Projects were selected not because of their short-term profitability, but because of their place within a matrix of political and industrial relations. This ultimately rendered a specific project profitable when parallel investments had also been made. The state classes invested rents, allowing them to select projects that were not otherwise immediately profitable.

In order to be politically successful, the state classes had to avoid privileging themselves too profligately, though no economic logic compelled them in this direction. Nonetheless, they had to develop internal mass markets. Poor households consume simple products. If demand is evenly distributed, many poor households consume large quantities of these simple products instead of a small number of more luxurious products. The use of traditional technology becomes possible. The first elements of a local investment goods industry emerge. In simple labour-intensive technology and mature capital-intensive technology (i.e., production of mass consumption goods), the comparative disadvantages of underdeveloped countries are rather low. In case of technically demanding products, the demand from poor households is directed to a small variety of products (e.g. refrigerators which reduce the deterioration of food). With the exception of crafts products, production for richer households requires expensive technologies for small markets. High costs are inevitable and starting costs for final and semi-final products tend to increase.

Politically, the centralisation of rents favoured the state classes. The absence of microeconomic controls meant that selection processes for investment were decided by negotiations between bureaucratic apparatuses even at the level of target definitions. If all segments of the state class accepted waste from other segments of the state class, a kind of conspiracy of silence could prevail, and conflicts within the state class could be downplayed. All elements of economic management—including the interpretation of goal attainment—could become politicised. This necessarily undermined the coherency of economic planning.

For Marxist, Keynesian, and Neoclassical economists in both East and West, this process was legitimised with reference to the apparent necessity of capital accumulation, which seemingly required a strong state. Social evils such as corruption and excessive privilege were criticised from the perspective of Western modernisation theory, especially in administrative science, and by non-Western theories of non-capitalist development paths. Both were agreed on the necessity of an essentially constructivist attempt to "improve" values, or to pique the revolutionary conscience of the (for Westerners) "new middle class", or (for non-Westerners) "national intelligentsia."

State classes tend to eliminate rivals or absorb them through clientelistic mechanisms. Opposition is disempowered and the formation of autonomous classes largely blocked. Resistance comes to emanate from the non-organised masses, the unstructured ranks of "the people."

Ironically, the inefficiency of state-led industrialisation policy resulted in the growth of small and middle industries. The state sector created more income than it produced goods. Consequently, a kind of excess of purchasing power emerged. Quite in line with Keynesianism, this excess was satisfied by small private enterprises which specialised in less demanding products. The more that demand came from lower incomes, the more these were efficient and independent from imports. To a certain degree, even underdeveloped economies reacted flexibly to market signals. Sometimes, this resulted from (even small) improvements in skills and infrastructure. State support could have been limited to narrow, strategically important inputs.

Facing the exhaustion of their financial resources, state classes intensified the demand for financial transfers. Hence the emergence in 1976 of the "New International Economic Order" with its Integrated Programme of Commodities. Before long, however, the state classes found themselves increasingly indebted to Western banks, which at this time faced excess liquidity due to the oil price increases of the 1970s. The global political basis for such an appropriation of rent vanished even before the fall of the Berlin wall. The collapse of some highly indebted economies of the Global South after 1982, coupled with the withdrawal of the Eastern Bloc as a serious competitor in 1989, served to re-establish Western political dominance.

As mentioned, inefficient state industrialisation provoked the emergence of a private sector. This sphere increasingly saw the state as a rapacious and parasitical burden. State classes increasingly used state financing to back politically useful but rather small groups, only adding to their growing reputation for corruption. Certainly, the state classes of the Global South were successful in expanding the school system.

However, when a more educated workforce appeared on the labour market, they were confronted by a neglected and shrunken formal economic sector. These newcomers positioned themselves against those in office by insisting on the importance of cultural identity and local language. This strange conglomeration—old and new small and middle business owners, an educated cohort with limited employment prospects, and broad sections of the once marginalised left—now constituted the social basis for the (re-)emergence of cultural nationalism. These new, "fundamentalist" cultural-identitarian political movements are strong where import-substituting industrialisation was attempted but proved too limited for the successful integration of the masses. Such conditions characterised parts of the Islamic world and India. Conversely, where development was more successful, these movements are much weaker. This can be seen from the examples of China, Vietnam or the Asian Tiger nations.

7. Globalisation and the permanence of rents

The new phase of globalisation will not fulfil Cobden's (1967 [1836]: 295) centuries-old neoliberal hope for an end to rent in the Third World and a global implementation of capitalism.

Per capita incomes at purchasing parity are two to seven times higher than those per capita incomes at the prevailing exchange rate. The success of the underdeveloped world in manufacturing exports is not due to lower real wages; it results from a lower international value of labour, and thus from lower exchange rates.[1]

At undervalued currencies, export sector workers cannot buy from the world market as much as they can buy locally. When households have low earnings, food accounts for approximately 50% to 60% of their consumption, necessitating a large proportion of locally produced industrial products consumed by poor households, such as clothing, furniture, shelter and transportation. Under such conditions, entry into export manufacturing by undervalued currencies requires the production of a local food surplus. It also needs a dynamic informal sector which is, however, rendered dynamic by the initially slow expansion of export sector employment. Among the leading manufacturing exporters of the Global South, the Green Revolution was especially successful in increasing yields.

Particularly noticeable were the cheap fingerprints of young women, whose income claims did not exceed their running subsistence costs. This was because women generally did not have to cover the whole cost of reproduction. They were supposed to earn only a rural by-income. Farms supply labour at wages marginally higher than their declining marginal product. Such workers are cheaper than landless industrial workers can be. The latter need to earn as much of their income per hour of work as this hour's share in their total time budget.

Devaluation is costly and implies income losses in the export of goods that would already sell at higher exchange rates. Successful manufacture-exporting countries have generally followed industrial policies for diversification instead of excessive devaluation. South Korea blocked the import of textile machinery when the demand for its textile exports became price inelastic. This was an appropriation of rent. South Korea could have taxed textile exports and financed a textile machinery development programme, much like an oil-producing country. Export upgrading depends on rent, which explains why they are generally positively evaluated by Asian observers (Khan/Jomo 2000b).

The developed capitalist world can tighten its belt and freeze wages, but this will not be successful in fighting devaluation-driven manufacturing exports. The only possible alternative to the "race to the bottom" is full employment in both the South and the West. In a convoy model of globalisation (Elsenhans 2006a), economic levels converge. This is precisely what occurred in the North Atlantic sphere during imperialism and after 1945. Lagging behind economies receive new export opportunities and can maintain the empowerment of their labour on the labour market.

If economies become increasingly important on the basis of devaluation-driven growth, the convoy model collapses. Lagging behind intermediate economies with full employment cannot maintain themselves in the face of competition from economies capable of unlimited devaluation. They cannot fall back on additional export opportunities from traditional or laggard lines of production for employment. They are trapped between the hammer of growth in the technically leading economies, and the anvil of devaluation-driven industrialising economies.

If we follow the theory of endogenous growth, then technical progress depends not on physical capital but rather on technical knowledge and skills. This is acquired through learning by doing, which results in the leading economy having comparative disadvantage in the newly emerging technology. In comparison to a developing country, the established economy benefits from hands-on experience with older leading technologies. However, it is not able to transfer this advantage entirely to the new technology, where neither the developing nor the established economy have learning by doing. Certainly, the established, leading economy also has productivity advances in the new technology, but not to the same degree as in the old leading technology. Following comparative advantage, the established economy inevitably specialises in the old leading technology, and leaves specialisation in new technologies to developing economies.

Dependency theory is blind to this phenomenon of catching-up economies. In the face of this threat, developed capitalist countries react with "strategic trade", i.e. industrial policy in order to maintain their lead and "be first". Temporary technical monopolies are used for rent appropriation in order to finance investment in (uncertain) future leadership positions. In this way, the West imports the rent-based politico-economic structures of the South.

Developed capitalist countries and the devaluation-driven, industrialising, but still underdeveloped countries all pursue parallel strategies of rent creation and appropriation. Mixtures of rent-based state intervention and competition tend to promote the globalisation of rent (Elsenhans 2004b). West and South limit the expansion of internal demand. Consequently, they trim mass incomes and promote rent by strengthening under-consumptionist tendencies.

Globalisation has not necessarily increased competition. In Germany alone, the number of large, worldwide automobile manufacturers is currently less than it was twenty-five years ago. Oligopolies serve to negate the capitalist sanction of falling profits in case of low net investment spending in the real economy. Profit rates of above 10% as a target are nothing more than the expression of limitations to competition, if considered in the light of the "golden rule of accumulation" (interest rate, profit rate and growth rate of the capital stock are equal). The neoliberal supporters of globalisation have registered no protest against this.

The monetary incomes of enterprises which are not used for net investment spending can instead be spent on financial assets. These incomes have no meaningful relationship with the real economy; they are based merely on an expectation of the continued influx of additional financial resources in search of financial assets. This is guaranteed by central banks through monetary easing (Elsenhans 2000a: 528-538). Here, high incomes are nothing more than politically created rents. They certainly render investment in the real economy more difficult. Moreover, however, they have served to propagate a certain contempt for productive work and a respect for speculation, which are entirely characteristic of rent-based economies.

Oligopolistic structures deepen under-consumptionist tendencies. These could be overcome only if marginality in the South were also overcome, and if the bargaining power of labour in the South and in the West were (re-)established. The transition to high levels of employment in the export-oriented developing countries would be accelerated through a more egalitarian distribution of income. Internal market-oriented sectors would grow through rising mass incomes. A burgeoning internal market-oriented industry would increase demand for investment goods. The share of the internal market was higher in Korea and Taiwan than it currently is in Germany. Rising real incomes have no influence on international competitiveness, which depends on the exchange rate.[2]

Globalisation is not the problem. The problem lies in the participation of marginality-ridden economies in the international division of labour in production lines that are important for employment. The much-vilified Hobson (1938: 313) pointed this out some eighty years ago when pointing to the use of cheap Chinese labour as a problem of imperialism.

For a convoy pattern of globalisation, there is no need to start with equal wages in the West and the marginality-ridden South. It is sufficient that, in both regions, high levels of employment are achieved. Keynes called for this in 1944/45.

However, the problem would persist for those countries that are unable to shift to overcoming marginality by devaluation-driven industrialisation. Some of these economies are not capable of self-centred development. There may be certain ecologically specific spaces that allow neither for export orientation nor internal market-oriented development, such as parts of sub-Saharan Africa.

The major responsibility for rising world demands lies with the West. If my alternative strategy of rising mass consumption in the South and in the West were implemented, it might shock financial markets, which would react with capital flight. This would be a problem for the underdeveloped world, which still imports its investment goods. Here, the balance of payments would deteriorate. However, for developed countries with their own investment goods production and low degrees of foreign indebtedness, capital flight would improve the competitiveness of the real economy because of a declining exchange rate. An operative local banking system can readily compensate declining access to international financial markets, because fiat money can be created nationally. Even in Korea, the share of international financial capital in investment financing is low.

8. Cooperation and fragmentation among rentiers in the international system

Transnational cooperation in order to achieve globally high levels of employment is improbable. Consequently, most countries of the Global South will surely opt for the second-best solution—the appropriation of rents in order to finance industrial policy.

The secular nationalists built post-colonial states based on state classes. These classes pursued policies of import substitution in the name of universal goals and norms, such as the right to development. From an early stage in this process, however, the state classes privileged the preservation and stability of their own power in foreign policy (an early example coming in the form of the Sino-Indian border conflicts of the 1960s). The accumulation of nuclear weapons was decided long before the end of the Cold War. The newly emerging powers of the BRIC (Brazil, Russia, India, China) pursue power politics inspired by realism. They openly show their disinterest in the liberal-constructivist outlook of Western European policy makers, which entails the assumed dominance of legal rules in international relations (Mohan 2003: 5).

The new cultural-identitarian political movements criticise the overextended state of the secularist state classes. They call for expanded markets and promote a "moral economy." At the same time, they engage in the liberalisation of their foreign economic sectors, though only if this promotes their economic and political interests (Elsenhans 2006b [2004]). When the foreign economic strategies of Chinese communists are compared to the new cultural-identitarian political movements of India or the Islamic world, and the neo-populist and moderate left in Latin America, then basic similarities are immediately apparent (Elsenhans 2004c).

We are living in a world economy that is characterised by rent appropriation and soft state interventionism. This corresponds to a state system based on power rivalries and a balance of power. Both structures reinforce each other and correspond to the goals of important social actors in the emerging powers, despite apparent ideological differences among them (i.e. between ex-communists, cultural nationalists, populists etc.).

In German academic circles, such foreign policy interpretations are rejected by constructivists, and by those who believe that power politics can and must be overcome through social or "identity-level" transformation. These positions are partly determined by an interpretation of the nineteenth century and its international balance of power as prone to violence. In fact, however, the Vienna system was based on the obligation of its members to observe good governance, which was defined at this time as monarchical principle. In contrast to the first half of the twentieth century, this system ensured a long period of peace. It succeeded in coordinating the great powers, though not in integrating the potential for peaceful change.

Because of nuclear armaments, a contemporary balance of power has to be based on defensive principles. At the end of the nineteenth century, the Vienna system departed from such principles. During the Cold War there was a problem around the credibility of nuclear deterrence. This was particularly true in terms of its protective value for non-sanctuary territories, such as the American nuclear guarantee for Western Europe. France abandoned Algeria when it became apparent that nuclear weapons only constituted a credible threat for the protection of "sanctified" metropolitan France (Elsenhans 2014 [1974]: 367-369). By contrast, foreign territories can be defended against internal rebels and external aggressors only with conventional forces. In this realm, the military advances of the great powers, especially the United States, are rather limited. Such wars can be waged only through the deployment of enormous and politically prohibitive personal resources—in Algeria between 1954 and 1962, for example, one soldier for five adult males. This challenge is alive and well in Iraq and Afghanistan.

Even for countries with enormous human resources, attempting to exercise political influence is far cheaper than a military occupation, which is also significantly easier in geographically close regions. A system is thus developing in which the great powers are regional hegemons, respected by other countries and dominant in their spheres of influence. Defensive, but compromise-ready great powers exercise strong influences over their neighbouring regions. Beyond these geographically delineated spheres of interest, however, the projection of military power has become challenging, even for the United States.

In the future international system, it is highly unlikely that armed conflict will arise over issues of resource distribution, the cost of environmental programs, or even trade. Much like the Vienna system, the capacity for solving such problems exists. In the nineteenth century, this system even allowed for the relatively peaceful (from the point of view of the West) resolution of essential issues for the balance of power, such as the colonial partition of the world. The only threat to peace was constituted by the possible emergence of an alliance of great powers. This had the potential to decisively alter the balance of power, resulting in the emergence of a hegemonic power.

The rationalisation of the state system could be useful for avoiding such instability. In the Arab and sub-Saharan spaces, there are no great powers. This is not dissimilar to the fragmentation of the political sphere on the Rhine after the decay of the German Empire subsequent to the peace of Westphalia (1648). Units formally became subjects of international politics which could only be objects of the great powers. A soft underbelly of the state system could once more provoke a race for distribution of spheres of influence between the great powers.

Long before the advent of constructivism as a viable theory of knowledge, other theories had already insisted on the primary causation of foreign policy behaviour by internal political and social contradictions. Such formulations included theories of imperialism, from the controversies between Kautsky and Lenin (Kautsky 1914; Lenin 1964 [1916] to the work of Kehr 1930: 264-271, 1970). In the 1950s and 1960s, the analysis of foreign policy decision-making processes showed that external aggressiveness was closely linked to social elites' perception of the domestic instabilities which confronted them. According to this perspective, international stability depends on resolving domestic contradictions, especially in the underdeveloped, rent-based systems.

Among the emerging powers, the larger ones are not really national states, in the sense that they represent the political organisation of ethnically united communities of identity. This is especially true of BRIC countries. These are multi-ethnic empires. The homogenisation of language characterises early bourgeois structures. This began before capitalism and, indeed, facilitated the transition to a capitalist economy. Contemporary structures of communication render such phenomena less important. Narrower ethnic identities based on language, religion, regional history, etc. can survive without compromising economic development and capitalist transformation. Unlike nineteenth-century European irridentism, ethnic groups with core languages, like Hindi or Mandarin, do not have large diasporas beyond the boundaries of their respective states that have to be liberated or unified. The emerging powers can be considered sated, at least in a territorial and ethnic-nationalist sense.

These states will be cautious in engaging in foreign-policy adventures because of the reduced homogeneity of their societies, and of their dominant classes. They perceive each other as rather unstable and are interested in stabilising power holders in their partner countries, even though these power holders may nominally be their rivals on the international stage. The goal is to ensure predictability, stability, and thus the preservation of their power. These elites reject dramatic social change. Democratisation has remained largely formal, without placing in question social and economic hierarchies. The constitution of autonomous social classes by the formation of strong labour movements would require full employment.

And so, the emerging state system of the twenty-firstcentury is characterised by stability and compromise between the great powers. Between these powers, there is rivalry, but also a kind of elite solidarity. Elites want to secure their military power, their economic resources, and their prestige. All participants are interested in avoiding serious military and ideological conflict, or conflict based on offenses to "national honour". No great power forces another to lose face, or decisively supports internal opponents in the other's sphere of high interest. China runs a low-profile in Kashmir or Assam, India in Tibet. Regressions from this principle are considered to jeopardise the stability of the system, which is a problem for elites of all nations, irrespective of their specific provenance and irrespective of their rivalries with each other.

The great powers will strenuously try to avoid being drawn into conflict with each other. They limit change in the power configurations of smaller powers. An example is the rigorously enforced closed door to the club of nuclear powers.

A multipolar balance of power system is not opposed to the constructivist hope that hostile perceptions of "enemies" can be modified and identities changed in order to promote international peace. The Vienna system already showed this.

A multipolar system of this nature can go also be accompanied by strong civil society networks. In the first half of the nineteenth century, Russia brought its dynastic influence to bear in order to shape Germany's internal politics. Perhaps the international system may be subverted—to a very marginal degree—by contemporary, international "civil society" actors grouped around non-governmental organisations. In microeconomic terms, however, these organisations swim very much within the mainstream. They adjust to the strategies of government and cannot counteract the logic of rent in relation to their target groups. They do not have strong support in the real civil societies of the rent-based emerging powers. Indeed, they tend to accommodate themselves to these structures. This does not exclude the fact that, in the area of "low politics", NGOs contribute to a thickening of legal norms. And yet the great powers will never abandon their sovereign right to be bound only by their own decisions and by power-political principles—they will never submit to majority voting. Smaller powers will prefer their own sovereignty and the putative, fundamental equality of states to majority decision-making in international fora, in an attempt to engineer a thin veil of protection against the infringements of the great powers.

Notes

1. Early on, Busch (1973) insisted on the importance of the exchange rate for competitiveness, although he did not analyse its relevance for economies with differential lags in productivity with respect to the industrial world.
2. I have formulated this alternative approach of development for mass production for the realm of mass consumption (Elsenhans 1975 [1974], 1982c). Despite the still existing references to dependency theory of the first version, I have argued against disassociation, which, in a non-precisely formulated version, appeared to me as problematic. I considered foreign economic strategy as secondary in relation to increasing mass demand as a condition for growth. Despite our differing positions on the relevance of the foreign economy element, Dieter Senghaas supported me against orthodox dependency opposition at that time.

References

Abbott, John C. (1967): Agricultural Marketing Boards in the Developing Countries. In: *Journal of Farm Economics* 49 (3), pp. 705-722.

Abdel-Malek, Anouar (1971): Ägypten—Militärgesellschaft. Das Armeeregime, die Linke und der soziale Wandel unter Nasser. Frankfort on Main: Suhrkamp.

Adamolekun, Ladipo (1986): Perspectives africaines en matière d'administration médiatrice. In: *Revue internationale des sciences administratives* 52 (1), pp. 69-73.

Ahmad, Aijiz (2008): Islam, Islamisms and the West. In: *Socialist Register* (44), pp. 1-37.

Ahmed, Iftikhar (1981): Technological Change and Agrarian Structure. A Study of Bangladesh. Geneva: International Labour Office.

Akyüz, Yilmaz; Gore Charles (1994): The Investment-Profits Nexus in East Asian Industrialization. Discussion Paper 91. Geneva: UNCTAD.

Alavi, Hamza (1972): The State in Post-Colonial Societies. Pakistan and Bangladesh. In: *New Left Review* (74), pp. 59-81.

Ali, Tariq (2002): Clash of Fundamentalisms: Crusades, Jihads and Modernity. London: Verso.

Allen, Robert C. (2009): British Industrial Revolution in Global Perspective. Cambridge et al.: Cambridge University Press.

Aly, Abd al-Monein Said; Wenner, Manfred W. (1982): Modern Islamic Reform Movements: The Muslim Brotherhood in Contemporary Egypt. In: *Middle East Journal* 36, pp. 336-361.

Amin, Samir (1973): Le développement inégal. Essai sur les formations sociales du capitalisme périphérique. Paris: Editions de Minuit.

Ammar, Hamid (1954): Growing Up in an Egyptian Village. Silwa, Province of Aswan. London: Routledge & Kegan Paul.

Amsden, Alice H. (1983): 'De-skilling', Skilled Commodities and the NICs' Emerging Comparative Advantage. In: *American Economic Review* 73 (2), pp. 333-337.

Anderson, Benedict (1983): Imagined Communities. Reflections on the Origin and Spread of Nationalism. London: New Left Library.

Andrzejewski, Stanislaw (1954): Military Organisation and Society. London: Routledge & Kegan Paul.

Anell, Lars (1981): Recession, the Western Economies and the Changing World Order. London: Frances Pinter.

Ardant, Gabriel (1975): Financial Policy and Economic Infrastructure of Modern States and Nations. In: Charles Tilly (ed.): The Formation of National States in Western Europe. Princeton, N.J.: Princeton University Press, pp. 164-242.

Arjomand, Said Amir (1984): Introduction: Social Movements in the Contemporary Near and Middle East. In: Arjomand, Said Amit (ed.): From Nationalism to Revolutionary Islam. London: Macmillan, p. 127.

Ashton, Thomas Southcliffe (1955): An Economic History of England. The 18th Century. London: Methuen.

Aukrust, Odd (1964): Factors of Economic Development. A Review of Recent Research. In: *Weltwirtschaftliches Archiv* 93 (1), pp. 23-43.

Auty, Richard M. (1991): The Resource Curse Thesis: Sowing the Oil Windfalls. In: *Courier* 130 (November-December 1991), pp. 68-70.

Aydalot, Philippe (1968): Essai sur les problèmes de la stratégie de l'industrialisation en économie sous-développée. L'exemple tunisien. In: *Cahiers du CERES*, pp. 1-175.

Baer, Werner; Figueroa, Adolfo (1982): State Enterprise and the Distribution of Income. Brazil and Peru. In: Thomas C. Bruneau; Philippe Faucher (eds.): Authoritarian Capitalism. Brazil's Contemporary Economic and Political Development. Boulder, Colo.: Westview Press, pp. 59-84.

Baer, Werner; Hervé, Michel E.A. (1966): Employment and Industrialisation in Developing Countries. In: *Quarterly Journal of Economics* 80 (1), pp. 89-107.

Bagchi, Amiya Kumar (1972): Private Investment in India 1900-1938. Cambridge: Cambridge University Press.

Bai, Moo-Ki (1982): The Turning Point in the Korean Economy. In: *Developing Economies* 20, 1 (March 1982), pp. 117-140.

Bairoch, Paul (1969): Révolution industrielle et sous-développement. Paris.

Balassa, Bela (1987): Les effets sur l'emploi des échanges de produits manufacturés entre pays développés et pays en développement. In: *Etudes internationales* 17 (2), pp. 285-304.

Bantiguy, Ludivine (2008): Que jeunesse se passe? Discours publics et expertises sur les jeunes après Mai 1968. In: *Vingtième siècle. Revue d'histoire* (98), pp. 7-16.

Baran, Paul A. (1952): On the Political Economy of Backwardness. In: *Manchester School of Economic and Social Studies* 20 (1), pp. 66-84.

Barber, Benjamin R. (1996): Jihad vs. McWorld. New York: Ballantine Books.

Bardhan, Pranab K. (1982): Unequal Exchange in a Lewis-Type World. In: Mark Gersovits (ed.): The Theory and Experience of Economic Development. Essays in Honor of Sir W. Arthur Lewis. London: Allen & Unwin, pp. 157-169.

Barkhausen, Max (1958): Staatliche Wirtschaftslenkung und freies Unternehmertum im westdeutschen und im nord- und südniederländischen Raum bei der Entstehung der neuzeitlichen Industrie im 18. Jahrhundert. In: *Vierteljahrschrift für Sozial- und Wirtschaftsgeschichte* 45 (2), pp. 168-241.

Bauer, Peter Tamás (1981): Equality, the Third World and Economic Delusion. Cambridge, Mass.: Harvard University Press.

Beattie, J.H.M. (1964): Bunyoro. An African Feudality. In: *Journal of African History* 5(1), pp. 25-35.

Becker, Walter; Gehrisch, Wolfgang (1977): Grundzüge der ökonomischen Entwicklung in den vorkapitalistischen Produktionsweisen. In: *Wirtschaftswissenschaft* 25 (9), pp. 1369-1384.

Bello, Walden (1998): East Asia: on the Eve of the Great Transformation? In: *Review of International Political Economy* 5 (3), pp. 424-444.

Benachenhou, Abdellatif (1971): Le renversement de la problématique ricardienne des coûts comparés dans la théorie économique contemporaine. In: *Revue algérienne des sciences juridiques, économiques et politiques* 8 (4), pp. 913-934.

Benot, Yves (1966): Développement accéléré et révolution sociale en Afrique occidentale. In: *La Pensée* (126), pp. 19-56.

Berger, Dieter (1954): Deutsche Muttersprache im Osten. In: Mackensen, Lutz (ed.): Deutsche Heimat ohne Deutsche: Ein ostdeutsches Heimatbuch.Braunschweig: Georg Westermann, pp. 83-90.

Berg-Schlosser, D. (1979): The Social Basis of Political Development in Kenya. A Structural and Cultural Analysis. Berkeley, Cal. et al.: University of California Press.

Berrill, K. E. (1960): International Trade and the Rate of Economic Growth. In: *Economic History Review* 12 (3), pp. 351-359.

Berument, Hakan; Pasaogullari, Mehmet (2003): Effects of the Real Exchange Rate on Output and Inflation: Evidence from Turkey. In: *Developing Economies* 41, 4 (December), pp. 401-435.

Bhagwati, Jagdish N. (1958): Immiserizing Growth. A Geometrical Note. In: *Review of Economic Studies* 25 (68), pp. 201-204.

Bhalla, Ajit S. (1960): On Nurkse's Concealed Saving Potential. In: *Indian Journal of Economics* 40 (159), pp. 305-310.

Bidwell, Percy Wells; Falconer, John I. (1968): Small Farmers of the New England and Middle Colonies. Pioneering in the Eighteenth Century. In: Alfred D. Chandler; Steward Bruchey; Louis Galambos (eds.): The Changing Economic Order. Readings in American Business and Economic History. New York: Harcourt & Brace, pp. 18-36.

Biggs, Margaret A. (1980): The Challenge. Adjust or Protect. Ottawa: North-South Institute.

Birdsall, Nancy; Ross, David; Sabot, Richard (1995): Inequality and Growth Reconsidered: Lessons from East Asia. In: *World Bank Economic Review* 9, 3 (September), pp. 477-508.

Bitar, Sergio (1979): Transición, socialismo y democracia. La experiencia chilena. Mexico: Siglo Veintiuno.

Blackhurst, Richard (1972): General Versus Preferential Tariff Reduction for LDC Exports. In: *Southern Economic Journal* 38 (3), pp. 350-362.

Bluestone, Barry; Harrison, Bennett (1982): The Deindustrialization of America. Plant Closings, Community Abandonment and the Dismantling of Basic Industry. New York, London: Basic Books.

Boatler, Robert W. (1975): Trade Theory Predictions and the Growth of Mexico's Manufactured Exports. In: *Economic Development and Cultural Change* 23 (4), pp. 491-506.

Boeckh, Andreas (2002): Die Ursachen der Entwicklungsblockaden in Lateinamerika. Einige entwicklungstheoretische Mutmaßungen. In: *Leviathan* 30 (4), pp. 509-529.

Bortkiewicz, Ladislaus von (1907): Wertrechnung und Preisrechnung im Marxschen System (3). In: *Archiv für Sozialwissenschaft und Sozialpolitik* 25 (2), pp. 445-489.

Bose, A. N. (1974): The Informal Sector in the Calcuttan Metropolitan Economy. World Employment Programme Research Working Paper No. 5. Geneva: International Labour Office.

Boutaleb, G. (1981): Les dangers de l'extraversion. In: *Révolution africaine*, pp. 23-45.

Brady, Dorothy (1964): Relative Prices in the Nineteenth Century. In: *Journal of Economic History* 24 (2), pp. 145-203.

Bredow, Wilfried von; Brocke, Rudolf H. (1987): Krise und Protest: Ursprünge und Elemente der Friedensbewegung in Westeuropa. Opladen: Westdeutscher Verlag.

Bresser Pereira, Luiz C. (1978): Les entreprises multinationales et le sous-développement industrialisé. In: *Tiers Monde* 19 (74), pp. 299-330.

Bronfenbrenner, Martin (1970): Radical Economics in America. A Survey. In: *Journal of Economic Literature* 8 (3), pp. 747-766.

Bruton, Henry J. (1968): Import Substitution and Productivity Growth. In: *Journal of Development Studies* 4 (3), pp. 306-326.

Bruton, Henry J. (1998): A Reconsideration of Import Substitution. In: *Journal of Economic Literature* 36 (2), pp. 903-936.

Buffie, Edward F. (1986): Devaluation, Investment and Growth in LDCs. In: *Journal of Development Economics* 20, 2 (March), pp. 361-379.

Busch, Klaus (1973): Ungleicher Tausch—Zur Diskussion über internationale Durchschnittsprofitrate, Ungleichen Tausch und komparative Kostentheorie anhand der Thesen von Arghiri Emanuel. In: *Probleme des Klassenkampfs* 3 (8/9), pp. 47-88.

Campbell, Mildred (1960): The English Yeoman and Elizabeth and the Early Stuarts. London: Merlin Press.

Caputo, Orlando; Pizarro, Roberto (1970): Desarrollismo y capital extranjero. Las nuevas formas del imperialismo en Chile. Santiago, Chile: Ediciones de la Universidad Técnica del Estado.

Cardoso, Fernando Henrique; Faletto, Enzo (1967): Dependencia y desarrollo en América Latina. Lima: Instituto de Estudios Peruanos.

Cardoso, Fernando Henrique; Faletto, Enzo (1977): Estado y proceso político en América Latina. In: *Revista Mexicana de Sociología* 39 (2), pp. 357-389.

Carlier, Omar (1992): De l'Islahisme à l'Islamisme. La thérapie politico-religieuse du FIS. In: *Cahiers d'études africaines*(June), pp. 185-219.

Carr, Edward Hallett (1966): The Twenty Years Crisis, 1919-1939. An Introduction to the Study of International Relations. London, New York.

Ceriello, Gustavo Rodolfo (1950): Nota. In: *I rimatori del dolce Stil nuovo.* Milan: Mondadori, pp. 5-12.

Chabal, Patrick (1986): Revolutionary Democracy in Africa. The Case of Guinea- Bissau. In: Patrick Chabal (ed.): Political Domination in Africa. Reflections on the Limits of Power. Cambridge: Cambridge University Press, pp. 84-108.

Chambers, James D. (1946): Enclosures and the Small Land-Owner. In: *Economic History Review* 10, 2 (November), pp. 118-127.

Chambers, James D.; Mingay, G. E. (1966): The Agricultural Revolution 1750-1880. London: Batsford.

Chen, Haichun; Gordon, M.J.; Zhiming, Yan (1994): The Real Income and Consumption of an Urban Chinese Family. In: *Journal of Development Studies* 31, 1 (October), pp. 201-213.

Cheng, Tu-Jen (1990): Political Regimes and Developmental Strategies: South Korea and Taiwan. In: Gereffi, Gary; Wyman, Donald L. (eds.): Manufacturing Miracles. Paths of Industrialization in Latin America and East Asia. Princeton, NJ: Princeton University Press, pp. 139-179.

Chinn, Dennis Leslie (1977): Distributional Equality and Economic Growth. In: *Economic Development and Cultural Change* 26 (1), pp. 65-79.

Chinweizu, A. (1987): The West and the Rest of Us. White Predators, Black Slaves and the African Elite. Lagos, Nigeria: Pero Press.

Chowdhuri, Satyabrata Rai (1976): Leftist Movements in India: 1917-1947. Calcutta: Minerva Associates.

Clague, Christopher K. (1967): An International Comparison of Industrial Efficiency. Peru and the United States. In: *Review of Economics and Statistics* 49 (4), pp. 487-493.

Clark, George (1961): The Seventeenth Century. Oxford: Oxford University Press.

Clark, W. Edmund (1978): Socialist Development and Public Investment in Tanzania, 1964-73. Toronto, Buffalo, London: University of Toronto Press.

Cline, William (1982): Can the East Asian Model of Development Be Generalized? In: *World Development* 10 (2), pp. 81-90.

Cobden, William (1967 [1836]): Russia: Protection of Commerce, in: Richard Cobden, Political Writings (1), William Ridgway: London, pp. 284-339.

Coghlan, T. A. (1918): Labour and Industry in Australia from the First Settlement in 1788 to the Establishment of the Commonwealth in 1901. Oxford et al.: Oxford University Press.

Condliffe, John Bell (1940): The Reconstruction of World Trade. A Survey of International Economic Relations. New York: W.W. Norton.

Cooper, Frederick (2002): Africa since 1940. The Past of the Present. Cambridge et al.: Cambridge University Press.

Crafts, Nicholas F. R. (1980): National Income Estimates and the British Standard of Living Debate. A Reappraisal of 1801-1831. In: *Explorations in Economic History* 17.

Crowder, Michael (1971): Introduction. In: Crowder, Michael (ed.): West African Resistance. The Military Response to Colonial Occupation. New York: Africana Publishing Co., pp. 1-18.

Davey, Brian (1975): The Economic Development of India. Nottingham: Spokesman.

David, Paul A. (1975): Technical Choice. Innovation and Economic Growth. Essays on American and British Experience in the Nineteenth Century. Cambridge: Cambridge University Press.

Davies, C.S.L. (1973): Peasant Revolts in France and England. A Comparison. In: *Agricultural History Review* 21 (2), pp. 122-134.

Deane, Phyllis (1965): The First Industrial Revolution. Cambridge: Cambridge University Press.

Deane, Phyllis; Cole, W. A. (1967): British Economic Growth 1688-1959. Trends and Structures. Cambridge: Cambridge University Press.

Denison, Edward F. (1967): Why Growth Rates Differ. Postwar Experience in Nine Western Countries. Washington D.C.: Brookings Institution.

Denitch, Bogdan (1970): La nouvelle gauche et la nouvelle classe ouvrière. In: *Homme et la société* (16), pp. 43-54.

Dessouki, Ali E. Hillal (1973): Arab Intellectuals and Al-Nakba: The Search for Fundamentalism. In: *Middle Eastern Studies* 9, 2 (April), pp. 187-195.

Deyon, Pierre (1972): La concurrence internationale des manufactures lainières aux XVIe et XVIIe siècles. In: *Annales. Economie, Société, Civilisation* 27 (1), pp. 20-32.

Digby, William (1901): 'Prosperous' British India. A Revelation from Official Records. London: T. Fisher Unwin.

Diwan, Ramesh (1995): Economic Reforms, Swadeshi and Foreign Investments. In: *The Hindu* 31 October 1995.

Dobb, Maurice Herbert (1951): Some Aspects of Economic Development. Three Lectures. Delhi: Delhi School of Economics. University of Delhi.

Dobson, C. R. (1980): Masters and Journeymen. A Prehistory of Industrial Relations. London, Totowa, N.J.: Croom Helm; Rowman & Littlefield.

Domar, Evsey D. (1961): The Capital-Output Ratio in the United States. Its Variation and Stability. In: F. A. Lutz; D. C. Hague (eds.): The Theory of Capital. Proceedings of a Conference Held by the International Economic Association. New York, London: Macmillan; St. Martins Press, pp. 95-117.

Donges, Jurgen B. (1971): Die Entwicklungsländer als Anbieter industrieller Erzeugnisse. In: *Weltwirtschaft* 21 (1), pp. 41-61.

Dumont, Louis (1970): Religion, Politics and History in India. The Hague, Paris: Mouton.

Dunham, Arthur Louis (1930): The Anglo-French Treaty of Commerce of 1860 and the Progress of the Industrial Revolution in France. Ann Arbor, Mich.: University of Michigan Press.

Dutt, Rajani Palme (1949): India Today. Bombay.

Dutt, Palme Rajani (1970): India Today [1949]. Calcutta: Manisha.

Ehrensaft, Philip; Armstrong, Warwick (1978): Dominion Capitalism. A First Statement. In: *Australian and New Zealand Journal of Sociology* 14 (3), pp. 352-363.

Einaudi, Jean-Luc (1986): Pour l'exemple, l'affaire Fernand Iveton: enquête.Paris.

Ekeh, Peter P. (1975): Colonialism and the Two Publics in Africa. A Theoretical Statement. In: *Comparative Studies in Society and History* 17 (1), pp. 91-112.

Elliott, John H. (1963): Imperial Spain (1409-1716). London: Edward Arnold.

Elsenhans, Hartmut (1974): Entwicklungstendenzen der Welterdölindustrie. In: Hartmut Elsenhans (ed.): Erdöl für Europa, Hoffmann & Campe: Hamburg, pp. 7-47.

Elsenhans, Hartmut (1975): Overcoming Underdevelopment. A Research Paradigm [1974]. In: *Journal of Peace Research* 12 (4), pp. 293-313.

Elsenhans, Hartmut (1976a): Ausbeutung und Unterentwicklung. Zur Entstehung des kapitalistischen Weltsystems. In: *Sozialwissenschaftliche Informationen für Unterricht und Studium* 5 (3), pp. 100-107.

Elsenhans, Hartmut (1976b): Klassenkämpfe—Zur Geschichte von Entwicklung und Unterentwicklung. In: José Linhard; Klaus Voll (eds.): "Weltmarkt und Entwicklungsländer. Berliner Studien zur Internationalen Politik. Schriftenreihe der Arbeitsstelle Internationale Politik und Schule" an der Pädagogischen Hochschule Berlin. Rheinstetten: Schindele, pp. 31-65.

Elsenhans, Hartmut (1976c): Lohnerhöhungen: Wachstumschance für den Kapitalismus. Eine Kritik am Gesetz vom tendenziellen Fall der Profitrate. In: *Forum DS. Zeitschrift für Theorie und Praxis des demokratischen Sozialismus* 1 (2), pp. 78-133.

Elsenhans, Hartmut (1976d): Neun Thesen zum Verhältnis von Staatsapparat und multinationalen Konzernen in der Dritten Welt. In: Dieter Senghaas; Ulrich Menzel (eds.): Multinationale Konzerne und Dritte Welt. Opladen: Westdeutscher Verlag, pp. 170-180.

Elsenhans, Hartmut (1976e): Zur Rolle der Staatsklasse bei der Überwindung von Unterentwicklung. In: Alfred Schmidt (ed.): Strategien gegen Unterentwicklung. Zwischen Weltmarkt und Eigenständigkeit. Frankfort on the Main, New York: Campus, pp. 250-265.

Elsenhans, Hartmut (1977): Ungleichheit und Unterentwicklung. Staat—Wirtschaft—Gesellschaft in der unterentwickelten Welt. Eine kommentierte Textsammlung. Rheinstetten: Schindele.

Elsenhans, Hartmut (1979): Agrarverfassung, Akkumulationsprozeß, Demokratisierung. In: Hartmut Elsenhans (ed.): Agrarreform in der Dritten Welt. Frankfort on the Main, New York: Campus, pp. 505-652.

Elsenhans, Hartmut (1981a): Commentaires. In: Arghiri Emmanuel: Technologie appropriée ou technologie sous-développée? Suivi d'une discussion avec Celso Furtado et Hartmut Elsenhans. Paris: Presses Universitaires de France, pp. 151-166.

Elsenhans, Hartmut (1981b): Egalitarisme social et critique des modes de production dans la périphérie au lieu d'antiimpérialisme et critique des rapports économiques entre le Centre et la Périphérie. In: EADI Working Group Multinationales et développement (ed.): Transfert de technologie et développement. Un débat. Symposium de Paris du 10 octobre 1980. Paris: Université de Paris, Institut d'Etudes du Développement Economique et Social, pp. 1-71.

Elsenhans, Hartmut (1981c): Social Consequences of the NIEO. No Change for Continued Reformist Strategies in the Centre without Structural Change in the Periphery. In: Egbert Jahn; Yoshikazu Sakamoto (eds.): Elements of World Instability: Armaments, Communication, Food, International Division of Labour. Proceedings of the Eighth International Peace Research Association Conference. Frankfort on Main, New York: Campus, pp. 86-95.

Elsenhans, Hartmut (1981d): Sur le bon emploi des schémas de reproduction. Contribution au Symposium de Paris sur l'ouvrage d'Arghiri Emmanuel 'Technologie Appropriée,

Mirage ou Réalité'. Working Group—Multinationales et Développement. European Association of Development Research and Training Institutes. General Conference 1981, Budapest, 11-14 November. Budapest: European Association of Development Research and Training Institutes.

Elsenhans, Hartmut (1982a): Capitalisme d'Etat ou société bureaucratique de développement. In: *Etudes internationales* 13, 1 (March), pp. 3-22.

Elsenhans, Hartmut (1982b): Contradictions in the Algerian Development Process: The Reform of the Public Sector and the New Approach to the Private Sector in Industry. In: *Maghreb Review* 7, 3/4 (May-August), pp. 62-72.

Elsenhans, Hartmut (1982c): Die Überwindung von Unterentwicklung durch Massenproduktion für den Massenbedarf—Weiterentwicklung eines Ansatzes. In: Dieter Nohlen; Franz Nuscheler (eds.): Handbuch der Dritten Welt (1): Unterentwicklung und Entwicklung—Theorien, Strategien, Indikatoren, Hoffmann & Campe: Hamburg, pp. 152-182.

Elsenhans, Hartmut (1983a): Croissance, développement, stratégies de satisfaction des besoins de base—ou pourquoi le développement doit être orienté vers les besoins des masses. Dakar: Ms. available at https://hartmutelsenhans.net/unpublished-papers-2/

Elsenhans, Hartmut (1983b): Le monde arabe et l'Europe dans la nouvelle division internationale du travail. In: Bichara Khader (ed.): Coopération Euro-Arabe. Diagnostic et Prospective (3). Actes du Colloque organisé à Louvain-la Neuve (2-4 décembre 1982) par le Centre d'Etude et de Recherche sur le Monde Arabe Contemporain de l'Université Catholique de Louvain. Löwen: CERMAC, pp. 34-123.

Elsenhans, Hartmut (1983c): Rising Mass Incomes as a Condition of Capitalist Growth: Implications for the World Economy. In: *International Organization* 37, 1 (Winter), pp. 1-38.

Elsenhans, Hartmut (1986): Der Mythos der Kapitalintensität und die notwendig falsche Technologiewahl der Entwicklungsländer. In: Beate Kohler-Koch (ed.): Technik und internationale Politik. Baden-Baden: Nomos, pp. 267-290.

Elsenhans, Hartmut (1987): Dependencia, Underdevelopment and the Third World State. In: *Law and State* 36, pp. 65-94.

Elsenhans, Hartmut (1992a): English Poor Law and Egalitarian Agrarian Reform in the Third World [1980]. In: Hartmut Elsenhans (ed.): Equality and Development. Dhaka: Center for Social Studies, pp. 130-162.

Elsenhans, Hartmut (1992b): Foundation of Development of the Capitalist World Economy [1979]. In: Hartmut Elsenhans (ed.): Equality and Development. Dhaka: Center for Social Studies, pp. 21-79.

Elsenhans, Hartmut (1993): Integrating Political Economy in the Comparative Study of Administration. In: Asmeron, Haile K.; Jain, Randhir Bahadur (eds.): Politics, Administration and Public Policy in Developing Countries. Amsterdam: Vrije Universiteit Press, pp. 16-35.

Elsenhans, Hartmut (1994a): Fundamentalismus in der Dritten Welt als Herausforderung an das internationale System des 21. Jahrhunderts. Kultursoziologie oder Politökonomie als Therapie. In: *Comparativ. Leipziger Beiträge zur Universalgeschichte und vergleichenden Gesellschaftsforschung* 4 (6), pp. 9-20.

Elsenhans, Hartmut (1994b): Rent, State and the Market: The Political Economy of the Transition to Self-sustained Capitalism. In: *Pakistan Development Review* 33, 4 (December), pp. 393-428.

Elsenhans, Hartmut (1996a): Gegen das Gespenst der Globalisierung. In: Werner Fricke (ed.): Jahrbuch Arbeit und Technik 1996. Zukunft der Industriegesellschaft. Bonn: Dietz, pp. 25-36.

Elsenhans, Hartmut (1996b): State, Class and Development [1981]. New Delhi, London, Columbia, Mo.: Radiant; Sangam; South Asia Books.

Elsenhans, Hartmut (1997): Rent and the Transition to Capitalism. In: *Asien—Afrika—Lateinamerika* 25, 6, pp. 651-686.

Elsenhans, Hartmut (2000a): Die Globalisierung der Finanzmärkte und die Entstehung einer neuen Rentenklasse. In: Ulrich Menzel (ed.): Vom Ewigen Frieden und vom Wohlstand der Nationen. Dieter Senghaas zum 60. Geburtstag, Frankfort on the Main: Suhrkamp, pp. 518-542.

Elsenhans, Hartmut (2000b): Globalisation in a Labourist Keynesian Approach. In: *Journal of Social Studies* (89), pp. 1-66.

Elsenhans, Hartmut (2000c): The Rise and Fall of Really Existing Socialism. In: *Journal of Social Studies* 87 (Jan.-March), pp. 1-16.

Elsenhans, Hartmut (2001a): Bedingungen des Politischen. Staat, Wirtschaft, Gesellschaft und Technik. In: Raban Graf von Westphalen; Volker Neßler (eds.): Deutsches Regierungsystem. Munich et al.: Oldenbourg, pp. 75-98.

Elsenhans, Hartmut (2001b): Renten in der exportorientierten Industrialisierung. Zur notwendigen und widerspruchsvollen Rolle des Staats. In: Peter Gärtner (ed.):

Staatlichkeit im Epochenbruch? Antworten aus der Perspektive des Südens und Ostens. Hamburg: Hamburgisches Welt-Wirtschafts-Archiv, pp. 251-296.

Elsenhans, Hartmut (2002): Macroeconomics in Globalization: Productivity, Wages, Profits, and Exchange Rates in an Era of Globalization. In: *Brazilian Journal of Political Economy* 22, 85 (January-March), pp. 53-78.

Elsenhans, Hartmut (2004a): Globalisation, Devaluation and Development. In: *Rajasthan Economic Journal* 27, 1 (October), pp. 1-14.

Elsenhans, Hartmut (2004b): Globalisierung von Profit oder Globalisierung von Rente. In: *Jahrbuch für Wirtschaftswissenschaften* 55 (3), pp. 263-289.

Elsenhans, Hartmut (2004c): Good Governance, Moral Economy, and the Shift from Secular State Classes to Identitarian Political Movements with Reference to Developing Countries. In: *Indian Journal of Political Science* 65, 4 (Oct.-Dec.), pp. 469-498.

Elsenhans, Hartmut (2005): A Benign Globalization vs. a Doomsday Scenario: How to Make Globalization in a Capital and Welfare Perspective. In: *Review of Global Politics* 10 (April), pp. 1-66.

Elsenhans, Hartmut (2006a): Globalization Between A Convoy Model and An Underconsumptionist Threat. LIT Verlag: Münster.

Elsenhans, Hartmut (2006b): The WTO, Globalisation and New Political Movements of the South. In: Elsenhans, Hartmut; Jain, Rajendra Kumar (eds.): India, the European Union and the WTO. New Delhi: Radiant Publishers, pp. 51-98.

Elsenhans, Hartmut (2007): Geschichte und Ökonomie der europäischen Welteroberung. Vom Zeitalter der Entdeckungen zum 1. Weltkrieg [1976]. Herausgegeben mit einem Vorwort von Matthias Middell, Leipziger Universitätsverlag: Leipzig.

Elsenhans, Hartmut (2012): The Rise of New Cultural Identitarian Movements in Africa and Asia in the Emerging Multipolar System. In: *Comparative Studies of South Asia, Africa and the Middle East* 32, 3 (Winter), pp. 642-661.

Elsenhans, Hartmut (2014): La guerre d'Algérie 1954-1962 [1974]. La Transition d'une France à une autre. Le passage de la IVe à la Ve République (2 vols.). Algiers: Dar el-Kitab el-arabi.

Elsenhans, Hartmut (2015a): Middle Classes and New Cultural-Identitarian Political Movements: Perspectives. In: Elsenhans, Hartmut; Ouaissa, Rachid; Schwecke, Sebastian; Tétreault, Mary Ann (eds.): *The Transformation of Politised Religion: Zealots Turned into Leaders.* Aldershot: Ashgate, pp. 143-162.

Elsenhans, Hartmut (2015b): Saving Capitalism from the Capitalists. A Contribution to Global and Historical Keynesianism. Beverly Hills, Cal., London, New Delhi: Sage.

Elsenhans, Hartmut (2019): The Impending Threat of Globalisation of Rent and the Defence of Capitalism by Labour. In: *International Studies* 56 (2), pp. 109-128.

Elsenhans, Hartmut (2020a): European Integration at the Crossroads (1). In: *Cultural World—Kul'tura Mira* 8 (22), pp. 37-66.

Elsenhans; Hartmut (2020b): European Integration at the Crossroads (2). In: *Cultural World—Kul'tura Mira* 8 (23), pp. 157-180.

Elsenhans, Hartmut (2020c): European Integration at the Crossroads (3). In: *Cultural World—Kul'tura Mira* 8 (24), pp. 270-306.

Elsenhans, Hartmut (2020d): Green Growth or the New Frontier of Capitalism: A Kaleckian Approach. In: Thomas Hickmann; Markus Lederer (eds.): Entwicklung, Verwaltung, Umwelt und Klima—Sozialwissenschaftliche Perspektiven aus Theorie und Praxis. Eine Festschrift für Harald Fuhr. Baden-Baden: Nomos, pp. 155-168.

Elsenhans, Hartmut (2021a): Capitalism, Development, Empowerment of Labour. A Heterodox Political Economy. London: Routledge.

Elsenhans, Hartmut (2021b): Overcoming Marginality as Objective of the Struggle against Poverty [1995]. In: Hannes Warnecke (ed.): Development, Capitalism, and Rent. The Political Economy of Hartmut Elsenhans. New York: Palgrave-Macmillan, pp. 101-133.

Elsenhans, Hartmut; Köpf, Rose (1981): Rohstoffpolitik im Spektrum des Nord-Süd-Dialogs. In: *Wochenschau für politische Erziehung, Sozial- und Gemeinschaftskunde* 32 (6), pp. 218-261.

Elshorst, Hansjörg (ed.) (1986): Entwicklungspolitik. Bilanz und Perspektiven. Zur Sache. Themen parlamentarischer Beratung 2/86. Saarbrücken-Schafbrücke: epi.

Emmanuel, Arghiri (1982): Appropriate or Underdeveloped Technology? Followed by a Discussion with Celso Furtado and Hartmut Elsenhans. Chichester et al.: John Wiley.

Engels, Friedrich (1972): Die Lage der arbeitenden Klasse in England. Nach eigner Anschauung und authentischen Quellen [1845]. In: Karl Marx und Friedrich Engels: Marx-Engels-Werke. Berlin: Dietz, pp. 225-508.

Engels, Friedrich (1972): Über den Verfall des Feudalismus und das Aufkommen der Bourgeoisie [1884]. In: Marx, Karl; Engels, Friedrich: Werke Band 21.Berlin: Dietz, pp. 392-401.

Erber, Georg; Hagemann, Harald (2012): Zur Produktivitätsentwicklung Deutschlands im internationalen Vergleich. Wiso Diskurs. Bonn-Bad-Godesberg: Friedrich-Ebert-Stiftung.

Ernst, Dieter (1983): The Global Race in Microelectronics. Innovation and Corporate Strategies in a Period of Crisis. Frankfort on Main, New York: Campus.

Ernst, Dieter (1994): Carriers of Regionalization: The East Asian Production Networks of Japanese Electronic Firms. Working Paper 73. Berkeley: Berkeley Round Table on the International Economy, November.

Evans, Peter B. (1979): Dependent Development. The Alliance of Multinational, State and Local Capital in Brazil. Princeton, N.J.: Princeton University Press.

Fabricant, Solomon (1959): Basic Facts on Productivity Changes. Occasional Paper 63. New York: National Bureau of Economic Research.

Falola, Toyin; Ihonvbere, Julius (1985): The Rise and Fall of Nigeria's Second Republic 1979-1984. London: ZED Books.

FAO: Yearbook of Food and Agricultural Statistics: Production. 1954 (8-1). Rome: Food and Agricultural Organisation.

Fatton, Robert (1985): The Political Ideology of Julius Nyerere. The Structural Limitation of African Socialism. In: *Studies in Comparative International Development* 20 (2), pp. 3-24.

Faujas, Alain (2008): Que ferions-nous sans la Chine? In: *Le Monde*, January 4th, p. 2.

Fauvet, Jacques (1959): La IVe République.Paris: Fayard, 1959.

Feis, Herbert (1940): The Changing Pattern of International Economic Affairs. New York, London: Harper.

Felix, David (1969): Economic Development. Take-Off into Unsustained Growth. In: *Social Research* 36 (2), pp. 266-293.

Fieldhouse, David Kenneth (1965): Die Kolonialreiche seit dem 18. Jahrhundert. Fischer Weltgeschichte Band 29. Frankfort on the Main: Fischer.

Fitch, Bob; Oppenheimer, Mary (1966): Ghana. End of an Illusion. In: *Monthly Review* 18 (3), pp. 1-130.

Fitch, Nancy (1992): Mass Culture, Mass Parliamentary Politics and Modem Antisemitism: The Dreyfus Affair in Rural France. In: *American Historical Review* 97, 1 (February), pp. 55-95.

Fitzgerald, Edmund V.K (1978): The State and Capital Accumulation in Mexico. In: *Journal of Latin American Studies* 10 (2), pp. 263-283.

Flinn, M. W. (1974): Trends in Real Wages, 1750-1850. In: *Economic History Review* 17 (2), pp. 395-413.

Fujita, Natsuki; James, William E. (1990): Export Oriented Growth of Output and Employment in Taiwan and Korea, 1973/74-1983/84. In: *Weltwirtschaftliches Archiv* 126 (4), pp. 737-753.

Furtado, Celso (1965): Development and Stagnation in Latin America. A Structuralist Approach. In: *Studies in Comparative International Development* 1 (11), pp. 159-175.

Furtado, Celso (1973): The Brazilian 'Model' of Development. In: Charles K. Wilber (ed.): The Political Economy of Development and Underdevelopment. New York: Random House, pp. 297-306.

Gadgil, D. R. (1971): The Industrial Evolution of India in Recent Times 1860- 1939. Bombay: Oxford University Press.

Ganiage, Jean (1968): L'expansion coloniale de la France sous la IIIe République 1871-1914. Avec la collobaration de Daniel Hémery: Indochine. Paris: Payot.

Gann, Lewis H.; Duignan, Peter (1978): The Rulers of British Africa 1870-1914. London: Croom Helm.

Gardner, Lloyd (1964): Economic Aspects of New Deal Diplomacy. Madison, Wis.: The University of Wisconsin Press, 1964.

Geiger, Theodor (1932): Die soziale Schichtung des deutschen Volkes. Soziographischer Versuch auf statistischer Grundlage. Stuttgart: Ferdinand Enke.

Georgescu-Roegen, Nicholas (1960): Economic Theory and Agrarian Economics. In: *Oxford Economic Papers* 12 (1), pp. 1-40.

Gereffi, Gary; Evans, Peter B. (1981): Transnational Corporations, Dependent Development and State Policy in the Semi-Periphery. A Comparison of Brazil and Mexico. In: *Latin American Research Review* 16 (3), pp. 31-64.

Gerschenkron, Alexander (1962): Economic Backwardness in Historical Perspective. Cambridge, Mass.: The Belknap Press of Harvard University Press.

Ghosal, H. R. (1966): Economic Transition in the Bengal Presidency 1793-1833. Calcutta: K.L. Mukhopadhyay.

Giersch, Herbert (1978): Zu den Forderungen nach einer neuen Weltwirtschaftsordnung. In: Herbert Giersch; Hans Günter Krüsselberg (eds.): Weltwirtschaftsordnung und Wirtschaftswissenschaft. Vorträge zum 450. Jubiläum der Philipps-Universität Marburg. Stuttgart: Gustav Fischer, pp. 18-29.

Giesen, Klaus-Gerd (1992): L'éthiques des relations internationales. Les théories anglo-américaines contemporaines.Brussels: Bruylant.

Gilboy, Elizabeth Waterman (1934a): Time Series and the Derivation of Demand and Supply Curves. A Study of Coffee and Tea. In: *Quarterly Journal of Economics* 48 (3), pp. 667-685.

Gilboy, Elizabeth Waterman (1934b): Wages in the 18th Century England. New York: Russell & Russell.

Gillis, Malcolm (1980): The Role of State Enterprises in Economic Development. In: *Social Research* 47 (2), pp. 249-290.

Gillman, Joseph (1965): Prosperity in Crisis. New York: Marzani & Munsell.

Goode, Richard; Lent, George E.; Ohja, P. D. (1966): The Role of Export Taxes in Developing Countries. In: *IMF Staff Papers* 13 (3), pp. 453-502.

Gorlin, Alice C. (1985): The Power of Soviet Industrial Ministries in the 1980s. In: *Soviet Studies* 37 (3), pp. 353-370.

Gould, Harold A. (1993): Mandai, Mandir and Dalits. Melding Class with Ethnoreligious Conflict in India's Tenth General Election. In: Gould, Harold A.; Ganguly, Sumit (eds.): India Votes: Alliance Politics and Minority Governments in the Ninth and Tenth General Elections. Boulder, Colo, et al.: Westview, pp. 293-340.

Grabowski, Richard (2018): Food Staple Production and Alternative Development Paths. India and China. In: *Journal of the Asia Pacific Economy* 23 (3), pp. 357-373. DOI: 10.1080/13547860.2018.1469588.

Grindle, Merilee Serill (1977): Power, Expertise and the 'Técnico'. Suggestions from a Mexican Case Study. In: *Journal of Politics* 39 (2), pp. 399-426.

Habakkuk, Hrothgar J. (1939): English Landownership 1680-1740. In: *Economic History Review* 10, 1 (November), pp. 2-18.

Habakkuk, Hrothgar John (1962): American and British Technology in the Nineteenth Century. The Search for Labour-Saving Inventions. Cambridge: Cambridge University Press.

Habermas, Jürgen (1965): Strukturwandel der Öffentlichkeit. Untersuchungen zu einer Kategorie der bürgerlichen Gesellschaft. Neuwied, Berlin: Luchterhand.

Hadwiger, Peter; Hippier, Jochen; Lotz, Helmut (1983): Kaffee. Gewohnheit und Konsequenz. Wuppertal, St. Gallen: Marandü Dia.

Hager, Wolfgang (1982): Protectionism and Autonomy. How to Preserve Free Trade in Europe. In: *International Affairs* 58 (3), pp. 413-428.

Haggard, Stephan Mark (1983): Pathways from the Periphery. The Newly Industrializing Countries in the International System. Berkeley, Cal.: Dissertation.

Hahn, Hans-Werner (1984): Hegemonie und Integration. Voraussetzungen und Folgen der preußischen Führungsrolle im Deutschen Zollverein. In: Berding, Helmut (ed.): Wirtschaftliche und politische Integration in Europa im 19. und 20. Jahrhundert. Göttingen: Vandenhoeck & Ruprecht, pp. 45-70.

Halbach, Axel J. (1983): Economic System and Socio-Economic Development of Developing Countries. A Statistical Analysis of World Bank Data. In: *Economics* 28, pp. 7-38.

Hallgarten, Wolfgang (1935): Vorkriegsimperialismus. Die soziologischen Grundlagen der Außenpolitik europäischer Großmächte bis 1914. Paris: Edition Météore.

Hanisch, Rolf; Tetzlaff, Rainer (eds.) (1980): Historische Konstitutionsbedingungen des Staates in Entwicklungsländern. Frankfort on Main: Alfred Metzner.

Hanley, Susan B.; Yamamura, Kozo (1977): Economic and Demographic Change in Pre-Industrial Japan. 1600-1868. Princeton, N.J.: Princeton University Press.

Hargreaves, John D. (1974): West Africa Partitioned. The Loaded Pause 1885-1889. London: Macmillan.

Harrod, Roy (1972): Economic Essays. London, New York.

Hartwell, Richard M. (1961): The Rising Standard of Living in England 1800-1850. In: *Economic History Review* 13 (3), pp. 397-416.

Hartwell, Richard M. (1964): The Standard of Living During the Industrial Revolution. A Discussion. In: *Economic History Review* 38 (1), pp. 135-146.

Haupt, Heinz-Gerhard (1974): Nationalismus und Demokratie. Zur Geschichte der Bourgeoisie im Frankreich der Restauration. Athenäum: Fischer.

Hein, Wolfgang (1985): Staatsklasse, Umverteilung und die Überwindung von Unterentwicklung. In: *Peripherie* 5 (18, 19), pp. 172-186.

Helmstädter, Ernst (1969): Der Kapitalkoeffizient. Eine kapitaltheoretische Untersuchung. Stuttgart: Gustav Fischer.

Hicks, John (1982): Money, Interest and Wages. Collected Essays on Economic Theory. Oxford: Basil Blackwell.

Hilferding, Rudolf (1968): Das Finanzkapital. Eine Studie über die jüngste Entwicklung des Kapitalismus [1909]. Frankfort on the Main: Europäische Verlagsanstalt.

Hirschman, Albert O. (1958): The Strategy of Economic Development. New Haven, Conn.: Yale University Press.

Hirschman, Albert O. (1968): The Political Economy of Import-Substituting Industrialization in Latin America. In: *Quarterly Journal of Economics* 82 (1), pp. 1-32.

Hirschman, Albert O. (1970): Exit, Voice and Loyality: Responses to Decline in Firms, Organizations and States. Cambridge, Mass.; London: Harvard University Press.

Hobson, John Atkinson (1938): Imperialism. A Study, Allen & Unwin: London.

Hodara, Isidoro (1985): Countertrade—Experiences of Some Latin American Countries. UNCTAD/ST/ECDC/27. Geneva: United Nations Conference on Trade and Development.

Hodne, Fritz (1975): An Economic History of Norway, 1815-1870: Tapir.

Holderness, B. A. (1976): Pre-Industrial England. Economy and Society 1500-1750. London, Totowa, N.J.. J.M. Dents & Sons; Rowman & Littlefield.

Holtgrave, Wilfried (1987): Industrialisierung in Singapur. Chancen und Risiken industrieorientierter Spezialisierung. Frankfort on Main, New York: Campus.

Hoskins, W. G. (1950): Essays in Leicestershire History. Liverpool: University of Liverpool Press.

Hostetler, Laura (2000): Quing Connections to the Early Modern World: Ethnography and Cartography in Eighteenth-Century China. In: *Modern Asian Studies* 34, 3 (July), pp. 623-662.

Howard, Earl Dean (1907): The Cause and Extent of the Recent Industrial Progress of Germany. Cambridge, Mass.: Houghton Mifflin.

Hsieh, Chang-Tai (1973): Measuring the Effects of Trade Expansion on Employment. A Review of Some Research. In: *International Labour Review* 107 (1), pp. 1-29.

Huntington, Samuel P. (1993): The Clash of Civilizations? In: *Foreign Affairs*72, 3 (Summer), pp. 22-49.

Hyden, Goran (1973): Efficiency Versus Distribution in East African Cooperatives. A Study in Organizational Conflicts. Nairobi, Kampala, Dar-es-salam: East African Literature Bureau.

Hyden, Goran (1983): No Shortcuts to Progress. African Development Management in Perspective. London: Heinemann.

Hymer, Stephen Herbert (1976): The International Operation of National Firms. A Study of Direct Foreign Investment. Cambridge, Mass., London: M. I. T. Press.

Ianni, Octávio (1965): Estado e capitalismo. Estrutura social e industrialização en Brazil. Rio de Janeiro: Civilição Brasileira.

Ianni, Octávio (1974): El colapso del populismo en Brasil. México: Universidad Nacional Autónoma de México.

Ibn Khaldûn, Abd-al-Rahman (1967): Discours sur l'Histoire universelle. Al-Muqaddima. Traduction nouvelle, préface et notes par Vincent Monteil, Sindbad: Paris.

Ikonicoff, Moïses (1973): Technologie et modèle de consommation dans le Tiers Monde. In: *Revue économique* 24 (3), pp. 619-640.

Ikonicoff, Moïses; Sigal, Silvia (1978): L'Etat-Relais, un modèle de développement des sociétés périphériques? Le cas de la Côte d'Ivoire. In: *Tiers Monde* 19 (76), pp. 693-706.

ILO (1973): Multinational Enterprise and Social Policy. Geneva: International Labour Office.

Jacoby, Henry (1985): The Bureaucratization of the Third World—The State Class. In: *Law and State* (31), pp. 102-116.

Jaspers, Karl (1949): Vom Ursprung und Ziel der Geschichte. Frankfort on Main: Fischer.

Jeanneney, Jean-Marcel (1978): Pour un nouveau protectionnisme. Paris: Seuil.

Jha, Prem Shankar (2003): India's Identity. New Delhi: Ms.

Jha, Prem Shanker (2000): The Fascist Impulse in Developing Countries: Two Case Studies.New Delhi: Ms.

Jones, Eric L. (1974): Agriculture and the Industrial Revolution. Oxford: Basil Blackwell.

Junge, Peter (1980): Asiatische Produktionsweise und Staatsentstehung. Zum Problem der logischen Analyse der Staatsentstehung mit Gemeineigentum. Bremen: Übersee-Museum Bremen.

Ka, Chih-Ming; Selden, Mark (1986): Original Accumulation, Equity and Late Industrialization: The Case of Socialist China and Capitalist Taiwan. In: *World Development* 14, 10/11 (October-November), pp. 1293-1310.

Kahn, Herman (1965): On Escalation: Methaphors, Scenarios. London: Pall Mall).

Kalecki, Michal (1942): A Theory of Profits. In: *Economic Journal* 52 (205-206), pp. 258-267.

Kant, Immanuel (1963): Zum ewigen Frieden. Ein philosophischer Entwurf. Herausgegeben von Thomas Valentiner. Stuttgart: Reclam.

Kantorowicz, Ernst H. (1963): Kaiser Friedrich II. Düsseldorf, Munich: Helmut Küppers.

Kasch, Volker (1984): Agrarpolitik in Malaysia. Baden-Baden: Nomos.

Kautsky, Karl (1914): Der Imperialismus. In: *Neue Zeit* 32 (2), pp. 908-922.

Kaviraj, Sudipta (1989): On State, Society and Discourse in India. Paper presented at the Conference on "Political Institutions in the Third World in the Process of Adjustment and Modernization" organized by DSE, Berlin, 4-7 July 1989. Berlin: Deutsche Stiftung für Entwicklungspolitik.

Kay, Cristóbal (2002): Why East Asia Overtook Latin America. Agrarian Reform, Industrialisation and Development. In: *Third World Quarterly* 23 (6), pp. 1073-1102.

Keddie, Nikki R. (1998): The New Religious Politics: Where, When, and Why Do 'Fundamentalisms' Appear? In: *Comparative Studies in Society and History* 40, 4 (October), pp. 696-723.

Kehr, Eckart (1930): Schlachtflottenbau und Parteipolitik 1894-1901. Versuch eines Querschnitts durch die innenpolitischen, sozialen und ideologischen Voraussetzungen des deutschen Imperialismus, Dr. Emil Ebering: Berlin.

Kehr, Eckart (1970): Englandhaß und Weltpolitik. In: Kehr, Eckart (ed.): Der Primat der Innenpolitik. Gesammelte Aufsätze zur preußisch-deutschen Sozialgeschichte im 19. und 20. Jahrhundert. Berlin: Walter de Gruyter, pp. 149-175.

Keil, Hartmut (1986): The Impact of Haymarket on German-American Radicalism. In: *International Labor and Working Class History* 29 (Spring), pp. 16-26.

Kellenbenz, Hermann (1963): Industries rurales en Occident de la fin du Moyen Age au XVIIIe siècle. In: *Annales. Economie, Société, Civilisation* 18 (5), pp. 823-883.

Kendrick, John W. (1961): Productivity Trends in the United States. A Study by the National Bureau of Economic Research. Princeton, N.J.: Princeton University Press.

Kenwood, Albert George; Lougheed, Alan L. (1971): The Growth of the International Economy. 1820-1960; An Introductory Text. London: Allen & Unwin.

Kepel, Gilles (2000): Jihad. Expansion et déclin de l'islamisme.Paris: Gallimard.

Kerr, Clark; Dunlop, John T.; Harbison, Frederick (1973): Industrialism and Industrial Man—The Problems of Labour and Management in Economic Growth. Harmondsworth et al.: Penguin.

Keyman, E. Fuat; Koyuncu, Berrin (2005): Globalization, Alternative and the Political Economy of Turkey. In: *Review of International Political Economy* 12, 1 (Spring), pp. 113-126.

Khan, Mushtaq H.; Jomo, Kwame Sundaram (2000a): Introduction. In: Khan, Mushtaq H.; Jomo, Kwame Sundaram (eds.): Rents, Rent-Seeking and Economic Development. Theory and Evidence in Asia. Cambridge et al.: Cambridge University Press, pp. 1-20.

Khan, Mushtaq H.; Jomo, Kwame Sundaram (2000b): Rents, Rent-Seeking and Economic Development. Theory and Evidence in Asia, Cambridge University Press: Cambridge et al.

Khelladi, Aissa (1992): Les islamistes algériens face au pouvoir. Algiers: Editions Alfa.

Kiersch, Gerhard (1972): Parlament und Parlamentarier in der Außenpolitik der IV.Republik.Berlin: Ph. D.

Kim, Hong Joo (1999): Kanalisierung von Renten und Transitionsproblematik—am Beispiel der Republik Korea. In: Zinecker, Heidrun (ed.): Unvollendete Demokratisierung in Nichtmarktökonomien. Die Blackbox zwischen Staat und Wirtschaft in den Transitionsländern des Südens und Ostens. Amsterdam: G+B Verlag Fakultas, pp. 57-70.

Kim, Sun-Hyuk (2000): The Politics of Democratization in Korea. The Role of Civil Society. Pittsburgh, Penn.: University of Pittsburgh Press.

Kindleberger, Charles P. (1961): Foreign Trade and Economic Growth. Lessons from Britain and France 1850-1913. In: *Economic History Review* 14 (3), pp. 289-305.

Klein, Burton H. (1959): Germany's Economic Preparations for War. Cambridge, Mass.: Harvard University Press.

Kohlmey, Gunther (1958): Entwicklungsprobleme des sozialistischen Wirtschaftssystems. Ein Diskussionsbeitrag. Berlin: Akademie-Verlag.

Kohlmey, Gunther (1962): Karl Marx's Theorie von den internationalen Werten mit einigen Schlußfolgerungen für die Preisbildung zwischen den sozialistischen Staaten. In: *Jahrbuch des Instituts für Wirtschaftswissenschaften*, pp. 19-122.

Koulakssis, Ahmed; Meynier, Gilbert (1985): Sur le mouvement ourvrier et les communistes d'Algérie au lendemain de la Première Guerre mondiale. In: *Mouvement social* 130 (January-March), pp. 3-32.

Krämer, Gudrun (1994): The Integration of the Integrists: A Comparative Study of Egypt, Jordan, and Tunesia. In: Salamé, Ghassan (ed.): Democracy Without Democrats? The Renewal of Politics in the Muslim World. London: I.B. Tauris, pp. 200-226.

Krasner, Stephen D. (1974): Oil is the Exception. In: *Foreign Policy* (14), pp. 68-83.

Krasner, Stephen D. (1977): US Commercial and Monetary Policy. Unraveling the Paradox of External Strength and Internal Weakness. In: *International Organization* 31 (3), pp. 635-671.

Krell, Gert (2004): Weltbilder und Weltordnung. Einführung in die Theorie der Internationalen Beziehungen. Baden-Baden: Nomos.

Krengel, Rolf; Baumgart, Egon R.; Boneß, Arthur (1974): Produktionsvolumen und Produktionspotential. Produktionsfaktoren der Industrie im Gebiet der Bundesrepublik Deutschland einschließlich Saarland und Berlin (West). Statistische Kennziffern, 15. Folge. 1962-1973. Berlin: DIW.

Krengel, Rolf et al. (1982): Produktionsvolumen und -potential, Produktionsfaktoren des Bergbaus und des verarbeitenden Gewerbes in der Bundesrepublik Deutschland. Statistische Kennziffern, 24. Folge, 1970-1981. Berlin: Deutsches Institut für Wirtschaftsforschung (DIW).

Kridl-Valkenier, Elizabeth (1985): Die Wirtschaftsbeziehungen der Sowjetunion zur Dritten Welt. Vom Optimismus zur Erleichterung. Geschichte, Probleme und aktuelle Entwicklungstendenzen in Theorie und Praxis. Ebenhausen: Stiftung Wissenschaft und Politik.

Kühne, Winrich (1980): Schwarzafrika und die Sowjetunion. Die Bedeutung der Rüstungs- und Militärhilfe als Instrument der militärstrategischen, ökonomischen und ideologischen Einflußsicherung. In: *Europa-Archiv* 35 (10), pp. 325-334.

Kulischer, Josef (1965): Allgemeine Wirtschaftsgeschichte des Mittelalters und der Neuzeit. Munich, Vienna: Oldenbourg.

Laaser, Claus-Friedrich; Schrader, Klaus (2009): Offshoring von Arbeitsplätzen. Ein empirischer Befund Für Deutschland. In: *Außenwirtschaft* 64 (2), pp. 183-204.

Lafay, Gérard (1996): Les origines internationales du chômage européen. In: *Revue d'économie politique* 106 (6), pp. 943-963.

Lamb, Geoff (1977): Neocolonial Integration of Kenyan Peasant. In: *Development and Change* 8 (1), pp. 45-59.

Lamchichi, Abderrahim (1990): Les Etats maghrébins face à l'islamisme. In: *Cahiers de l'Orient* 18, pp. 133-165.

Landsberger, Henry A.; MacDaniel, Tim (1976): Hypermobilization in Chile, 1970-1973. In: *World Politics* 28 (4), pp. 502-541.

Langer, William Leonard (1936): The Diplomacy of Imperialism 1890-1902 (1). New York: Alfred A. Knopf.

Laszlo, Ervin; Baker, Robert; Eisenberg, Elliott (1978): The Objectives of the New International Economic Order. New York, et al.: Pergamon Press.

Lazonick, William (1974): Karl Marx and Enclosures in England. In: *Review of Radical Political Economics* 6 (2), pp. 1-53.

Leff, Nathaniel H. (1964): Economic Development Through Bureaucratic Corruption. In: *American Behavioral Scientist* 8 (3), pp. 8-14.

Lehmann, Hartmut (1980): Das Zeitalter des Absolutismus. Gottesgnadentum und Kriegsnot. Stuttgart, Berlin, Cologne: Kohlhammer GmbH.

Lembke, Hans H. (1980): Die Grundbedürfnisrelevanz ländlicher Elektrifizierungsprogramme in Thailand. Ein Beitrag zur Methodik der Grundbedürfnisorientierten Evaluierung. In: Hans Gsänger (ed.): Grundbedürfnisorientierte ländliche Entwicklungspolitik. Berlin: Deutsches Institut für Entwicklungspolitik, pp. 155-192.

Lenin, Vladimir Ilyich (1960): The Development of Capitalism in Russia [1899]. The Process of the Formation of the Home Market for Large-Scale Industry. In: Vladimir Ilyich Lenin: Collected Works (3). Moscow: Progress Publishers, pp. 21-607.

Lenin, Vladimir Ilyich (1964): Imperialism, the Highest Stage of Capitalism. A Popular Outline [1916]. Lenin Collected Works (22). In: Vladimir Ilyich Lenin: Collected Works 22. Moscow: Progress Publishers, pp. 187-304.

Leontief, Wassily (1951): Input-Output Economics. In: *Scientific American* 185 (4), pp. 15-21.

Leontief, Wassily (1954): Domestic Production and Foreign Trade. The American Capital Position Re-Examined. In: *Economia Internazionale* 7 (1), pp. 9-38.

Leontief, Wassily (1956): Factor Proportions and the Structure of American Trade. Further Theoretical and Empirical Analysis. In: *Review of Economics and Statistics* 38 (4), pp. 386-407.

Lewis, William Arthur (1954): Economic Development with Unlimited Supply of Labour. In: *Manchester School of Economic and Social Studies* 33 (2), pp. 139-191.

Lewis, William Arthur (1978): The Evolution of the International Economic Order. Princeton, N.J.: Princeton University Press.

Liebermann, Sima (1970): The Industrialization of Norway 1800-1920. Oslo: Universitätsforlaget.

Limaye, Madhu (1989): Indian National Movement. Its Ideological and Socio-Economic Dimensions. New Delhi: Radiant.

Linden, Marcel van der (1988): The Rise and Fall of the First International: An Interpretation. In: Holthoon, Frits Van; Linden, Marcel van der (eds.): Internationalism in the Labour Movements 1830-1940 (1). Leiden: Brill, pp. 321-335.

Logan, Bernard I. (1987): The Reverse Transfer of Technology from Sub-Saharan Africa to the United States. In: *Journal of Modern African Studies* 25 (4), pp. 597-612.

Lokanathan, P. S. (1935): Industrial Organization in India. London: Allen & Unwin.

Lord Ernle (1961): English Farming. Past and Present. With Introductions by G. E. Fussell and O.R. McGregor. London, Melbourne: Heinemann; Frank Cass.

Lucchini, Riccardo (1969): Le sous-développement économique et social et le système corporatif. Considérations tirées de l'exemple portugais. In: *Vierteljahresberichte der FES—Probleme der Entwicklungsländer* (35), pp. 35-46.

Ludloff, R. (1956): Industrial Development in 16th-17th Century Germany. In: *Past and Present* (10), pp. 58-75.

Lusso, Joyce (1965): La question kurde. In: *Revue Internationale du Socialisme 2* (11/12), pp. 689-697.

Luxemburg, Rosa (1951): The Accumulation of Capital [1912]. London: Routledge & Kegan Paul.

Luxemburg, Rosa (1963): Die russische Revolution. In: Luxemburg, Rosa: Die russische Revolution. Eingeleitet und herausgegeben von Ossip K. Flechtheim [1918]. Frankfort on the Main: Europäische Verlagsanstalt, pp. 45-80.

Lydall, Harold (1977): Distribution during the Process of Development. Geneva: International Labour Office.

Lydall, Harold F. (1975): Trade and Employment. A Study of the Effects of Trade Expansion on Employment in Developing and Developed Countries. Geneva: International Labour Office.

MacCloskey, Donald W. (1975): The Economics of Enclosure. A Market Analysis. In: William N. Parker und Eric L. Jones (eds.): European Peasants and Their Markets. Essays in Agrarian Economic History. Princeton, N.J.: Princeton University Press, pp. 123-160.

Machowski, Heinrich; Schultz, Siegfried (1985): Soviet Economic Policy in the Third World. In: *Vierteljahreshefte zur Wirtschaftsforschung* (4), pp. 406-417.

Mahajan, V. S. (1960): The Terms of Trade Between Primary Producing and Manufacturing Countries and Economic Development. In: *Indian Journal of Economics* 40 (159), pp. 357-360.

Mahon, James E. (1992): Was Latin America Too Rich to Prosper? Structural and Political Obstacles to Export-Led Industrial Growth. In: *Journal of Development Studies* 28, 2 (January), pp. 241-263.

Mährdel, Christian (1957): Zur Entstehung des Feudalismus in Ostafrika. In: *Wissenschaftliche Zeitschrift der Karl-Marx Universität Leipzig* 7 (1/2), pp. 130-131.

Mamdani, Mahmood (1976): Politics and Class Formation in Uganda. London: Heinemann.

Mantoux, Paul (1905): La Révolution industrielle au XVIIIe siècle. Essai sur les commencements de la grande industrie moderne en Angleterre. Paris.

Mantoux, Paul; Rappard, William E.; Bourguin, Maurice (1938): La crise mondiale. Zurich: Institut Universitaire de Hautes Etudes Internationales, Editions Poligraphiques.

Martinez, Luis (1998): La guerre civile en Algérie.Paris: Karthala.

Marx, Karl (1959): Capital (3). The Process of Capital Production as a Whole [1894]. New York: International Publishers.

Marx, Karl (1965): Capital (1). The Process of Production of Capital [1867]. Moscow: Progress Publishers.

Marx, Karl (1972): Das Elend der Philosophie. Antwort auf Proudhons "Philosophie des Elends" [1847]. In: Karl Marx und Friedrich Engels: Marx Engels Werke. Band 21. Berlin: Dietz, pp. 63-182.

Marx, Karl (1972): Zur Kritik der Hegelschen Rechtsphilosophie. Einleitung [1844]. In: Karl Marx und Friedrich Engels. Marx Engels Werke. Band 1. Berlin: Dietz, pp. 378-391.

Marx, Karl (1973): Grundrisse. Fundamentals of the Critique Political Economy [1857-1861] (Rough Draft). Harmondworth: Penguin.

Matter, Konrad (1976): The Effects of Foreign Private Enterprise on Development. The Case of Colombia. Sankt Gallen: Dissertation.

Mawhood, Philip (1982): The Place of Traditional Political Authority in African Pluralism. In: *Civilisations* 32 (2-1), pp. 109-240.

Mayer, Jörg; Butkevicius, Arunas; Kadri, Ali (2002): Dynamic Products in World Exports. Geneva: UNCTAD).

Medard, Jean-François (1982): The Underdeveloped State in Tropical Africa. Political Clientelism or Neo-Patrimonialism. In: Christopher Clapham (ed.): Private Patronage and Public Power. London: Frances Pinter, pp. 162-192.

Meillassoux, Claude (1978): Kinship Relations and Relations of Production. In: David Seddon (ed.): Relations of Production. Marxist Approaches to Economic Anthropology. London: Frank Cass, pp. 289-330.

Menzel, Ulrich; Senghaas, Dieter (1983): Autozentrierte Entwicklung in historischer Perspektive. In: Hans-Dieter Evers, Dieter Senghaas; Huberta Wienholtz (eds.): Auf dem Weg zu einer Neuen Weltwirtschaftsordnung. Baden-Baden: Nomos, pp. 77-96.

Meo, G. D.; Jambes, J. P.; Guerrero, R. (1985): Dynamique socio-énergétique à Dakar. Dakar: ENDA.

Michels, Robert (1925): Zur Soziologie des Parteiwesens in der modernen Demokratie. Untersuchungen über die oligarchischen Tendenzen des Gruppenlebens. Leipzig: Kröner.

Mitchell, Tony (1988): From a Developing to a Newly Industrialised Country: The Republic of Korea, 1961-82. Geneva: International Labour Office.

Mohan, C. Raja (2003): Crossing the Rubicon: the Shaping of India's New Foreign Policy, Viking: New Delhi.

Mokyr, Joel (2009): The Enlightened Economy. An Economic History of Britain 1700-1850. New Haven, Conn. et al.: Yale University Press.

Momayezi, Nasser (2001): Islam and the Democratic Movement in Iran. In: *International Studies* 38, 4 (October-December), pp. 341-362.

Morkre, Morris E. (1979): Rent-Seeking and Hongkong's Textile Quota System. In: *Developing Economies* 17 (1), pp. 110-118.

Morris, Morris David (1965): The Emergence of an Industrial Labor Force in India. A Study of the Bombay Cotton Mills, 1854-1947. Berkeley, Cal., Los Angeles: University of California Press.

MPAT, Ministère de Planification et de l'Aménagement du Territoire (1980): Synthèse du bilan économique et social de la décennie 1967-1978. Algiers.

Mukherjee, Santosh (1978): Restructuring of Industrial Economies and Trade with Developing Countries. Geneva: International Labour Office.

Mukhia, Harbans (1985): Peasant Production and Medieval Indian Society. In: *Journal of Peasant Studies* 12 (2/3), pp. 228-252.

Müller, Herta (2002): Marktwirtschaft und Islam. Ökonomische Entwicklungskonzepte in der islamischen Welt unter besonderer Berücksichtigung Algeriens und Ägyptens. Baden-Baden: Nomos.

Müller-Plantenberg, Urs; Hinkelammert, Franz (1973): Condiciones y consecuencias de una política de redistribución de ingresos. In: *Cuadernos de la realidad nacional* 16 (2), pp. 203 228.

Murray, Roger (1967): Second Thoughts on Ghana. In: *New Left Review* (45), pp. 25-39.

Musson, Albert E. (1978): The Growth of British Industry. London: Batsford.

Myrdal, Gunnar (1970): The 'Soft State' in Underdeveloped Countries. In: Paul Streeten (ed.): Unfashionable Economics. Essays in Honour of Lord Balogh. London: Weidenfeld & Nicolson, pp. 227-243.

Mytelka, Lynn Krieger (1985): The Transfer of Technology: Myth or Reality?Bruges: manuscript.

Mytelka, Lynn Krieger (1986): The Transfer of Technology. Myth or Reality? In: Carol Cosgrove; J. Jamar (eds.): The European Community's Development Policy: The Strategies Ahead. Conference organised at the College of Europe, Bruges, 4-6 July 1985. Brugge: De Tempel, pp. 243-281.

Najmabadi, Afsaneh (1987): Iran's Turn to Islam: From Modernism to a Moral Order. In: *Middle East Journal* 41, 2 (Spring), pp. 202-217.

Nakamura, James I. (1966a): Agricultural Production and the Economic Development of Japan 1873-1922. Princeton, N.J.: Princeton University Press.

Nakamura, James I. (1966b): Meiji Land Reform, Redistribution of Income and Saving from Agriculture. In: *Economic Development and Cultural Change* 14 (4), pp. 428-439.

Nef, John U. (1940): Industry and Government in France and England 1540-1640. Philadelphia, Penn.: The American Philosophical Society.

Nell, Edward J. (1967): Economic Relationships in the Decline of Feudalism. An Examination of Economic Interdependence and Social Change. In: *History and Theory* 6 (3), pp. 313-350.

Nelson, Richard R. (1968): A 'Diffusion' Model of International Productivity Differences in Manufacturing Industry. In: *American Economic Review* 58 (5), pp. 1219-1248.

Nerfin, Marc (1974): Entretiens avec Ahmed Ben Salah sur la dynamique socialiste en Tunisie dans les années 1960. Paris: Maspéro.

Newfarmer, Richard S.; Mueller, Willard F. (1975): Multinational Corporations in Brazil and Mexico: Structural Sources of Economic and Noneconomic Power. Report to the Subcommittee on Multinational Corporations of the Committee on Foreign Relations. United States Senate. Washington: United States Government Printing Office.

Niebuhr, Reinhold (1949): The Nature and Destiny of Man: A Christian Interpretation: 2. Human Destiny. New York: Charles Scribner's Sons.

Nohlen, Dieter (1974): Die wirtschaftlichen Gründe des Scheiterns von Salvador Allende. In: *Hamburger Jahrbücher für Wirtschafts- und Gesellschaftspolitik* 19, pp. 43-66.

Nohlen, Dieter; Sturm, Roland (1982): Über das Konzept der strukturellen Heterogenität. In: Dieter Nohlen and Franz Nuscheler (eds.): Handbuch der Dritten Welt (1). Unterentwicklung und Entwicklung—Theorien, Strategien, Indikatoren. Hamburg: Hoffmann & Campe, pp. 92-116.

Nolte, Hans-Heinrich (2003): Jüdischer Widerstand und der Beginn des Partisanenkriegs im Rußlandfeldzug. In: *Mitteilungen der Stiftung Deutsches Holocaust Museum* 12 (March), pp. 22-27.

Noreng, Øystein (1980): The Oil Industry and Government. Strategy in the North Sea. London: Croom Helm.

Northedge, F.S. (1966): The Troubled Giant. Britain among the Great Powers. 1916-1938. London: Bell.

Nurkse, Ragnar (1953): Problems of Capital Formation in Underdeveloped Countries. New York: Oxford University Press.

O'Donnell, Guillermo A. (1973): Modernization and Bureaucratic-Authoritarianism. Studies in South American Politics. Berkeley, Cal.: University of California—Institute of International Studies.

O'Donnell, Guillermo A. (1977): Corporatism and the Question of the State. In: James M. Malloy (ed.): Authoritarianism and Corporatism in Latin America. Pittsburgh, Penn.: University of Pittsburgh Press, pp. 47-88.

OECD (1979): The Impact of Newly Industrializing Countries on Production and Trade in Manufactures. Report by the Secretary General. Paris: Organisation for Economic Cooperation and Development.

OECD (1985): Costs and Benefits of Protection. Paris: Organisation for Economic Cooperation and Development. International Labour.

OECD (2018): Perspectives on Global Development 2019. Rethinking Development Strategies. Paris: OECD.

Okishio, Nobuo (1961): Technical Change and the Rate of Profit. In: *Kobe University Economic Review* 7, pp. 85-99.

Oloruntimehin, B. Olatunji (1971): Senegambia-Mahmadou Lamine. In: Crowder, Michael (ed.): West African Resistance. The Military Response to Colonial Occupation. New York: Africana Publishing Co., pp. 80-110.

Önis, Ziya (1997): The Political Economy of Islamic Resurgence in Turkey: The Rise of the Welfare Party in Perspective. In: *Third World Quarterly,* 18, 4 (October 1997), pp. 743-766.

Oshima, Harry T. (1971): 'Labour-Force Explosion' and the Labour Intensive Sector in Asian Growth. In: *Economic Development and Cultural Change* 19 (2), pp. 161-183.

Ostrogorski, Moisei (1903): La démocratie et l'organisation des partis politiques.Paris: Calmann-Lévy.

Pang, Eng Fong; Lim, Linda Y. C. (1989): High Tech and Labour in the Asian NICs. In: *Labour and Society* 14, pp. 43-57.

Pant, Girijesh (2001): Islamic Resurgence and Neoliberal Economic Reforms in West Asia. In: *International Studies*38, 4 (October-December), pp. 323-340.

Parker, R. S. (1949): Australian Federation. The Influence of Economic Interests and Political Pressure. In: *Historical Studies, Australia and New Zealand* 4 (13), pp. 1-24.

Pasinetti, Luigi L. (1974): Growth and Income Distribution. Cambridge: Cambridge University Press.

Petras, James F. (1980): Neo-Fascism. Capital Accumulation and Class Struggle in the Third World. In: *Journal of Contemporary Asia* 10 (1/2), pp. 119-129.

Pfaller, Alfred (1983): The New Protectionism and the Limits to Structural Adjustment. In: *Intereconomics* 18 (5), pp. 218-224.

Pietsch, Anne-Jutta (1978): Der Arbeitsplatzwechsel als Konfliktmanifestation in der Sowjetunion. In: Elsenhans, Hartmut (ed.): Migration und Wirtschaftsentwicklung. Frankfort on the Main, New York: Campus, pp. 257-282.

Poidevin, Raymond (1970): Finances et relations internationales 1887-1914.Paris: Armand Colin.

Pollard, Sidney (1968): The Genesis of Modern Management. A Study of the Industrial Revolution in Great Britain. Harmondsworth: Penguin.

Posthuma, Anne Caroline (1995): Restructuring and Changing Market Conditions in the Brazilian Auto Component Industry. LC/R1484. Santiago: Economic Commission for Latin America and the Caribbean.

Prebisch, Raül (1962): The Economic Development of Latin America and its Principal Problems. In: *Economic Bulletin for Latin America* 7, 1 (February), pp. 1-22.

Primack, Martin L. (1966): Farm Capital Formation as a Use of Farm Labor in the United States 1850-1910. In: *Journal of Economic History* 26 (3), pp. 348-362.

Prothero, I. J. (1971): London Chartism and the Trades. In: *Economic History Review* 24 (2), pp. 202-219.

Qiu, Peng (1999): Ausländische Direktinvestitionen im chinesischen Transformationsprozeß. Amsterdam: G+B Verlag Fakultas.

Quijano Obregón, Aníbal (1971): Nacionalismo, Neoimperialismo y Militarismo en el Perú. Buenos Aires: Ediciones Periferia.

Rader, Trout (1971): The Economics of Feudalism. New York, London, Paris: Gordon & Breach.

Ranke, Leopold von (1957): Französische Geschichte vornehmlich in sechzehnten und siebzehnten Jahrhundert (1). Hamburg: Standard Verlag.

Raup, Philip M. (1967): Land Reform and Agricultural Development. In: Herman M. Southworth; Bruce F. Johnston (eds.): Agricultural Development and Economic Growth. Ithaca, N.Y.: Cornell University Press, pp. 267-314.

Redford, Arthur (1964): Labour Migration in England 1800-1850. Edited and Revised by W.H. Chaloner. Manchester: Manchester University Press.

Renan, Emest (1996): Qu'est-ce qu'une Nation? [1882]. In: Renan, Emest: Qu'est-ce qu'une Nation? Et autres écrits politiques. Paris: Imprimerie Nationale, pp. 223-243.

Rey-Goldzeigner, Annie (1977): Le Royaume Arabe. La politique algérienne de Napoléon III 1861-1870.Algiers.

Reza, Sadrel; Mahbubul Alam, A.H.M.; Ali Rashid, M. (1987): Private Foreign Investment in Bangladesh. Dhaka: University Press.

Riegler, Claudius H. (1978): Emigrationsphasen, Akkumulation und Widerstandsstrategien. Zu einigen Beziehungen der Arbeitsemigration von und nach Schweden 1850-1930. In: Hartmut Elsenhans (ed.): Migration und Wirtschaftsentwicklung. Frankfort on the Main, New York: Campus, pp. 31-69.

Riesebrodt, Martin (2000): Die Rückkehr der Religionen. Fundamentalismus und der „Kampf der Kulturen". Munich: C. H. Beck.

Riggs, Fred W. (1960): Prismatic Society and Financial Administration. In: *Administrative Science Quarterly* 5 (1), pp. 1-46.

Rittenberg, Libby (1986): Export Growth Performance of Less Developed Countries. In: *Journal of Development Economics* 24, 1 (November), pp. 167-177.

Rivière, Claude (1985): Rites de la démocratie et de l'autocratie en Afrique. In: *Cultures et développement* 17 (3), pp. 453-471.

Robinson, Joan Violet (1978): The Organic Composition of Capital. In: *Kyklos* 31 (1), pp. 5-20.

Robinson, Joan Violet (1979): Aspects of Development and Underdevelopment. Cambridge: Cambridge University Press.

Rodrik, Dani (2008): Why Do More Open Economies Have Bigger Governments. In: John Gerard Ruggie (ed.): Embedding Global markets. An Enduring Challenge. Aldershot: Ashgate, pp. 113-144.

Röpke, Jochen (1978): Probleme des Neuerungstransfers zwischen Ländern unterschiedlicher Entwicklungsfähigkeit. In: *Ordo Jahrbuch für die Ordnung von Wirtschaft und Gesellschaft* 29, pp. 244-279.

Rosenberg, Nathan (1969): The American System of Manufactures. The Report of the Committee on the Machinery of the United States and the Special Reports of George Wallis and Joseph Whitworth 1854. Edited With an Introduction by Nathan Rosenberg for the University Press. Edinburgh: Edinburgh University Press.

Rosenstein-Rodan, P. N. (1943): Problems of Industrialization of Eastern and South Eastern Europe. In: *Economic Journal* 53, 210/201 (June-September), pp. 202-211.

Rotfels, Hans (1956): Die Nationalidee in westlicher und östlicher Sicht. Osteuropa und der deutsche Osten. Reihe I, Buch 3. Cologne, Braunsfeld: Verlagsgesellschaft Rudolf Müller.

Rothbarth, Erwin (1946): Causes of the Superior Efficiency of US Industry as Compared with British Industry. In: *Economic Journal* 56 (233), pp. 383-390.

Rowlands, Marie B. (1975): Masters and Men in the West Midland Metalware Trades Before the Industrial Revolution. Manchester: Manchester University Press.

Rudolph, Lloyd I.; Hoeber Rudolph, Susanne (1987): In Pursuit of Lakshmi Political Economy of the Indian State.Chicago, Ill.; London: University of Chicago Press.

Safir, Nadji (1980): Absentéisme et mobilité du travail dans l'industrie algérienne. Note pour une problématique. Equipe 'Procès du travail'. Algiers : Centre de Recherches en Economie Appliquée (CREA).

Salter, Wilfried E. G. (1960): Productivity and Technical Change. Cambridge et al.: Cambridge University Press.

Samraoui, Mohammed (2003): Chronique des années de sang. Algérie: comment les services secrets ont manipulé les groupes islamistes.Paris: Denoël.

Sandmeyer, Udo (1976): Wahl der industriellen Technologie in Entwicklungsländern. Diessenhofen, Schweiz: Ruegger.

Saul, John S. (1974): The State in Post-Colonial Societies. Tanzania. In: *Socialist Register* 11, pp. 349-372.

Saville, John (1969): Primitive Accumulation and Early Industrialization in Britain. In: *Socialist Register* 6, pp. 247-271.

Schirazi, Asghar (1995): Gegenkultur als Ausdruck der Zivilgesellschaft in der Islamischen Republik Iran. In: Ibrahim, Ferhad; Wedel, Heidi (eds.): Probleme der Zivilgesellschaft im Vorderen Orient. Opladen, pp. 135-164.

Schmitz, Hubert (1984): Industrialisation Strategies in Less Developed Countries: Some Lessons of Historical Experience. In: *Journal of Development Studies* 21, 1 (October), pp. 1-21.

Schorske, Carl E. (1965): German Social Democracy, 1905-1917. The Great Schism. Cambridge, Mass.: Harvard University Press.

Scott, Ian (1980): Party and Administration under the One-Party State. In: William Tordoff (ed.): Administration in Zambia. Manchester: Manchester University Press, pp. 139-161.

Scott, James C.; Kerkvliet, Benedict J. (1973): How Traditional Rural Patrons Lose Legitimacy. A Theory with Special Reference to Southeast Asia. In: *Cultures et développement* 5 (3), pp. 501-540.

Senghaas, Dieter (1972): Editorisches Vorwort. In: Dieter Senghaas (ed.): Imperialismus und strukturelle Gewalt. Analysen über abhängige Reproduktion. Frankfort on the Main: Suhrkamp, pp. 7-25.

Senghaas, Dieter (1974): Vorwort. Elemente einer Theorie des peripheren Kapitalismus. In: Dieter Senghaas: Peripherer Kapitalismus. Analysen über Abhängigkeit und Unterentwicklung. Frankfort on the Main: Suhrkamp, pp. 7-36.

Senghaas, Dieter (1977): Weltwirtschaftsordnung und Entwicklungspolitik. Plädoyer für Dissoziation, Frankfort on the Main: Suhrkamp.

Senghaas, Dieter (1982): Von Europa lernen. Entwicklungsgeschichtliche Betrachtungen. Frankfort on the Main: Suhrkamp.

Seton-Watson, Robert William (1937): Britain in Europe, 1789-1914: A Survey of Foreign Policy. Cambridge.

Shapiro, Gilbert; Markoff, John; Weitman, Sasha R. (1974): Quantitative Studies of the French Revolution. In: *History and Theory* 13 (2), pp. 163-191.

Sherry, Stephenson (2013): Addressing Local Content Requirements. Current Challenges and Future Opportunities. In: *Biores—Analyses and News on Trade and Environment* 7 (3).

Shih, Chien-Sheng (1968): Economic Development in Taiwan After the Second World War. In: *Weltwirtschaftliches Archiv* 100 (1), pp. 112-134.

Shivji, Issa G. (1980): The State in the Dominated Social Formations of Africa. Some Theoretical Issues. In: *International Social Science Journal* 32 (4), pp. 730-742.

Sid Ahmed, Abdelkader (1987): Du 'Dutch Disease' a 'l'OPEC Disease'. Quelques considérations théoriques autour de l'industrialisation des pays exportateurs de pétrole. In: *Tiers Monde* (112), pp. 896-908.

Sideri, Sandro; Johns, Sheridan (1980): Introduction. In: Sandro Sideri and Sheridan Johns (ed.): Mining for Development in the Third World. Multinational Corporations, State Enterprises and the International Economy. New York, et al.: Pergamon Press, pp. 1-22.

Siedschlag, Alexander (2001): Einführung—Internationale Politik als skeptische Gegenwartswissenschaft und die Münchner Schule des Neorealismus. In: Alexander Siedschlag (ed.): Realistische Perspektiven internationaler Politik. Festschrift für Gottfried-Karl Kindermann zum 75. Geburtstag. Opladen: Leske & Budrich, pp. 13-66.

Singer, Hans Wolfgang (1949): Post-war Price Relations in Trade between Underdeveloped and Industialized Countries. E/CN.1/Sub.3/4.5. New York: United Nations.

Singer, Hans Wolfgang (1950): U.S. Foreign Investment in Underdeveloped Areas. The Distribution of Gains between Investing and Borrowing Countries. In: *American Economic Review* 40, 2 (May), pp. 473-485.

Singer, J. David; Small, Melvin (1968): Alliance Aggregation and the Onset of War 1815-1945. In: David J. Singer (ed.): Quantitative International Politics. Insights and Evidence. New York: Free Press, pp. 247-286.

Singh, A. (1979): North Sea Oil and the Reconstruction of UK Industry. In: Frank Blackaby (ed.): De-Industrialisation. London: Heinemann, pp. 202-224.

Sinn, Hans Werner (1975): Das Marx'sche Gesetz des tendenziellen Falls der Profitrate. In: *Zeitschrift für die gesamte Staatswissenschaft/Journal of Institutional and Theoretical Economics* 131 (4), pp. 647-696.

Smaldone, Joseph (1972): Firearms in the Central Sudan. A Reevaluation. In: *Journal of African History* 13 (4), pp. 591-607.

Smiley, Robert H.; Ravid, S. Abraham (1983): The Importance of Being First. Learning Price and Strategy. In: *Quarterly Journal of Economics* 98 (2), pp. 359-362.

Smith, David A. (1997): Technology, Commodity Chains and Global Inequality. In: *Review of International Political Economy* 4 (4), pp. 734-762.

Smith, Thomas C. (1968): The Japanese Village in the Seventeenth Century. In: John Whitney Hall; Marius B. Jansen (eds.): Studies in the Institutional History of Early Modern Japan. Princeton, N.J.: Princeton University Press, pp. 263-282.

Solow, Robert M. (1957): Technical Change and the Aggregate Production Function. In: *Review of Economics and Statistics* 39 (3), pp. 312-320.

Sopade (1980): Deutschland-Berichte der Sozialdemokratischen Partei Deutschlands (Sopade) 1934-1940 (6): 1939. Frankfort on the Main: Petra Nettelbeck.

Squire, Lynn (1981): Employment Policies in the Developing Countries. New York: Oxford University Press.

Steglich, Walter (1960): Eine Streiktabelle für Deutschland 1864 bis 1880. In: *Jahrbuch für Wirtschaftsgeschichte* 1 (2), pp. 235-282.

Strack, Dieter; Helmschrott, Helmut; Schönherr, Siegfried (1997): Internationale Einkommensvergleiche auf der Basis von Kaufkraftparitäten. Das Gefälle zwischen Industrie- und Entwicklungsländern verringert sich. In: *IFO Schnelldienst* 50 (10), pp. 8-14.

Strayer, Joseph R. (1992): The Albigensian Crusades.Michigan.

Stürmer, Wilhelmine (1968): Die Entwicklungskomponenten des Kapitalkoeffizienten. Dargestellt am Beispiel des Maschinenbaus und der chemischen Industrie der Bundesrepublik. In: *Mitteilungen des Rheinisch-Westfälischen Instituts für Wirtschaftsforschung* 19 (1), pp. 13-28.

Sumption, Jonathan (2000): The Albigensian Crusade.London; Boston, Mass.: Faber & Faber.

Sun, Haishun (1996): Direct Foreign Investment and Linkage Effects: The Experience of China. In: *Asian Economies* 25, 96 (May), pp. 5-29.

Szentes, Tamás (1971): The Political Economy of Underdevelopment. Budapest: Akadémiai Kiadó.

Tandon, Rameshwar (1986): Balance-of-Payments Adjustment and Financing in Devloping Countries. In: *Foreign Trade Review* 21 (2), pp. 193-204.

Temin, Peter (1966): Labor Scarcity and the Problem of American Industrial Efficiency in the 1850's. In: *Journal of Economic History* 26 (3), pp. 277-298.

Thakre, K. S. (1998): Gandhinagar, National Council Session, 3-4. May 1998. In: Thakre, K. S.: President's Addresses—K.S. Thakre—1998-1999. New Delhi: Office Secretary, B.J.P.

Thirsk, Joan (1978): Economic Policy and Projects. The Development of a Consumer Society in Early Modern England. Oxford: Clarendon Press.

Thompson, E. P. (1975): The Making of the English Working Class. Harmondsworth et al.: Penguin.

Tibi, Bassam (2001): Die neue Weltunordnung: Westliche Dominanz und islamischer Fundamentalismus.Munich: Ullstein.

Tökei, Ferenc (1982): Some Contentious Issues in the Interpretation of the Asiatic Mode of Production. In: *Journal of Contemporary Asia* 13 (3), pp. 294-303.

Tönnies, Ferdinand (1935): Gemeinschaft und Gesellschaft. Grundbegriffe der reinen Soziologie. Berlin: Curtius.

Treitschke, Heinrich von (1953): Anfang, Mittel und Ende. Das Werden der deutschen Einheit. Rede, gehalten in Leipzig am 5. August 1863 zur 50-Jahr-Feier der Befreiungsschlacht. In: Treitschke, Heinrich von: Freiheit, Einheit, Völkergemeinschaft: eine Auswahl aus Reden und Schriften.Munich: Walter Verlag, pp. 15-24.

Trinquier, Roger (1961): La guerre moderne. Paris: Table Ronde.

Trinquier, Roger (1980): La guerre. Paris: Albin Michel.

Tunzelmann, G. N. von (1979): Trends in Real Wages, 1750-1850, Revisited. In: *Economic History Review* 32 (1), pp. 33-49.

UNCTAD (1978): Draft of an International Code of Conduct on the Transfer of Technology. Geneva: UNCTAD.

UNCTAD (1982): The Feasibility of Measuring International Flows of Human Resources. Geneva: UNCTAD.

United Nations (1949): Relative Prices of Exports and Imports of Underdeveloped Countries. New York: United Nations.

Upadhyaya, Deendayal (1968): Integral Humanism. Noida: Jagriti Prakashan.

Uzoigwe, G.N. (1985): European Partition and Conquest of Africa: An Overview. In: Boahen, A. Adu (ed.): Africa under Colonial Domination 1880-1935. London, Paris: Heinemann, UNESCO, pp. 19-44.

Vakil, C. N.; Brahmananda, P. R. (1956): Planning for an Expanding Economy. Accumulation, Employment and Technical Progress in Underdeveloped Countries. Bombay: Vera.

van Klaveren, Jacob (1964): Die Problematik der Manufaktur - Erscheinung im Ancien Regime. In: *Zeitschrift für die gesamte Staatswissenschaft / Journal of Institutional and Theoretical Economics* 120 (2), pp. 317-328.

Varoufakis, Yanis (2021): Capitalism has become 'techno-feudalism'. The world-renowned economist explains how tech companies and the pandemic have made the rich richer and poor poorer. Online available at https://www.aljazeera.com/program/upfront/2021/2/19/yanis-varoufakis-capitalism-has-become-techno, downloaded 15-03-2021.

Varshney, Ashutosh (2002): Ethnic Conflict and Civic Life: Hindus and Muslims in India.New Haven, Conn., et al.: Yale University Press.

Vellas, François (1981): La fonction de pays relais dans les échanges Nord-Sud. Le cas de la Côte d'Ivoire. In: *Tiers Monde* 22 (85), pp. 120-139.

Venkatasubiah, Hiranyappa (1958): Indian Economy since Independence. London, New York, Bombay: Asia Publishing House.

Vernon, Raymond (1966): International Investment and International Trade in the Product Cycle. In: *Quarterly Journal of Economics* 80, 2 (May), pp. 190-207.

Vernon, Raymond (1973): Does Society Also Profit. In: *Foreign Policy* (13), pp. 103-122.

Vernon, Raymond (1974): Competition Policy Towards Multinational Corporations. In: *American Economic Review* 64 (2), pp. 276-282.

Vries, Jan de (2008): The Industrious Revolution. Consumer Behavior and the Household Economy, 1650 to the Present. Cambridge: Cambridge University Press.

Wälde, Thomas (1983): Permanent Sovereignty over Natural Resources. Recent Developments in the Mineral Sector. In: *Natural Resources Forum* 7 (3), pp. 239-251.

Wallerstein, Immanuel Maurice (1974): The Modern World-System. Capitalist Agriculture and the Origins of the European World-Economy in the Sixteenth Century, Academic Press: New York, Orlando, Fla.

Warren, Bill (1973): Imperialism and Capitalist Industrialisation. In: *New Left Review* (81), pp. 3-44.

Webb, Steven B. (1980): Tariffs, Cartels, Technology and Growth in the German Steel Industry, 1879 to 1914. In: *Journal of Economic History* 40 (2), pp. 309-329.

Wittfogel, Karl August (1931): Wirtschaft und Gesellschaft Chinas. Versuch der wissenschaftlichen Analyse einer großen asiatischen Agrargesellschaft. Leipzig: C.L. Hirschfeld.

Wittfogel, Karl August (1957): Oriental Despotism. A Comparative Study of Total Power. New Haven, Conn. et al.: Yale University Press.

Wittfogel, Karl August (1969): Results and Problems of the Study of Oriental Despotism. In: *Journal of Asian Studies* 28 (2), pp. 357-365.

Woodward, Donald (1981): Wage Rates and Living Standards in Pre-Industrial England. In: *Past and Present* (91), pp. 28-46.

World Bank: Global Consumption Data Base. Washington: World Bank. Online available at http://datatopics.worldbank.org/consumption/country/India.

Yacine, Tassadit (1998): The HAMAS Movement: A Moderate Face of Algerian Islamism. In: *ISIM Newsletter* 1 (October); p. 10.

Yamamura, Kozo (1979): Pre-Industrial Land-Holding Patterns in Japan and England. In: Albert M. Craig (ed.): Japan. A Comparative View. Princeton, N.J.: Princeton University Press, pp. 276-323.

Yang, Dennis Tao (2012): Aggregate Savings and External Imbalances in China. In: *Journal of Economic Perspectives* 26 (4), pp. 125-146.

Yi, Guk-Yueng (1988): Staat und Kapitalakkumulation in ostasiatischen Ländern: Ein Vergleich zwischen Korea und Taiwan. Saarbrücken: Breitenbach.

Ziebura, Gilbert (1955): Die deutsche Frage in der öffentlichen Meinung Frankreichs von 1911-1914. Studien zur europäischen Geschichte (1). Berlin: Colloquium.

Ziemer, Klaus (1984): Demokratisierung in Westafrika? Die politischen Systeme von Senegal, Elfenbeinküste und Togo nach zwei Jahrzehnten Unabhängigkeit. Paderborn: Schöningh.

Zinecker, Heidrung (2011): Gewalt- und Friedensforschung—funktioniert der entwicklungspolitische Kompass. In: Peter Schlotter und Simone Wisotzki (eds.): Friedens- und Konfliktforschung. Baden-Baden: Nomos, pp. 137-182.